One Blue Bonnet

Nov 91.

Frank Coutts

One Blue Bonnet

A Scottish Soldier Looks Back

Brigadier Frank Coutts

B+W PUBLISHING · EDINBURGH

First published 1991
by B+W Publishing
7 Sciennes
Edinburgh
© Frank Coutts 1991
ISBN 1 873631 04 9

British Library Cataloguing in Publication Data:
A catalogue record for this book is available from the British Library

Printed by Billings of Worcester

Contents

The cover drawing of the author, sketched in a slit trench somewhere east of the Rhine in March 1945, is by the late Captain Peter White KOSB.

Acknowledgements

The author expresses his sincere thanks to the following for their assistance:

• to the Trustees of the 52nd (Lowland) Division and the next of kin of the late Lieutenant Colonel G.W.I. Scott for permission to use photographs and maps taken from *Mountain and Flood*, the official history of the 52nd (Lowland) Division 1939-45 by the late George Blake (Jackson, Son & Company, Glasgow, publishers to the University, 1950)

• to the President and Committee of the Scottish Rugby Union for approval and checking of rugby episodes in Chapters Seven and Eleven.

• to Lieutenant General Sir Derek Lang KCB, DSO, MC, DL for his most generous Foreword.

• to Major The Earl Haig OBE, KStJ, DL, Jack Webster of the *Glasgow Herald*, and to Andy Irvine MBE for their commendations.

• to John M. Pearson for the map of 'sHertogenbosch

• to Mrs Elizabeth White for permission to use extracts and a drawing from the late Captain Peter White's unpublished book *With the Jocks*.

• to Sir Charles Fraser for his help and advice.

Foreword

by
Lieutenant General Sir Derek Lang KCB DSO MC DL
formerly GOC-in-C Scottish Command and
Governor of Edinburgh Castle

A Scottish journalist wrote recently: "Every old soldier has a bash at writing his memoirs". Such memoirs provide a useful record for future generations but few outside the family read them. *One Blue Bonnet* however is different and should not be confined to the family bookshelves, dedicated to grandchildren, but should reach a wide Scottish public and those interested in Scotland beyond its borders, for it is a good read and fulfils an important purpose.

This son of the manse records his three careers - policeman before the war, soldier during and after it and military administrator and charity organiser in retirement over the last two decades - with enthusiasm and feeling.

Events in his life are described vividly. The book is full of amusing anecdotes and is well balanced with illustrations. As a Scottish rugby international he deserves and is likely to have readers from devotees of the great game.

His wartime and post-war military experiences in Britain, North West Europe and the Far East are told graphically, perceptively and wittily. He records, from first hand knowledge, matters of historical significance on the demise of the Empire overseas in the fifties and draws valuable conclusions from them. He was at the centre of affairs in Scotland when major reductions were forced on the Army politically and on Scotland's Regiments in the sixties and pulls no

punches in expressing his views on what happened. The subject is topical today, as this book goes to print, with more changes in the offing. It should therefore be read by all concerned for and interested in our Military Heritage.

Frank Coutts writes sympathetically with a light easy style. There is not a dull moment in the pages of *One Blue Bonnet*.

I commend it to you strongly.

Preface

Dear Neil and Kirsty

You said: "Why are you writing a book Grandad?" Good question. Vanity? Not entirely. Heredity is so important. As you get older you begin to ask: "Who am I?", and I think we have a duty to set down for future generations what we know about our times. Anyway, I thought you would like to know about life in the 20th century, when so many momentous things happened, from someone whom you have known well in the early years of your life.

Scribbling seems to run in the family. The first book on record is one about my great-grandfather, Francis Coutts (1805-1887) written by one of his sons, John Coutts, in 1907. Francis Coutts, my namesake, was born on a farm called Cuttleburn in the clachan of Coull near Tarland, Aberdeenshire, which is Coutts territory.

Uncle Pip did some research into the family roots and discovered that our ancestors were 'out' with the Farquharson clan in the '45 - that is the 1745 uprising which culminated in the defeat of the clans at Culloden. Apparently, they never got to the battle in time. They were delayed, carousing in the tavern at Auldearn, far from the fray. Knowing your grandfather, I can hear you sniggering: "That figures!" Not so, because that Francis Coutts was a fierce teetotaller.

Life at Cuttleburn was hard, there was barely a living to be had for a family of six and it came to an end abruptly when the local minister (of all people), "a kind man and affectionate towards the poor", claimed half of Cuttleburn for the manse glebe and was successful. The Coutts family had to move to a farm at Cults near Aberdeen, but young Francis prospered, turned to what we now call physiotherapy and became famous as originator of the Acid Cure, the Spinal System of treatment and many other cures that were highly regarded by the medical profession. Much of his success was achieved among The Good and The Great at Melrose Hydropathic where, in those days, people went for the cure. He was a highly respected figure in Aberdeen, led a very virtuous Christian life, and, the Memoirs record, "he was faithful to the motto of the Coutts clan Esse Quam Videre (To be, rather than to seem).

My father, Dr Jack Coutts (1875-1957), was a minister of the Church of Scotland in Coldstream, Rangoon, Aberdeen, Glasgow, Milngavie and Melrose. No wonder we have itchy feet! He was a lovely man - a great preacher, a kindly pastor of his flock, and a man of many parts. He was Padre (Chaplain) to the 13th Battalion of the Royal Scots in the 1914-18 war, a talented pianist (entirely by ear), totally impractical (like me, he couldn't even knock in a nail straight); he couldn't even drive a car! He pranged it so often that he gave up. The last occasion was at a right angled bend between Amulree and Dunkeld when he accelerated at the corner and went right through the fence. He was so charming to the poor lady occupier that she more or less apologised for having her fence in the wrong place.

Dad. *This photograph was widely displayed throughout drawing rooms in Milngavie. At ladies' bridge parties it was known as 'Jack's the boy' - and turned to the wall so as not to witness the gambling.*

Grandad Coutts wrote several books on religion. They are very learned and I find them tough going. They all reveal his very deep religious faith. In the 1930's he even wrote one called *The Church and the Sex Question*. That was pretty 'with it' for these days. Don't rush to read it; there's nothing very revealing. His childrens' sermons were excellent, and he edited the Church of Scotland youth magazine *Greatheart* for many years.

His wife Rose (Fleming) was a remarkable lady. Of course you knew her well as Granny Rose. She lived to be nearly 101 (1886-1987). She lived through three world wars, raised six children, was a model minister's wife, a rotten cook, a good horsewoman and she set down her memoirs in an (unpublished) manuscript called *Horse Trot to Moon Walk*. It's well worth reading.

Granny Rose's father, Sir John Fleming LLD (1851-1925), was Lord Provost of Aberdeen and Liberal MP for West Aberdeen. Don't get the idea that he reached these high offices from any inherited wealth or status. Far from it. He was brought up on a wee farm called Middleton of Dulrulzion on the Blackwater, about half-way between Blairgowrie and what you now call the Glenshee Ski Centre at the Devil's Elbow.

His memoirs, *Looking Backwards for Seventy Years 1921-1851*, are fascinating. One remark in the book struck me very forcibly: "One learns more after leaving school than at it". Too true. Have a look at the Dux board at any school and work out how many got to the top of their profession.

Life must have been hard in the glen. Three of his sisters and one brother died of what they called the 'croup', now called Diptheria, for which there was no known cure. Describing a hard days work in the fields he said: "Fed all day on oatcakes and cheese, we supped our porridge at night with gusto". And later, when he started work in Dundee, he would think nothing of walking eleven and a half miles home from Blair to Dalrulzion.

"Where did you get that hat?" Dragon, friend, Mother. New Milton, c.1938

You must have read of the Tay Bridge disaster when on a wild Sunday night in 1879 the Tay Bridge (there was only a railway bridge then) blew down and with it fell a complete passenger train. John Fleming and his wife (Elizabeth Dow) were out for a walk that evening and they actually saw a shower of sparks as the train fell into the river with appalling loss of life. He worked in Dundee for many years, first in jute and eventually in timber in which he became an expert, travelling often to the Baltic for supplies. The business expanded and he moved to Aberdeen where he founded the family business of John Fleming & Co. Ltd, now run by Mark Fleming, our cousin.

One of Sir John's sons, Robert Fleming (1883-1963) - my Uncle Bob - also set down his memoirs in a paperback aptly called *Leaves Off a Family Tree*. He was educated at Aberdeen Grammar School and Fettes College and became a civil engineer. In 1905 he emigrated to Canada and worked for years on the Canadian Pacific Railway which was then pushing west from Sudbury and Saulte Saint Marie ('The Soo') in Ontario. It was a real bushwacker's life - competing with forests, swamps, wild rivers, mosquitos, grizzly bears and difficult Clerks of Works! When he was working on the Algoma Central Railway from Sudbury down to Little Current on Manitoulin Island (Lake Huron) he met and married a local girl, Bess Patten, the girl singing in the choir at the Presbyterian Church.

Uncle Bob and Aunt Bess were very special friends of Granny Rose, and mine. On her death bed in Crieff, Granny said to me: "Never forget the Canadian connection, Francis." We won't. Aunt Bess came over to stay with Granny Rose at St Fillans when Bob Fleming was in France with the Canadian troops in World War I. While stationed at a place called Vimy Ridge, a name sacred to the Canadians because they lost so many casualties there, he received a telegram from his father-in-law, T. J. Patten in Little Current: "Care to go halfers on a small island at McGregor Bay (Lake Huron)? Your share fifty dollars" He did - and today it must be worth at least a million.

Coming more up to date, your Uncle Ben Coutts has made a great name for himself as a BBC broadcaster on farming matters. He has recently published his autobiography, *Bothy to Big Ben*, which describes his rise from humble beginnings, through horrific war experiences, to live a very full life of considerable distinction. He followed that book with another containing some of his notable broadcasts, called *Highland Air*. And we now have a real live author in the family! Sheena's husband, Alastair Scott, has written four fine travel books and we hope that there will be many more to come.

They have a saying down on the Borders at the Common Ridings: "Haud up yer heids ye gallant lads, ye cam' frae naethin' sma'". That's my wish for you two. Take pride in your fine McCallum ancestry, and the future will hold no fears for you.

I hope you enjoy reading these musings. They come to you with all my love and the very best wishes for your future in the 21st century.

Frank Coutts
Gharb
Gozo
Malta GC
1991

To my long suffering ladies:
Morag, Fiona and Sheena.

Chapter One
'Smiles Better
(1918-1936)

I was between a man and a boy,
a hobble de hoy, a fat, little, punchy
concern of sixteen
R.H. Barham - *Aunt Fanny*

Back in the 1920's no one needed to tell us that Glasgow was miles better. We knew it for sure. Mind you, we didn't know anywhere else. There were blemishes of course. You could see kids going about the streets barefoot, there were too many men with war medals selling matches in the gutter, the weather wasn't all that hot (with paralysing fogs in the winter), but it was a fine city, the Second City of the Empire, with all those magnificent ships lying on the Clyde waiting to sail to exotic ports all round the world, and the Glaswegians were so chummy. Most of all, it was home.

Home was St Luke's Manse, a fine sandstone building on the Strathblane Road high above Milngavie, facing south with a fine view of the experimental Bennie Railplane at Burnbrae which was intended to revolutionise our rail transport. Only the Germans were clever enough to make use of it. It speaks volumes for the liberality of the United Free Church of Scotland that they could afford such a splendid home for their minister, his wife and six kids. They even added to it while we were there! It was a lovely spot to grow up in, on the edge of the country, adjacent to the big

1

City of Glasgow Waterworks. There was a huge garden with a lawn big enough to act as a mini-rugby field and trees straight enough to act as goal posts. Endless goal-kicking was the order of the day - with second-hand balls, practically round, bought from Old Joe at Anniesland for five bob at the end of the season. Many's the altercation we had with neighbours when the ball went o'er the dyke.

School was the Glasgow Academy at Kelvinbridge on the Great Western Road, a fine institution. Goodness knows how Dad afforded the fees for five of us - his salary was never more than £600 per annum - but there were generous concessions for the manse. The Academy specialised in the three R's - Religion, Rugby and Regimental Preparation. I jest of course, but these three subjects did play a significant part in our lives.

Religion comprised principally of morning prayers in the gym at the top of the building for the whole of the senior school - hundreds of boys crammed into a wood-lined structure with only two small exits - on reflection, it must have been a horrific fire risk. It was a simple routine: a Bible reading, a Psalm read verse about by Rector and boys and a prayer followed by notices for the day. It left a deep impression, and I always felt sorry for the Jewish boy who for some reason wasn't there for prayers. Indiscipline was punished 'instanter' by lurking prefects who administered a well aimed kick on the backside. This will horrify modern educationalists, but it was extremely effective and I cannot recall any case of physical injury, student resentment or parental complaint.

Rugby Football was the second religion. There was no choice. In the summer, instead of cricket, one could opt for shooting, tennis or golf, but the winter game, autumn and spring was rugby for all. The Glasgow Academicals had been one of the eight founder members of the Scottish Rugby Union in 1873; indeed the inaugural meeting of the S.R.U. was held in the old Academy building in Elmbank Street. Also, the Academical XV in the 1920's and 30's had an unprecedented run of success with the names of Herbert Waddell, Jimmy Nelson, Max Simmers, Jimmy Dykes et al as every schoolboy's heroes. Nevertheless, one

2

couldn't help feeling sorry for those who shivered miserably at New Anniesland and loathed the game. They didn't even have the consolation of a hot bath afterwards, for the facilities were woefully inadequate. Even at the opening of the ground in 1925 the Hawick Captain was heard to exclaim as he surveyed the cracked basins and the cold, muddy water: "If this is *New* Anniesland, goodness knows what *Old* Anniesland is like!" Up at 'The Alps', the new extension on the Dalmuir Road, conditions were even more primitive. Wearing your big brother's hand-me-down boots, and with snow in the air on a February day, rugby was certainly a character-forming game!

Hawick were the side whom everyone loved to hate, because they were so consistently successful. Their star at that time was Jock Beattie, an awesome forward who played 21 times for Scotland. He was my hero. After one game at Anniesland I burst into the manse shouting "He spoke to me, he spoke to me." Dad said: "Who spoke to you?"

"Jock Beattie of Hawick"

"What did he say?"

"It's bluidy cauld the day". I told that story in Hawick in 1973 when I had the honour of proposing the health of the Hawick Rugby Football Club at their centenary dinner. Jock Beattie was there in fine fettle.

Rugby was so important that boys discovered that they could knock at the Rector's door and say "Please Sir, I've left my rugby kit at home" to which Dr Edwin Temple ("Ted"), a saintly man, would reply: "Silly boy, silly boy - go home and get it". Since most of the boys came from the 'sooth'-side, i.e. the south side of the River Clyde, it meant virtually a day off school.

There was a lot of travelling involved. Just after 8 o'clock, lunch-time piece firmly in the school bag, we ran all the way to Milngavie Station to catch the 8.27 train to Charing Cross, thence a hurried walk up Woodlands Road to reach prayers, breathless. Getting to Anniesland was by the famous Glasgow trams with their instantly recognisable colour codes - Green for Anniesland, Blue for Kirklee, White for the University - and so on. To prevent us from squandering our fare money on tuck we were issued with plastic tokens. It worked fine until an ingenious sweetie shop man at Anniesland defeated the system by accepting tokens for sweets.

Motor Transport in the early 20's was pretty scarce. Rankin's bus came to Milngavie and on to Balfron - driven by some sort of steam traction. In the mid-20's Mother became the proud possessor of a *car* - a bull-nose Morris with the spare wheel and spare petrol can strapped to the running board. It was open to the wind and rain, apart from a rather complicated waterproof cover on struts which clamped on to the front windscreen. It was a joy to drive and we all learned illicitly, on side roads long before the legal age limit. I took my driving test out of Croall Bryson's Garage in Kelso in 1935, the same year compulsory tests were introduced. It took about 10 minutes; smugly, I think I was a better driver than the instructor.

There was one snag about the car. Come the General Strike in 1926, we were driven to school by car when most of the other boys stayed away. Bobby and Fleming said their chums had put down tacks on the road to give us a puncture - perfidious brothers; nothing happened at all.

Nothing can be more boring in an account of schooldays than an endless recitation about our 'wonderful teachers', but by any standards, there were one or two teachers at the Academy then who were quite exceptional. Many of the masters came from English Universities, a deliberate policy, because we all had the most ghastly Glasgow accents - with glottal stops galore - and they tried valiantly to get us to 'talk proper'. One such was Captain Jack Coleman Smith ('Coley'). He had served in India with the British or Indian Army and, from all accounts, had pacified The Khyber Pass entirely single-handed - at least that was the schoolboy version of his prowess. I don't think he'd ever played the game of rugby but he turned out to be a brilliant coach. I had the good luck to be in his under-13 side and he coached us through to an undefeated 1st XV in 1934-1936, though we never managed to beat Heriot's: a subject of frequent controversy with my contemporary, Sir John Orr of Heriot's.

Coley didn't pull his punches. In a 1st XV match in front of

Coley's Juniors, Glasgow Academy Junior XV 1930-31
Played 8, won 8; points for 318, points against 27
(Left to right) **Back Row:** *W. McMillan, Bill Leggat-Smith, Billy McDowall,*
Hamish McBean, Captain Jack Coleman-Smith, W.C. Wishart, Jim Henderson*,
A.M. McAuly. **Middle Row:** *George Norton, F.H.C.*, Miffy Smith, Charlie*
Anderson, Russell Bruce*, Bill Russell, W.T. Ritchie. **Front Row:** *Ian Goodall,*
H.L. Gardiner   **Internationalists*

a sizeable crowd he shouted at brother Wally from the stand:
"Coutts, your bottom's as high as the grandstand". Coleman
Smith went on to make a name for himself in the early years of
the war as a competent broadcaster with a programme of early
morning physical exercises to music, which was a novelty at the
time.

We did actually do some work! There was a long tradition of
the classics and our master was one of the Old School - 'Lanky'
Robertson. He was nearly stone deaf, but operated one of the
early hearing aids with an ear plug in one ear and a hand-held
mike thrust into the terrified student's face. We were all scared
stiff of him, but he was a wonderful teacher of both Latin and
Greek. Despite his deafness no one dared take advantage of him
and you could hear a pin drop as he called us out in turn to

translate from Virgil, Livy or Xenophon. He wielded the best strap in school - rumour had it that he hardened it with methylated spirits. If you qualified for six of the best from Lanky Bob you didn't offend again in a hurry.

'Geordie' Moffat, the Maths master was another character, a Scot with a real sense of humour. In my illustrious great-grandfather's memoirs, it was recorded that he never "mastered the mathematics". Heredity is all. I don't know of a single member of the clan since who has managed to muster more than a minimal pass in mathematics. After Geordie had painstakingly explained a problem on the black-board over and over again, he asked the class if they all understood it. Sheepishly, up went the Coutts hand. "Well, Coutts, we'll do it all again *just* for you". Walter Richmond, a class-mate of these days and a close Army colleague, also related by marriage, used to retell that tale with great relish.

Regimental Preparation was in the compulsory Officers Training Corps. The Glasgow Academy is a War Memorial Trust, and our memories of the 327 old boys who had died in the recent World War were very real. We were often in uniform - H.L.I. Mackenzie kilt and glengarry - and we prided ourselves on our meticulous salute to the War Memorial at the west end of Kelvinbridge - "Up 1-2-3-4-5 Down". Whilst enjoying the training, and particularly shooting, brother Ben and I were attracted by the opportunity to learn the pipes. We were very lucky in our instructors. The great John MacColl at his home and his son of the same name at school were of the very top class.

Any activity after school carried the attraction of High Tea, that particularly Scottish institution, at Hubbard's for all of one and threepence - a real tuck in. Although the band was a bit of a skive, we worked jolly hard and blew mightily when we marched the Contingent to the annual church parade, to the ranges at Dechmont near Cambuslang, or to St Enoch Station for annual camp at Gailes near Troon. At camp we had to take our turn as Duty Band, playing Reveille and Lights Out. One morning, having slept in, we were playing Reveille - *Hey Johnny Cope are ye wakin' yet?* - attired in pyjamas instead of full uniform when we were of course spotted by Captain Frank Batchelor, a charming officer, who had suffered shell-shock in the First War. His rebuke was fulsome and concluded: "It was also a dreadful insult to the memory of the late General Sir John Cope". Since Cope was the enemy (at Prestonpans) we couldn't see that it mattered much.

It horrifies me to recall how free and easy we were with arms and ammunition. We took our rifles and bayonets home with us in the train (to the undoubted detriment of the rolling stock in the London and North Eastern Railway). I don't suppose we were meant to have ammunition, but we did, and frequently fired it into the bank in the manse garden. Boys will be boys.

Although it can be claimed that cadet training at school can teach lessons which have to be unlearned in the Services, the advantages are considerable - pride in school, uniform and self and a willingness to obey orders, the forerunner of the right to give them.

There wasn't much time for what is now called leisure. The biggest excitement in the year was undoubtedly *Hengler's Circus* somewhere in Sauchiehall Street. Kids nowadays just don't know what fun a good circus can be. And this was on a stage, complete with water scene - magic! The Christmas Carnival at Kelvin Hall was also fun. One needed a Sugar Daddy as guide - with a constant supply of sixpences and thripennies. A kindly neighbour, Mr Wallace, obliged.

The winters were undoubtedly colder then. Every year, it seemed, the cry went through school "Tannoch's bearing!" (Tannoch Loch was the tiny piece of water at the back of the Milngavie reservoir.) True to form the benign Rector would declare a skating holiday, and all day long we would scoosh about the ice on our rickety skates held together by a screwing mechanism - playing ice hockey and at night "canoodling" in the bushes at the end of the loch. Tannoch had its tragic side too. In February 1928 the ice caved in and two young people were drowned. Brothers Bobby and Fleming were given life-saving awards from the Boys' Brigade and Boy Scouts respectively for repeatedly diving under the ice to save life.

Another diversion was radio, then called 'the wireless'. Dad was selected to give one of the first religious broadcasts in Scotland. Bobby, the only technician in the family, had to assemble the 'cat's whiskers' apparatus which would bring Dad's voice magically across the ether. I'll never forget the look of disappointment on Mother's face when, after thirty minutes frantic twiddling, the announcer was clearly heard to say: "...and you have just been listening to a religious broadcast by the Reverend J. W. Coutts".

I don't know whether you could call the Boys' Brigade leisure. It is a Church-based organisation, founded in Glasgow and still doing sterling work. The Minister's laddies had, ex-officio, to be members, although somehow or other Wally landed up in the more up-market Boy Scouts. It was in the B.B. that one learnt for the first time what the expression "Jock Tamson's Bairns" was all about, for one met on equal terms with boys from very humble homes and could go to these houses without the slightest feeling of condescension. It was a real privilege. These Friday evening drills, pipe band practice, annual inspections, church parades, and annual camps at Lamlash were the best possible character training for a callow youth.

Sunday was one long round of duty. Boys Brigade bible class, church once and often twice were relieved only by a health-giving walk round the Waterworks in the afternoon. The Manse pew at St Luke's was, of course, right at the front. Mother used to marshal her troops, all six of them, mostly kilted, at the front door and then march them down the aisle. It was a real *tour de force*, indicating no doubt that "the service may now begin." But the effect was somewhat blurred by the fact that on arrival most of the boys, instead of bowing their heads in prayer, were to be seen making signs of triumphalism - or dejection - to the Buchanan boys in the Laird's Loft, depending on the result of yesterday's Academy-High School match.

Quite often we had a visiting minister as a weekend guest. Meeting one at the station and carrying his bags (a good mile) to the manse, I was heard to exclaim: "He's got simmits made o' concrete!" Once we had a slow-spoken MacLeod from Skye. At

John William Coutts	Rose (Fleming) Coutts
Robert Fleming	Bobby
Walter Fleming	Wally
John Burnaby Fleming	Ben
Francis Henderson	Fat (later Frank)
Jean Mary	Mick
Philip Gordon	Pip

St Luke's Manse, Milngavie, c.1928
Every one a nickname

Sunday evening supper, which was always rather a special meal at the manse, Mother looked up to see that the table was totally bare and Mr MacLeod hadn't yet eaten a morsel!

We were always hungry. The faithful Ally, the Aberdonian maid, standing arms-akimbo beside her blackened range and beneath a forest of washing on the double pulley, was always good for a "piece" or even a fly sixpence for the pictures which was all the more iniquitous because she was only paid about £30 a year.

I hate to say it but sister-baiting was another pastime. We really were horrid to poor Maisie. I really can't understand why; we were a fairly civilised bunch and yet we gave her a dog's life throwing her Teddy out of upstairs windows and making her invariably play the role of goalkeeper where she was known as "Sparra" because of her legs which were spindly in comparison to our oak trees. She doesn't seem to have held it against us. Entirely different in temperament, she is now a very successful painter.

Holidays at St Fillans were bliss. Wally has described them in *A Scottish Childhood* (p 44). "Figgs" had everything - a lovely stone Victorian house with a superb view up Loch Earn, boating and sailing (no centre board and sails made of old sheets), the loveliest 9-hole golf course in the world, magnificent hills to climb, and even 'the girl next door'. Holidays or no, Dad insisted on morning prayers after breakfast - a simple prayer and reading attended by all including Ally. Typically, my principal memory is the experience of keeking through one's prayerful fingers at the photographs in that prince of all newspapers *The Bulletin* which was the standard accompaniment to the more serious *Glasgow Herald*. A fortune awaits the newspaper man who can recapture the universal appeal it had in the 30's.

Living right on the loch we were hardly ever out of it. Discipline was strict. No one could take the boat out alone until they were capable of swimming the width of the loch - about 100 yards at that point. One of the incentives was that berthed right opposite Rath Erenn on the south shore was the steamer which plied the loch to Lochearnhead and back three times a day. Bill, the skipper, seemed to be glad of our company and we were all capable of taking the wheel for the 7-mile journey "nae bother". The smell of the coke fire in the crew's cabin forrard, laced with the reek of tobacco and whisky, is with me yet. I cannot understand why the Scottish Tourist Board does not encourage more of these delightful cruises today; they seem anxious only to rush people from place to place.

Certain walks became annual pilgrimages. Ben Vorlich, the only Munro in the area was a 'must', Glenartney to visit the Macnabs, Loch Baltachan, forming up place for the famous clan raid on Neish island, The Birran - all had their place in our annual ritual.

Maturity gradually advanced, without too many complications. Girlie adventures were about par for the course and mainly associated with the Douglas Cinema in Milngavie which then provided chummy seats where a boy and girl could enjoy the "big picter" in ecstasy. One night could have caused a parental breakdown. On a hot summer's evening a Midnight Matinee was on offer. Parental permission was of course refused. The rebellious reaction was to squeeze out of the manse annexe by ladder and so to enjoy the forbidden fruit. So far as I know we were undetected - but I wouldn't be too sure!

But all good things come to an end. Nemesis arrived in the form of a very smart car with a KS registration (Roxburghshire) and strange faces dotted round the kirk - a badly camouflaged Vacancy Committee. The inevitable result was a unanimous call for Dad to St Aidan's Church in Melrose, to which delightful place we all moved in 1935. I stayed on at the Academy Boarding House in Colebrooke Terrace under the parental guidance of Coley and Ethel, and flourished. Ted's successor, Dr Roydon Richards, made the classics come to life, and the school captain Billy McDowall, a future Judge in The Sudan, became a friend for life.

When Postie arrived at St Aidan's Manse in Melrose with the first mail for mother he enquired: "Any boys that play rugby?"

"Yes; five," she said.

Postie flung his hat in the air.

We were Borderers.

11

Chapter Two
The Year In Between
(1936-1937)

Who came? Who went?
How many days were spent
In this calm solitude?
The Ojibway knows.
Louis A. Nees - McGregor Bay: The Quiet Paradise

Most boys at the Academy went into medicine, law, account-
ancy or their father's business. Since my father's business was
Our Father's business it wasn't an easy decision and certainly one
which he insisted must come from above and not from within.
None of us was ever "anti"; the truth was that none of us would
have dared try to follow such a brilliant act. There were no
Careers Masters, university entrance was increasingly being
encouraged, but one had to possess brains or money, preferably
both. I had neither. School reports didn't make encouraging
reading. "What does 'lethargic' mean, Dad?" Another, which I
treasure, said: "This boy cannot *even* play Rugby Football".
Nevertheless, I did manage a group of Highers and Lowers which
were considered to be a passport to some kind of employment.
The trouble was that we were, as usual, in the middle of a good-
going recession; no one was likely to take on someone who didn't
even know what he wanted to do.

Dad in his usual wisdom summed the situation up. "There's
a hundred pounds in the kitty for you. Use it as you will. After

12

that you're on your own". Thinking of the time some years back when Mother and Granny Fleming had slipped off to Canada for a month or two, leaving the Dragon Aunt (of whom more anon) in charge, I opted for a trip to Canada for what is now tactfully called 'the year in between', a must for late developers.

So it was that, round about my 18th birthday, I embarked at the Tail o' the Bank (Greenock to the uninitiated) on the good ship *Duchess of Bedford*, Canadian Pacific, for passage to Montreal. Up to the Second World War, ships left regularly from Southampton, Liverpool and the Clyde for the New World. Steaming out on the packet steamer one couldn't help thinking about the thousands of Scots families who had taken this route in the Clearances. Who knows? I might have been a potential migrant myself. That night, homesick and sea-sick as the coast of Ulster heaved up and down, I would fain have been back in sunny Melrose under the Eildons. Next morning, fresh as a daisy, we were marching round the decks led by me as piper, and taking part in those ludicrous games like shuffleboard which keep passengers from utter boredom. There was of course the obligatory shipboard romance when one pledged undying devotion under the moonlight on Boatdeck 3B to someone, sadly, never to be seen again.

*Tourist passengers route march on the **Duchess of Bedford***

People who charge across the Atlantic in aeroplanes can have no idea of the dignified pleasure of sailing up the St Lawrence River, calling at that permanent reminder of French presence, Quebec, (where a dockyard matey nicked my camera) and passing with a salute the Heights of Abraham where British soldiers won the day using all the traditional military virtues of surprise, fitness and courage.

As the sleeper train trundled westwards from Montreal I couldn't help thinking that Uncle Bob and his pioneers had driven in every bolt to secure our safe passage. In the morning Sudbury, the nickel town and not the most picturesque town in Canada, rudely called Mudbury by my relatives, was looking its most unglamorous under a freak invasion of moths which were lying six-inches deep on the station platform. There on the branch line stood the waiting carriages of the Algoma Eastern Railway. It took off on the long run down the Algoma peninsula with me sitting bolt upright, all alone, sweating profusely as the temperature rose above the 100 mark; I couldn't possibly take off my new tweed sports jacket - must arrive "proper"! As the morning wore on we stopped at stations with euphonious names like Espanola, Fox Lake, and Whitefish Falls, eventually arriving to a rapturous welcome at Birch Island from Uncle Bob, Aunt Bess, Jock (16) and Bobby (14), my second family.

I was now in the "Quiet Paradise" - McGregor Bay. We travelled for about an hour in the Mail Boat through a bewildering succession of islands and channels. Fifty years later I saw Jock traverse the route on a pitch black night in a rainstorm; he knows every rock and every tree. Our destination was, of course, the aforesaid Vim or Vimy Island where Uncle Bob had established the most perfect holiday home, built with their own four hands. He could rightly call himself 'The Laird'. He called it Vimy, I'm sure, but Aunt Bess preferred the wise-crack Vim because of all the cleaning it took.

Originally the home of Ojibway Indians, McGregor Bay had been by-passed by French and British missionaries until it was discovered in the 1920's as a holiday paradise. There is a small store serving the islanders, manned in my day by Henry Silva and

Ethel. It really was our life-
line, and could be reached
in 30 minutes in a canoe
from Vim. Since the war, a
charming little church has
been built on the rocks
above the store. Like most
holiday places, McGregor
Bay runs very much on tradition, and the No.1 tradition is the Sailing Race on
Saturday. All ages and
classes are catered for and
it is a great social occasion.
The Flemings carried off
most of the loot.

'The Laird'. Uncle Bob Fleming
in his trail blazing days c.1910

The next two months comprised the most exotic adventure
holiday any schoolboy could devise. From the compulsory
"skinny" dip at reveille until dropping exhausted into Coutts
Cottage at day's end, it was one long round of swimming,
canoeing, sailing and adventure round the countless islands and
channels of this superb corner of Canada.

A work-up period for the raw-boned Scot was clearly required.
Lesson 1: "Paddle your own canoe". A birch bark canoe is a
fickle performer, very light and liable to capsize at the slightest
shift in weight. There was of course the odd disaster; was my face
red when I turned a canoe upside down with a "kicker" (out-
board motor) on the back? We were now ready for a trial run, a
48-hour exercise on "Baldy", our tame "mountain" - all of 800ft
- on the mainland. Baldy is the home of the most delicious
blaeberries, called "blueberries" in Canada. We picked baskets
of them and flogged them the next day to the Yanks in their huge
holiday yachts.

I was soon deemed fit for Lesson No.2 - a week long
expedition into the outback. No wonder there was a look of
parental concern as we set off loaded with a week's rations. There
was just one inch of freeboard as we headed off round Iroquois

Island and into North Bay. The interior at this point is studded with lakes and the object of the expedition was to take a wide anti-clockwise sweep via Kirk Creek, Long Lake and Hourie Creek back to Whitefish Falls on the main drag and thence via friendly territory to The Potholes, a favourite picnic spot where a parental rendezvous had been arranged. Canoeing on the lakes was pure pleasure, far from the madding crowd, but the "portaging" in between them was back-breaking toil in very high temperatures. The first trip was the two-man lift of the canoe and paddles, then back to base for two or more return trips for tent, bedding and stores. As some of the portages were a mile or more, it took a long time.

Always on the look-out for bears, we could hear them at night, none too reassured by the belief that they are more frightened of us than the other way round. The first sighting of a moose was an excitement, bringing to mind the Punch zoo joke: Keeper: "There's a moose loose". Gentleman on park bench: "Are you Scots or English?" We were armed with a .22 rifle in case of emergencies, but the real enemy was the mosquito, fortunately non-malarial; they attacked my rich Scots blood with gusto, day and night.

I had often heard the expression "busy as a beaver", but to understand it one had to see the astonishing skill displayed in the construction of a beaver dam. Another interesting find was a deserted gold mine called Bousquet. Uncle Bob later said that it was quoted on the stock exchange and we should have had a gamble - but it didn't look a good bet to me.

Feeding was basically out of tins, not a very clever decision in view of our weight problems, but our culinary skills were exiguous. The zenith of our cooking art was a North American delicacy out of a packet called Aunt Jemima's Pancake Mixture, taken with loads of maple syrup. Later, I discovered Pumpkin Pie which is mouth watering.

We didn't see a single soul for the whole week and were quite relieved to make the rendezvous with civilisation on schedule. I admired Jock immensely. He was so like his father and so practical with his hands in contrast to my clumsiness. We have

16

been life-long friends. I never got to know Bobby so well. He was a much more effervescent character but, tragically, he was killed leading his platoon of the Queens Own Rifles of Canada soon after the Normandy landings in 1944.

Come September, the boys had to get back to school at Upper Canada College in Toronto and we moved down en bloc to 61 Foxbar Road in the trusty Packard, parked at Birch Island. The bay freezes up in the winter. Our eldest daughter Fiona went up there from Grenada at Christmas 1972 and skied over the ice from White-fish. It was a question whether she or Angus the dog would collapse first!

Jock & Bobby,
Upper Canada
College OTC, 1936

I had to be found employment, and the first choice was brilliant - a three month typing and shorthand course at a small college nearby. Every morning I set off to join my class of 29 Canuck lassies and me. It was the best course I ever undertook. The shorthand deserted me years ago but touch-typing has been a life-long boon and undoubtedly got me through Staff College when the time came, for my writing is awful. The second choice was German, taught by a White Russian emigre

called Anatole Panovsky. He was a fascinating man who introduced me to the life of these unfortunate people who had been hounded from their native land by the Bolsheviks.

Rugby in Canada was still in its infancy but there were three teams in Toronto - the University, Toronto Irish and the Wanderers, who were the boys for me. They were a cheerful bunch, nearly all Brits who had recently emigrated. The standard can't have been very high because I was picked for the Provincial

Anatole Panovsky

side, Ontario, and travelled down to Montreal for the annual blood match against Quebec. It was pretty fierce stuff.

On another occasion I travelled down to Ottawa with my uncle and aunt to see the capital and on to Montreal. We drove down the Ottawa River on a Sunday morning when the French Canadians were pouring into chapel with their huge families in tow. My Presbyterian hosts had very strong feelings about the French influence in Canada. Aunt Bess was particularly vociferous, for the Pattens had been much longer in Canada than the Flemings, and later insisted that I read a book called *Bilingual today; French tomorrow*. The tension is still apparent today. Recently, when flying down from Sudbury to Toronto the hostess started her safety announcement in French and the whole plane exploded in derisory laughter.

Niagara was another 'must' on more than one occasion. Truly, one of the wonders of the world. That, plus all the delights of the Toronto autumn season - American Football with cheer leaders, ice hockey (The Maple Leafs, not Leaves), St Andrew's Church, country dancing with the 48th Highlanders, and the St Andrew's Ball in the Royal York Hotel were all very well, but, despite the warmth of my family ties I was outstaying my welcome. It was time to return to base. With commendable thrift Uncle Bob arranged a cheap excursion to New York, complete with sight-seeing tours, from which I would not return, but instead head back for Scotland on the *Lancastria*, a sad ship which was to meet its fate under German bombs after the fall of Dunkirk.

It was indeed a sad withdrawal to be leaving such splendid friends. The international scene was gloomy too. Hitler was on the march and for weeks *The Globe and Mail*, the Toronto newspaper, had contained rumours of the "Mrs Simpson affair". I left the U.S.A. under King Edward VIII and arrived in Scotland in the reign of King George VI. It was a gloomy voyage too. The only port of call was Halifax, Nova Scotia which was commemorating - on a Sunday - the anniversary of the huge explosion there in the First War.

Britain was in crisis and so was I.

Chapter Three
The Policeman's Lot
(1937-1940)

When constabulary duty's to be done, to be done
A Policeman's lot is not a happy one....happy one.
Gilbert & Sullivan

I'd had my fun, now I had to get a job. My three older brothers were all settled in their careers. Bobby, born deaf and fiercely independent, had completed his apprenticeship with Albion Motors and was moving on to diesels in Manchester, Fleming (Wally) had graduated from St Andrews with distinction and was now a District Officer in Kenya, and Ben was learning agriculture the hard way in Sussex, as recorded in his book *Bothy to Big Ben*. Maisie was at Esdaile, the ministers' daughters college in Edinburgh, and Pip had just won a scholarship from St Mary's, Melrose, to Fettes. Meantime, I was eating my head off at the manse, playing Rugby for Melrose 3rd XV and revelling in my second-row partnership with Adam Crawford.

Generations of Crawfords, Allans, Bunyans and Fraters have been the backbone of Melrose rugby. "Big Yid" was the youngest of the Crawford clan. Like them all, rugby was his life. Something of a place-kicker, and in the days when the scrum-half held the ball for the kicker, Adam is alleged to have invited his astonished scrum-half in a match at Hay Lodge Park, Peebles to align the

"Ba' a wee bit mair Tweed-wards". In his shop in the High Street of Melrose he is now one of the great characters on the Border scene.

It was a joy also to get to know the glorious Borderland on foot, to climb the Eildons and sing in the choir at St Aidan's, poodlefaking with the sopranos. My parents, bless 'em, never showed one sign of irritation or frustration with their unemployed son. They even seemed quite proud when I got a part-time job as extra-duty postman at Christmas time!

I had no chance of entering the Army and the Colonial Police forces showed little interest. There had been much talk in the papers about the new Metropolitan Police College at Hendon, instituted by Lord Trenchard with an officer entry equivalent to Sandhurst. Entry was either by

    (a) University degree

    (b) open exam or

    (c) through the ranks of the Metropolitan Police.

I decided to have a bash at (b) via (c) and went down to London for interview. I'd never been to London before. The splendid Waverley Line, so cruelly axed by Beeching, took us right from Melrose to St Pancras and I stayed with Billy and Anne Harding-Thompson, a cousin of Dad's, in Chelsea. Getting the Underground to Westminster was almost as frightening as the interview. The Dragon Aunt (of whom more anon) had an ex-boyfriend (she had many) who was a high-ranking Police Officer and he had advised her that the trick question was: "What is the difference between a 'lintel' and a 'lentil'?" I think it was a leg-pull; needless to say the question was not posed. There were over 60 of us for interview - 3 were offered Permanent Appointments, all of them ex Police Cadets, and 10 of us were offered Short Service Appointments (10 years - all rapidly converted to permanent when the threat of war became obvious). I wired home: "Lentils victorious".

Peel House, the Metropolitan Police Training School, named after its illustrious Founder, was in Horseferry Road, Westminster. The initial training was eight weeks. As is usual in these establishments, the instructors were the cream of the Force and

*Postcard of Peel House Training Squad 1937. (F.H.C. behind
The Grandee.) Message on the back: "8th July 1937, I saluted
Princess Marina, Duchess of Kent, three times today."*

they did a great job with pretty raw material. The syllabus was
based on the "I. B.", the Instruction Book, a forbidding black
hard cover loose leaf which we were constantly amending. This
was the law simply (?) explained for ordinary coppers. It was
tough going and a lot of it had to be learned by rote. Our
instructor, Sergeant Dewar, a steely-eyed Scot right out of Walter
Scott or John Buchan, stood no nonsense. As important as the
law was the general training - Drill, PT, First Aid etc. We lived
in cubicles and the grub and administration were pretty good.
Those who had been away from home before had few complaints.

We were a very cosmopolitan bunch. Like National Service,
it was very good for everyone to "muck in" and learn how the
other half lives. Very few of the trainees were Londoners and we
were fascinated by the Cockney patter of some of the instructors.
Everyone was "mate" or "chummy" - "yes, mate"; "give us a
hand, chummy". Two of our instructors were Olympic Wrestling
champions. One, dear Sergeant 'inchcliffe was in charge of PT
and Games. The sports grounds were out at Hendon and he was
forever encouraging us out there for voluntary games with the

cry: "Anybody 'ere for 'endon?" Those with an eye to their future inevitably went to 'endon.

Our intake of about 30 had a particular aim in view. If we progressed sufficiently well we would be put into uniform early and let loose on the great British public on the occasion of the Coronation of King George VI on 12 May 1937. We made it and were posted for the day to "O" Division, a non-existent part of the Met. I took to the streets at 3 am as PC 640 "O". It was an historic occasion and I was privileged to watch it from the Embankment in front of the RAF memorial where there were hordes of schoolchildren. We were on duty for 17 hours. No one had taught us how to slip off to spend a penny so we were legs-crossed all day, but there was always something happening and the kids were marvellous. The King and Queen were at their most relaxed as they were on the way back from the Abbey.

The training course fell a bit flat after that. I took an instant dislike to the First Aid instructor and was not surprised when I failed and had to re-sit my exam. There was a commendable amount of practical work. Simulated traffic accidents were always approached with the same ludicrous stock question: "And what has happened here, Sir, please?" There was no wireless, nor anything remotely connected with real crime, its prevention, detection and punishment. We were trained to be staunch upright London coppers, worthy of the Americans' accolade: "We think your Policemen are wonderful!"

We were duly inspected by some grandee and split up to our various Divisions. From our training we knew where most of the tough Divisions were which required the strong arm men, but on the periphery of London there were still reasonably rural beats which were referred to as the "Birds Nesting Divisions". I was posted as PC 220 'B' to Gerald Road Police Station, (near Victoria Station), a sub-Division of 'B' Division which covered Belgravia and Chelsea. Gerald Road had 18 beats, nine of them in fashionable Belgravia and nine in not so fashionable Pimlico.

People who think that pounding a beat is some sort of romantic occupation should think again. It is the most mind-bogglingly boring duty known to man. But it is what the Police is all about - the prevention of crime. I'm not surprised that there are hardly any policemen seen on the beat nowadays. They prefer to drive around in Panda cars and arrive after the crime has been committed. I would never claim to have been a good policeman but at least we did our bit by just being there. The powers-that-be were not, in my opinion, all that clever. We clocked in at 5.45am (for early turn), 1.45 for the late turn and 9.45 pm for night duty and solemnly marched out of the station in true Gilbert and Sullivan fashion under the Section Sergeant while the beatmen we were relieving were lurking round near the station ready to book out. Any criminal in his senses would know that this was the time to operate. Even the criminals were a bit thick in these days - perhaps there was a sense of fair play? In due course staggered hours came into force. This didn't please the Duty Sergeants who loved the 15-minute briefing session when we solemnly wrote down the registration numbers of all the cars stolen in the past 24 hours. I still have a fantastic memory for car numbers. Special announcements were also read out concerning persons and property requiring special attention, and then we were required to show our 'appointments', whistle, truncheon and notebook. The truncheon slid down a special pocket behind the right trouser pocket. As the ultimate deterrent it served its purpose well. With my chum from Shetland, Jim Wishart, we found it the ideal instrument for silencing caterwauling cats in Sloane Square in the small hours of the night. I did once use it in anger against one of Sir Oswald Mosley's stormtroopers. We were only allowed to draw our truncheons on the order of a superior or when under personal physical threat, and its use was limited to a blow on the shoulder or arm - never the head. In this case it was most effective in breaking up an ugly mob of Fascist yobbos. A few well-aimed swipes in the area of the elbow and they were on the run.

There was accommodation above the Police Station for only a small number of single men, so we stayed in digs nearby, at 8 Hugh Street with the portly Mrs Rae, a kindly Scot who looked after about 15 boarders including a number of SMT bus drivers, all of us working very irregular hours. She charged £1.10/- per week, all in, three meals a day. That was 50% of our pay which was £3.3/- per week, without change for three years. There was no cost of living allowance or automatic rises for inflation in these days. Although all uniform was provided free, one had, sensibly, to buy one's own boots and an allowance of 1/- (5p) per week was made for this. We wore through a lot of shoe leather!

For the first month new boys went out on the streets under instruction of an "old sweat", some of whom were cooperative and a fund of information, others who were resentful of this constant companion. In truth, they were reluctant to disclose the sources of their illicit cups of tea and other comforts. Later the new intake carried out short attachments to the CID, the traffic branch and the office, no doubt all part of an assessment programme.

In due course we were on our own. Like most things in life, the more you put into a job, the more you get out. Working a beat was a wonderful opportunity to meet people from every walk of life. Although the Old Sweats looked on me as an upstart Public Schoolboy, albeit with a Scots accent, I had the advantage over them of having been brought up in a totally classless society - the "in" thing in 1991, but pretty rare in the 1930s. I loved chatting up the costermongers in Pimlico - and the next day doffing one's hat with a smart salute to the Duke of Kent in Belgrave Square or Lord Halifax, the Foreign Secretary, in Eaton Square. That could be followed by a sordid suicide. Sunday afternoons were the worst - usually the gas oven which is clean and tidy. I will spare the reader alternative methods.

I reckon that on the whole "lawr'n order", that phrase which the English can never pronounce properly, was pretty well established in B Division, but the seamy side of life was never far removed. Dad had warned me that ladies of ill repute would possibly offer their services in return for protection from the law. As a Scottish parson he cannot - very properly - have had any idea of the incredibly mangy, crumby assortment of "Toms" (police slang for prostitutes) who patrolled our patch at the back of Victoria Station. His rosy-cheeked son was perfectly safe. The doyen of the pack was a formidable character nicknamed by us

"Frostie Fanny". She must have been old enough to draw her pension - but with high-heeled shoes, a slinky figure and subdued lighting, she must have had her admirers. "Chacun à son goût".

Along with the problem of the oldest profession inevitably came, and new to me, that of homosexuality. As an innocent teenager I had naively believed that sexual intercourse between males was physically impossible. I was in for a shock. Policemen aren't meant to blush, but on one of my first visits to Court to give evidence in some very simple traffic offence I heard a Police Surgeon in the witness box say: "I inspected the accused's anus, your worship, and found it to be funnel-shaped and spongy". About the same time I was actually importuned myself by a society toff in a dinner jacket in the small hours of the morning in Belgravia. I suppose if I'd hit him I would have been charged with assault. It was even more revealing to discover that these disgusting practices were also indulged in by the female sex. A visit to the Black Museum at Scotland Yard disclosed the tools of their trade. Short pause for nausea. Whilst in this state the reader might as well be informed that we often had to accompany the drunks to St George's Hospital at Hyde Park Corner and there to help the long-suffering nurse to apply a stomach pump. A messy business.

Rather like war, police work consists of long periods of boredom followed by incidents of intense activity and excitement. I was plodding down Buckingham Palace Road one day when I suddenly saw a naked woman on the topmost ledge of the Grosvenor Hotel outside Victoria Station. Decisions, decisions.... do I race to the top of the Hotel, or wait for the "marmalade" at the bottom? Have a go - race for the lift - which floor? - arrive there gasping to find a young Austrian girl sedately wrapped in a blanket. Another victim of the Anchluss, Hitler's invasion of Austria. At that time a lot of refugees from Europe were pouring into the country. Call an ambulance and get down to the paperwork - lots of it. A more congenial duty was the daily escort for Her Majesty's Guard as it marched up Buckingham Palace Road from Chelsea Barracks to The Palace. Happiness is operating the traffic lights on manual control.

One of the most congenial duties was "schools". Each beat was affiliated to one or more schools and it was a point of honour and duty to be at tricky road crossings to see the kiddies across in safety. This was long before the days of 'Lollipop' men and women. Was it not a mistake to take this duty away from the force? Toddlers became used to the local bobby; he was a friend to be trusted. As the youngsters grew older and cheekier, it was possible to do a little firm correction. Nowadays, the Police are always banging on about 'community involvement'. This was where it all started and a precious liaison has been lost.

Pimlico had its own "Speakers' Corner" where the Communists and Fascists each had their soapbox sessions, one just round the corner from the other. It was almost like a play with a predetermined climax because the evening had to conclude with a punch-up between the two groups. We solemnly intervened and separated them - just another part of the play. One evening, in the back streets of Westminster not far from the House of Commons, Sir Oswald Mosley was blasting off on a podium when a lady on a top flat above emptied a full chamber pot on his head with deadly accuracy. What a critic! It is pathetic now to think of these two ideologies, totally discredited in 1991, attracting the support of highly intelligent people in the 1930's and since.

Rivalries of a different kind were the order of the day at Stamford Bridge, Chelsea's football ground, which was outside our "patch", but where we often did duty of a Saturday. As I was totally uninterested in the round ball game I was happy to take the less popular duties outside the ground, where most of the action took place anyway, and leave soccer-loving coppers to patrol the terraces and get in peoples' way. On the few occasions I was on duty at Twickenham, it didn't seem to work the other way round! But I did see Wilson Shaw's try there in 1938 as an ordinary spectator, a moment of sheer bliss. Off-duty, I also saw Sir Len Hutton make his historic 364 runs at the Oval in 1938.

A lot of time - too much - was spent on traffic duty. Traffic lights had been introduced but some junctions were considered too complicated for lights - Victoria Station, Ebury Street/

Grosvenor Gardens, Hyde Park Corner, Knightsbridge/Sloane Street, and, a real brute, Chelsea Bridge/Embankment. About every three months one spent a whole month on point duty: 8 am-4 pm one week, and 4-12 the next. It was very taxing both physically and mentally, but stimulating; one couldn't relax for a moment. In August 1938 I was on Chelsea Bridge during the holiday rush. Towards the end of the month when it was getting dark earlier in the evening and the cars were tearing back from the coast it was really hair-raising. I went home absolutely played out - social life nil. Victoria Station was more fun. The traffic was slow-moving and one had to deal at the same time with a constant barrage of questions from tourists. We had a totally inadequate information guide and sometimes one felt obliged to say, in a strong Scots accent: "Sorry, mate, I'm a stranger here myself!" Since the "other half" of that traffic point was taken by an 'A' Division man (from the neighbouring Division), there was no time for boredom and for 8 hours solid one was subjected to a solid diet of bus exhaust fumes. It didn't seem to do much harm.

Night duty (10 pm-6 am) came round every third month. It took a week to get used to sleeping by day. Thereafter, it was fairly relaxing. Time goes very slowly between 2 am and 6 am. We weren't supposed to "gossip" with neighbouring beatmen - but rules are made to be broken. Some of our pranks would not have pleased the Home Secretary. A favourite one was to stand by an empty taxi rank and when the phone rang at about two in

P.C. 220 'B' on point duty

the morning we would stifle our giggles and say: "This is the Fire Station - where is the fire?" or "This is the Cat and Dog Home". Naughty, naughty. We did cover the ground and we did protect property - but the dawn was always welcome.

One of the banes of a policeman's life is attending Police Court. If you arrested a drunk at 1 am he had to appear in court at 10 o'clock in the morning. The drunk sleeps it off in the cell while the policeman continues to plod his beat - with no sleep in the morning and the rest of his day ruined. There is a lot of hanging about and in the end the chap probably pleads guilty, no evidence is required and he gets a caution and, who knows, "a pound out of the Poor Box". The Magistrates at Horseferry Road were a courteous and impressive team. It was always a pleasure to see them administer justice so fairly.

Most of the cases I took to court were for traffic offences of the pettiest kind - parking in ridiculous places like King's Road, Chelsea, opposite Peter Jones or failure to show Road Fund Licences. We were encouraged to give a lot of cautions rather than prosecute but every now and then we would be reminded that one hadn't submitted many cases recently. One couldn't be too soft-hearted; records were kept and one's performance was being assessed.

When we were really pushed for a summons or two we would catch pedal cyclists hanging on to the back of lorries on the Embankment, a favourite means of locomotion for young Londoners in these days. The offence was known as "causing oneself to be drawn", a form of words whose *double entendre* caused many a bellylaugh among the old sweats.

From time to time we would have a blitz. In the early days of traffic lights people were very bad about shooting over on the red light - particularly taxi drivers, not the policeman's best friends. It was so easy to catch them. Jim Wishart would stand at the light in plain clothes watching the red light. If anyone transgressed by more than 5 yards he held up his hand and I, in uniform, stopped the vehicle on the other side of the lights. A day's catch of 20 would make a visit to court worthwhile.

The reader could be thinking at this point that we were

nothing more than glorified traffic wardens, but that wouldn't be fair. There was a lot of routine preventive work the whole time. True, one didn't effect any brilliant apprehension of criminals - that was mainly handled by the CID - but hardly a day passed without a brawl of some kind. One was also conscious of being part of a community, admittedly a very cosmopolitan one, and we were the eyes and ears of authority. Nothing much went on that we didn't know about. One of the saddest statistics was that most of the turmoil was within families and in these cases we were expressly forbidden from taking sides or from prosecuting. It's heartening to see that this policy is now being reviewed. The clear evidence of child abuse has brought people up with a start. In our case, it was normally the disgruntled husband back from the pub taking a swipe at his missus, as of right, as it were.

Working shifts made one's social life chaotic or non-existent. My main relaxations were rugby and music. Sport was very much encouraged and it didn't take me long to discover that playing Rugby for "B" Division was worth a half-day off. That led fairly

Twelve Taffies, two Jocks and one Sassenach.
Met Police Rugby XV, Aldershot 1939.

29

soon to selection for the Met Police 1st XV which was a very good one with its fine ground at Imber Court, Thames Ditton and an impressive fixture list. There was a very strong Welsh influence - 12 of them, supported by one Sassenach and two Scots - a grand bunch and we had a lot of fun up and down the country. Our Captain was Arthur Rees, Cambridge Blue and Welsh Internationalist, one of Lord Trenchard's new Station Inspectors, fresh from the Hendon College, a grand chap and a fine leader. Unfortunately his Welsh blood carried him a bit far one day at Nottingham and he was sent off for a quite unnecessary piece of "aggro" - splendid upper-cut, Sir. In 1990 I asked him at the Barbarians Centenary Dinner if there had been any disciplinary consequences; he couldn't think of any and it certainly didn't do his career any harm as he later served with the Royal Air Force and became Chief Constable of Staffordshire. The last Calcutta Cup match (Scotland v England) before the war was at Murrayfield in 1939. The Met Police side took on the Edinburgh City Police team that morning and I regret to say they defeated us. Not for the first time I was up against my future Scotland colleague, PC John Orr, later Chief Constable of Edinburgh and Borders.

I had always been fond of music and as a boy had regularly attended the Scottish Orchestra's concerts in the old St Andrew's Hall, alas no more. My father pointed out that the brilliant Sir John Barbirolli was very openly devoted to his leading oboist Evelyn Rothwell. How right he was! He eventually married her. In London the choice was enormous. The only concerts I could afford were the Proms in the old Queen's Hall. I teamed up with an Ayrshire Scot PC 226 Johnnie Johnson who was a devotee. Gosh, we must have been fit to stand for hours on end after an 8-hour day on the beat. No wonder I have varicose veins!

My social life wasn't entirely restricted to rugby and music. The best pubs in London were those purveying the admirable Scots ale of Messrs McEwan and Younger. Starting at the Bag o' Nails in Buckingham Palace Road there were McEwan pubs all over London. In fact, they issued a map of them and this acted as a challenge to some of us to sample every one in an evening! I'm afraid we never made it. We always seemed to get stuck when we ran into some good Scots folk and had a good blether.

Our days-off routine was very odd. Monday one week, Wednesday the next, then Friday/Sunday (useless), followed by Tuesday, Thursday and Saturday/Sunday - one proper weekend in eight. These I would spend either with Ben on the stud at Petworth or with the Dragon Aunt at New Milton near Bournemouth. Ah! I promised the reader to divulge more about The Dragon. She was Aunt May, my mother's youngest sister. She had suffered the loss of several fiances in the First War in which she was an active VAD nurse (and again in The Second). She often came to look after us at Milngavie when the folks were away and pretended to be very fierce (hence "Ye Dragone"), but in fact she had a heart of gold. She eventually married my father's brother, Walter, who had a throat complaint which only enabled him to speak in a whisper. The poor chap was horribly hen-pecked.

To get to New Milton on Friday night the only train stopped at Brockenhurst leaving the weary copper a 10-mile walk through the New Forest at 2 am. Going to Ben's was easier. PC Gwyn Moses and I had gone half-shares in an Austin 7 which cost us £4 each. Here she is in a Sussex lane:

Wish we had kept her. She would be worth a packet today. Police work was physically and, to a certain extent, mentally demanding, but I had to bear in mind the aim which was to get to the Police College at Hendon either by open exam or by selection. I went to evening classes which were well run (and almost free) in Westminster, but I couldn't attend when I was on "the back shift". Eventually the exam was on me. The results did not surprise.

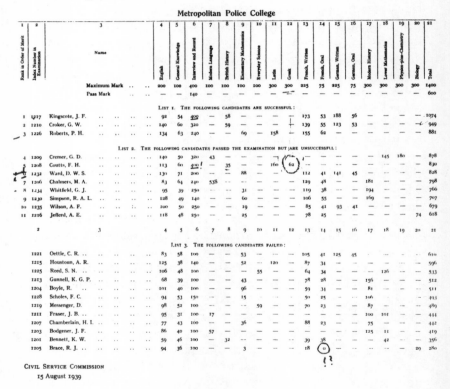

Metropolitan Police College

1 Rank in Order of Merit	2 Index Number in Examination	3 Name	4 English	5 General Knowledge	6 Interview and Record	7 Modern Language	8 British History	9 Elementary Mathematics	10 Everyday Science	11 Latin	12 Greek	13 French, Written	14 French, Oral	15 German, Written	16 German, Oral	17 Modern History	18 Lower Mathematics	19 Physics-plus-Chemistry	20 Biology	21 Total
		Maximum Mark ..	200	100	400	100	100	100	100	300	300	225	75	225	75	300	300	300	300	1400
		Pass Mark ..	—	—	140	—	—	—	—	—	—	—	—	—	—	—	—	—	—	600
		LIST 1. THE FOLLOWING CANDIDATES ARE SUCCESSFUL:																		
1	1217	Kingscote, J. F.	92	54	400	—	58	—	—	—	—	173	53	188	56	—	—	—	—	1074
2	1210	Croker, G. W.	140	60	320	—	59	—	—	—	—	139	55	123	53	—	—	—	—	949
3	1226	Roberts, P. H.	134	63	240	—	—	69	—	158	—	155	62	—	—	—	—	—	—	881
		LIST 2. THE FOLLOWING CANDIDATES PASSED THE EXAMINATION BUT ARE UNSUCCESSFUL:																		
4	1209	Cremer, G. D.	140	50	320	43	—	—	—	—	—	—	—	—	—	—	145	180	—	878
5	1208	Coutts, F. H.	113	60	400	—	35	—	—	160	62	—	—	—	—	—	—	—	—	830
6	1232	Ward, D. W. S.	130	71	200	—	—	88	—	—	—	112	41	141	45	—	—	—	—	828
7	1206	Chalmers, M. A.	83	64	240	538	—	—	—	—	—	129	48	—	—	181	—	—	—	798
8	1234	Whitfield, G. J.	95	39	250	—	—	31	—	—	—	119	38	—	—	194	—	—	—	766
9	1230	Simpson, R. A. L.	128	49	140	—	—	60	—	—	—	106	55	—	—	169	—	—	—	707
10	1235	Wilson, A. F.	100	50	250	—	—	19	—	—	—	85	41	93	41	—	—	—	—	679
11	1216	Jefferd, A. E.	118	48	250	—	—	25	—	—	—	78	25	—	—	—	—	—	74	618
	2	3	4	5	6	7	8	9	10	11	12	13	14	15	16	17	18	19	20	21
		LIST 3. THE FOLLOWING CANDIDATES FAILED:																		
	1221	Oettle, C. R. ..	83	58	100	—	—	53	—	—	—	105	41	125	45	—	—	—	—	610
	1215	Houstoun, A. R.	125	38	140	—	—	52	—	120	—	87	34	—	—	—	—	—	—	596
	1225	Reed, S. N. ..	106	48	100	—	—	—	55	—	—	64	34	—	—	—	126	—	—	533
	1213	Gunnell, K. G. P.	68	39	100	—	—	43	—	—	—	78	28	—	—	156	—	—	—	512
	1204	Boyle, R. ..	101	40	100	—	—	96	—	—	—	59	34	—	—	81	—	—	—	511
	1228	Scholes, F. C.	94	53	150	—	—	15	—	—	—	50	25	—	—	106	—	—	—	493
	1219	Messenger, D.	98	52	100	—	—	—	59	—	—	70	23	—	—	87	—	—	—	489
	1211	Fraser, J. B. ..	95	31	100	17	—	—	—	—	—	—	—	—	—	100	101	—	—	444
	1207	Chamberlain, H. I.	77	43	100	—	—	36	—	—	—	88	23	—	—	75	—	—	—	442
	1203	Bodgener, J. F.	86	40	100	57	—	—	—	—	—	—	—	—	—	125	11	—	—	419
	1201	Bennett, K. W.	59	46	100	—	32	—	—	—	—	39	38	—	—	—	42	—	—	356
	1205	Brace, R. J. ..	94	36	100	—	—	3	—	—	—	18	0	—	—	—	—	—	29	280

CIVIL SERVICE COMMISSION
15 August 1939

The interview mark was encouraging. I always remember the question which stumped me - "describe how you would lay out a new two-lane highway" (once again the emphasis on traffic not crime). What they were looking for was a cycle lane as in

Holland. Despite much prompting I just couldn't get it. The marks in Greek were depressing - though what use ancient Greek would have been in a constabulary career one fails to understand! But a decent mark might have achieved the aim. In any case, the outlook for the College was not encouraging. There was a lot of opposition to the Sandhurst-type entry within the Force and its future was doubtful. In fact, the College closed at the outbreak of war to be replaced after the war by the Bramshill Police College for selected serving officers and specialist courses. Personally, I very much regretted the demise of the College. The arrival of the first batch of Junior Station Inspectors ex-Hendon was a breath of fresh air. The long-serving Inspectors were decent enough chaps, but they were pretty thick, inflexible and very low on man-management skills. The new boys got out and about more and were very approachable. The argument still rages in the correspondence columns of *The Times* and *The Telegraph* although my letters have never been published!

In the summer of 1938 it seemed that war was inevitable. Then came Chamberlain's dramatic meeting with Hitler at Munich which seemed to have gained us a reprieve. I was on duty in Sloane Street at the junction of Pont Street on the night he returned, proudly waving the piece of paper which sadly meant nothing for it signified only the end of the civilised world as we knew it.

From then on it was a mad rush to prepare for war. Air Raid Precautions in every form became top priority - the construction of shelters, mainly above ground, the issue of gas masks and decontamination suits, the enlistment and training of Police War Reserves - it was all go. The reaction of Londoners to these events was remarkably stoic, especially when one considers that it was a mere 20 years since "the war to end all wars". The League of Nations had been a fiasco and Britain was anxious not to be beastly to the Germans. It would be true to say that no one was greatly surprised or alarmed. As the 1930's developed the warnings became obvious. The pity is that so few people had the guts to do anything about it. I was hardly out of my teens and merely reacted enthusiastically to the excitement of it all. The atmosphere of friendliness and "we're all in it together" was very evident in Pimlico. I can't remember any anti-war demonstrations of any kind. No one wanted war - but it became inevitable.

With the chances of a police career nullified my thoughts turned more and more to the army. I had tried to enlist in The London Scottish TA, but was refused permission by the Met Police. On 8th July 1939 my age group was notified for conscription, but I was deferred as the Police was a reserved occupation.

When the sirens eventually wailed out in earnest on 3rd of September I was in church at St Columba's Pont Street which I had joined when first coming to London. Dr Archie Fleming closed the service with a prayer and bid us return to our homes in calmness and confidence. I ran all the way to my digs in Eaton Terrace and changed into uniform. At the nick we were told to go home and carry on as usual.

The first three months of the war were very frustrating. The Phoney War was so unreal, drinking endless cups of tea at ARP posts. I remember one particular night in Royal Avenue, Chelsea when the news of our victory at the Battle of the River Plate and the sinking of the Graf Spee came through. Our elation was unbounded. So far the war had been a complete damp squib. It would never be won without offensive action. This was further proof that the Royal Navy were the best in the world.

I applied formally to leave the Force and was granted an interview with Superintendent Honour of "B" Division (I'm afraid we called him "Dishonour", probably quite unfairly) - but he turned me down, saying with some justification that our training as policemen was of much more value to the nation than the need for soldiers who were "two a penny". By December 1939 the need for RAF pilots was so acute that one or two PCs were released for this purpose. I saw a chink in the armour of top brass and applied again - this time with success. I would still be a member of the Met, but would forego pension rights for the period of absence.

My boots were wearing thin, my bicycle was creaking and I handed in my Police uniform with the only regret that I was temporarily leaving a fine Force and a great bunch of chaps.

Chapter Four
Gang Fur A Sudger
(1940-1941)

And some will go sudgering far from their hame.
Bonnie Strathyre

You would think it would be the easiest thing ever to join the Army four months after the start of a major war. Not so. I reported to the Recruiting Office in Galashiels and asked to join the local Regiment, The King's Own Scottish Borderers. They regretted that the KOSB had stopped recruiting "as there were no rifles". "That's a fine way to run a railway", I thought and went home, dejected. However, help was at hand - it's not *what* you know, it's *who* you know that counts. Our near neighbour in Melrose was Colonel McLaren, a distinguished retired KOSB officer who was the Recruiting Officer for the area. (His son, Duncan, died gallantly in Burma in command of the 2nd Battalion KOSB). The Colonel soon reported that The London Scottish had vacancies so I checked in again at the Volunteer Hall in Gala and after a cursory medical by our own Melrose doctor received the King's shilling early in 1940.

It was something of a disappointment to be directed back to London again, but the faithful Waverley Line took me back to St Pancras - this time by Government Warrant - thence to report to the well known Buckingham Gate HQ of The Scottish, just a stone's throw from the old nick at Gerald Road. In that cavernous building a draft was forming, some volunteers, some conscripts, and after the minimum of paperwork we were taken by

"Wha sunk the bloody Emden?"

train to Pinner near Harrow to join the 2nd Battalion London Scottish. (I little thought that 30 years later I would be back at Buckingham Gate as Inspecting Officer).

In 1938 the Territorial Army had been doubled, each unit throwing off another and being obliged to shed a fair share of its officers and NCOs for the purpose. The 2nd Battalion shared all the pride of a Regiment which had gained a magnificent reputation in the South African and 1914-18 wars. My father used to tell how the troops in France were very jealous of the publicity which invariably surrounded the exploits of The Scottish. The Jocks would say: "Wha sunk the bloody Emden?" "The London Scottish of course."'

We raw recruits were soon made aware of this pride which

was very evident among our NCOs who were in the main London businessmen from middle-management who had joined the Terriers pre-war, and quickly learned to be proficient soldiers. Our long-suffering Sergeant Butt was a pure Cockney but he wore his kilt with a swagger and RSM Kelly was soon to be held in awed admiration. The officers looked splendid in their hodden grey uniform. I knew a few of them from pre-war rugby encounters, and when I went in for my medical, wearing only a towel round my waist, I realised that the Medical Officer facing me was R.O. Murray, the Cambridge University and Scotland hooker. He looked up and said; "Aren't you the Coutts who played for the Met Police?" There followed an animated Rugby chat and precious little medical examination.

The Recruit Company was billeted in private houses which had been requisitioned. We slept on palliasses filled with straw, about six to a room. We really were a Heinz variety. On one side of me was Donald Morrison, a Fettesian and double-first from Oxford, on the other Jock McLarty, a Glasgow keelie, whom even I found hard to understand. The dining hall was in a manor house nearby. The first meal on arrival was kippers - but unfortunately the QM's store was right out of cutlery for the new intake so we just had to eat them with our fingers. Of the countless improvements which have taken place in the Army during my 40 years the creation of the Army Catering Corps was undoubtedly No.1. Until they were formed in 1942, the grub, cooked by regimental cooks, was appalling. If Superintendent Honour thought that I had joined the Army for fame and fortune - as he suggested - he was a long way off the mark! The first pay day was no surprise either - two bob a day, 14/- a week with deductions of 3/6d, which included a voluntary allotment of half-a-crown back to the manse, making a grand total of 10/6d a week or $52^1/_2$ pence in today's money. Yet it ran to an ounce of pipe tobacco a week and at least one good night out in the pub. By this time the sensible battle dress had been issued and it stood the test for many years to come. On each shoulder we had a hodden grey patch with a blue thistle superimposed and, underneath, the Bow Bells sign of the 47th (Second London) Infantry Division. (The

1st London Scottish were in the Black Cat 56th Division which subsequently saw admirable service in Italy). We were encouraged to buy - from Hobson's in London - a service dress jacket and hodden grey kilt. These were second hand, first war, stocks and, by an astonishing coincidence, my jacket still had the Divisional signs of the 52nd Lowland Division with which I was later to spend a large part of my service. My parents must have stumped up for this finery, but it was dirt cheap and it was certainly good for morale to have a change for walking out.

There were no barrack squares in Pinner so our training was carried out in suburban back streets, devoid of traffic because of the petrol shortage. The drill, weapon training, P.T. etc came easily, and the discipline was more relaxed than the Police. After a few weeks we were more or less up to 50% of the Trained Soldier standard nowadays. Suddenly, the tempo of life changed. Germany invaded Norway and the sorry saga of events leading up to Dunkirk unfolded. The prospect of an invasion of Britain suddenly became very possible and our weapon training took on a new reality. The weapon in question was the P14 rifle, a Canadian First War affair with a very awkward magazine, which only held 5 rounds, and had a brute of a bolt action. Nevertheless, we were part of an active Division and from this point on we were rushed all over East Anglia, for the most part guarding R.A.F. aerodromes which were reckoned to be a prime target for bombing or parachutists. During this phase the Recruit Company were stationed in a good hutted camp at Epping; one of the companies nearby was bombed and suffered casualties. The guarding of R.A.F. Stations was by no means an unpopular duty as there were lovely ladies of the Womens Royal Air Force in fair numbers - and they took a liking to the kilt. During the period of the Dunkirk evacuation I reckon we must have moved at least a dozen times. The Army was clearly in disarray, and 47 Div was very low in the pecking order. The only time we settled for any recognisable period was in Cambridge where we mounted a ceremonial guard on the Post Office. In off-duty hours a visit to King's College Chapel and kilted punting on the Backs were pleasant diversions.

Next, the Battalion was banished to the Midlands into quite the worst camp of all time at Rugeley in Staffordshire. Sir William Deedes, the former Editor of *The Daily Telegraph*, confirmed this in a 1990 article. He was an officer in the same Brigade. The entire Brigade was in white bell tents on a bare hillside which was an industrial slag heap. The Luftwaffe could have had a field day. After a few excruciating days sanity prevailed and we were moved to the delightful Shugborough Hall, home of the Earl of Lichfield, where the parkland provided adequate camouflage and a pleasing camp site.

Everyone's thoughts now turned to defeating the Hun if he dared to attack Britain. Churchill's speeches and the R.A.F.'s brilliant Battle of Britain successes had us all on our toes and eager to do our bit. If the German tanks ever got ashore we had at that time practically no guns capable of stopping them. But necessity is the mother of invention. Each Battalion formed a Tank Hunting Platoon which was equipped with push bicycles - brand new they were, right out of the factory at Brum. How do you knock out a tank with a bike? 'Seasy. The bikes gave the necessary mobility to get into a position to ambush the tanks - a defile or a narrow street. The weakest part of a tank is its engine, particularly the air intake, and the means of attack was the so-called Molotov cocktail - a lethal mixture of petrol and adhesive oil. These, with a lighted fuse, could brew up a tank nicely. Needless to say, there was no shortage of volunteers for this new-style guerilla warfare. The oldest joke in the Army is "Anyone here ride a bike?" when the Sergeant wanted fatiguemen to dig latrines. The Platoon was soon a going concern with 2885443 Private Coutts F. H. and sundry other Good Time Charlies culled from the whole Battalion. The Platoon Commander was Ian MacKenzie, the genial scrum half of The London Scottish and a purveyor of sherry wine.

In the Army you don't just ride a bike, you have to do it by numbers. What fun we had, falling in, in straight lines and obeying Cavalry orders like: "Half Sections Right - Walk march" "Prepare to mount" "Mount" Wobble, wobble, wobble. It wasn't long before the next move was ordered - to South Wales.

The Tank Hunting Platoon of course had to go by bike. It took us four days and I don't think I've ever laughed so much in all my life. At lunch-time each day we stopped at a wayside pub and partook of the local cider which was vicious. Fortunately, there was next to no traffic and we stuck to minor roads because our cavalry formations were distinctly eccentric for the first hour after the break.

Our destination was Ham Castle in Llantwit Major, Glamorgan, a gloomy sort of place enlightened only by my selection for a Non Commissioned Officers Cadre. If ever there were a turning point in my life, this was it. Sergeant Rennie, a regular Gordon Highlander, was our instructor and he was an inspiration. One began to see the reason for every lesson and understand, too, what true professionalism meant. Colonel Tommy Lamb, Queen's Own Highlanders, a life-long friend, was on the same course, so Sgt Rennie got a reasonable return for his labours. After the Lord Mayor's Show, it was back to Dining Room Orderly and washing greasy pans with cold water and no soap powder.

At Llantwit, we were bombed for the first time. Returning from the pub, someone said "What's that funny whistling noise?" In one second flat we were all in the ditch, one on top of the other. Another lesson learned.

In the autumn of 1940 we would have to move out of tents and into winter quarters, like the Armies of old. Where would it be this time? Horse boxes! We moved en bloc to Chepstow Racecourse where we slept eight to a horsebox in considerably less comfort than the previous occupants, but there was no shortage of straw. On the way there - no bikes this time - we marched, and when we got to Cardiff we were invited to march through the City headed by the Pipe Band. The streets were lined with cheering spectators, and one dear old lady pressed a packet of fags into my palm on its rifle butt. Sgt Rennie would not have approved.

Chepstow in Monmouthshire gave The Scottish a great welcome. Everyone had a home to go to for baths and meals and the Till family were my hosts. The Bn Concert Party put on an uproarious Pantomime at Christmas and in no time we had put together a good rugby team. With that rascal Trevor Thom many afternoons were spent goal-kicking. Every Saturday we piled into the back of a 3-tonner and went to play one of the Valley XVs which were still going strong as the miners were vital to the war effort and reserved. We had some memorable battles - Usk, Abertillery, Cymbran, Pontypool and so on. They were all good teams and we were pushed to hold them. Later we were invited to play none other than the great Cardiff on the famous Arms Park ground. There had been a heavy air raid the night before and the pitch was littered with particles of glass. The iodine bottle was in full use after a great match. Wilfred Wooller who was with the local anti-aircraft Artillery was a notable member of the Cardiff team. They must have entertained us well; on the way back Dusty Millar, an aristocratic Private soldier louped a dyke to spring a leak and fell 30 ft on to a railway line. He was feeling no pain and joined in the general hilarity.

We did train hard for war too, and took part in regular exercises on the Brecon Beacons. Active service seemed as remote as ever for a Battalion which was itching to show its paces. In the spring of '41 we were at least moved to the front line of the anti-invasion defences - to Brighton where we were billeted in the prestigious girls' school, Roedean. The bell in each room which invited us to "Ring if you require a mistress in the night" sadly brought no response. Each morning on muster parade we presented arms to Hitler across the channel. The beach defences were gaining in strength each day, and we helped to improve them and trained realistically on the lovely Sussex Downs. A good report on the NCOs cadre brought its reward and I was now Lance Corporal Coutts, the hardest rank in the Army, particularly when one's charges were good friends of a year's standing. The promotion party went on a little too long in Brighton and we were all put on a "fizzer", Army Form 252, by the Guard Commander for being a few minutes late back to camp. My visions of rapid promotion took an overnight slump, but the Company Commander on orders the next day was the jovial Major "Hearty" Henderson and he let us off with a wigging.

There were obviously a large number of potential officers in the Battalion, and although we all wanted to stick together as a combatant unit, we feared that the Powers-That-Be would use us as a training and officer-producing unit. Our fears were justified for in due course batches of potential officers were put before a selection board. My turn came and I was persuaded that it would be unpatriotic to resist. The initial interview was with the Commanding Officer, Lieutenant Colonel Maxwell, who later became our Chief Staff Officer in 52 Div, and after the war, head of the London Passenger Transport Board. Supported by one or two regimental officers, he seemed satisfied and the next stage was interview by the Brigadier of which I have absolutely no recollection whatsoever. Thirty of us were selected in that batch. After a few days leave we were to report to the 167 Officer Cadet Training Unit at Malvern in Worcestershire.

The camp at Malvern Wells had been newly knocked together and was comfortable enough by the standards of the day - six to a room in double bunks. My room mates were all London Scottish from the 2nd Bn - Andy Anderson, who had been an outstanding Motor Transport NCO in the Bn and later first editor of the Soldier magazine in Brussels and editor of the *Daily Record* in Glasgow, Douglas Ramsay, "Scratcher" Elliot ("Scratcher" was our name for bed, or "the pit", and he loved it), Dickie Bird with gigolo moustaches and Iain Alexander. The authorities made the crass error of putting all 30 London Scots in the same Company and we simply took the show over. The staff were only fair to middling; some of the lecturers were charming "re-treads" (retired officers, re-employed), but the tactical training was years out of date. The scandalous run-down of the Forces in the 1920's and 30's had taken its toll. We actually spent days constructing a First War trench system, which would have done credit to the Battle of the Somme. There was too much drill and not enough weapon training, minor tactics and leadership training, but as the minor tactics for World War II had not yet evolved it was perhaps just as well. There was a good deal of physical training and we flogged up and down the Malvern Hills till we knew every nook and cranny.

It had recently been ruled that all officers should be able to ride a motor bike so we were let loose in a field under instruction. It was surprising how many officer cadets hadn't the ability to perform this simple task, and it was just as well they were in a field with a soft landing.

Once again the local people were very welcoming. We had no baths in the camp so we were allocated in pairs to families in the town. Duggie Ramsay and I went every week to the Pilkingtons (glass makers), where we were met by the butler with two gleaming white towels over his arm. We then removed our Army boots and walked in our socks to the most glamorous bathroom. Once we were cleansed we were ushered in to the lady of the house to enjoy a glass or two of delicious sherry.

One evening about six of us were walking down the road to our local, "The White Swan", all in the kilt, arrogant as you like when, coming the other way, was a group of nuns. After we had passed, Andy said: "I don't mind you chatting up the girls, Frank, but I draw the line at nuns. That end one definitely winked at you." We stopped and turned round. They too had stopped and one came forward. She was Barbara Bryce-Buchanan, an "old flame" from Milngavie. She told me she was blissfully happy in an Anglican seminary. You can be sure I had my leg pulled over that. Also, over an incident in an exercise when the Section I was temporarily commanding was accused by an old lady of eating spring onions out of her garden. As Section Commander I had to take the rap. The punishment was just: "Go back to the old lady tonight in walking out uniform and apologise." She was absolutely charmed and gave me a delicious tea.

It was a three months course and it gradually became clear that, barring disasters, we would be passing out soon as commissioned officers. There were a few disasters for some. The dreaded initials "R.T.U." (Returned To Unit) were frequently bandied about by the instructors and some cadets fell by the wayside.

Eventually the great day came when we were invited to bid for our Regiments - three choices. It was an easy choice for me: 1) KOSB, 2) Royal Scots, 3) Gordon Highlanders, the parent

Regiment of The Scottish. I guess that Colonel McLaren had been at work behind the scenes and my number one choice came up - another landmark in my life. Nearly everyone seemed to be satisfied. Andy went to his beloved Gordons, Duggie to The Lovat Scouts, and so on. Then the uniform wallahs descended; in the case of the Scottish Regiments, Messrs William Anderson of George Street, Edinburgh, the beginning of a happy association. We were fitted out for our service jackets, trews and other accoutrements, a proud day.

In the final drill competition I was delighted to pip a Coldstream Guardsman for first place and the next day we passed out with valedictory good wishes from the Commandant. Homeward bound, we wore our regimental uniforms with aplomb. At Carlisle station I suddenly realised that a soldier had saluted me. No British soldier ever received a smarter or more grateful acknowledgement from a "one pipper".

Chapter Five
All The Blue Bonnets
(1941-1944)

March! March! Ettrick and Teviotdale!
Why the deil dinna ye march forward in order?
March! March! Eskdale and Liddesdale
All the Blue Bonnets are over the Border.
Sir Walter Scott

Ravensdowne Barracks in Berwick-Upon-Tweed is the oldest occupied barracks in Britain. It has been the home of the 25th of Foot, The King's Own Scottish Borderers since 1881 after an unseemly wrangle with the War Office who wanted to base the Regiment in York. This proposal was anathema to the officers and men of a Scottish regiment which had been raised by beat of drum in the City of Edinburgh by David, 6th Earl of Leven in 1689 for the defence of the city. Today, 302 years later, the KOSB are one of only six Regiments of the Line which have retained their identity completely unchanged since their formation (see Postscript).

We are sometimes teased by other Scottish Regiments for having our Headquarters 'in England', but Berwick is rather a special place. Having survived for centuries being pounded by the English and Scots in turn and having been governed by both, it is now pleasingly neutral. The KOSB barracks and the T.A. Centre of the Royal Northumberland Fusiliers stand side by side and the Wallace Green Church of Scotland and the Church of England are just across the way. The Borderers have the Freedom of the Royal Burgh (1947) and are always made most welcome.

From Berwick the Regimental recruiting area spreads west-wards - across the six counties of the Scottish border to Stranraer 192 miles away, through Berwickshire, Selkirkshire, Dumfries-shire, the Stewartry of Kirkcudbright and Wigtownshire. It is a huge area where the communications are poor and run from north to south, not from east to west. The difference in character between the eastern and western counties is very real - Mosspaul between Hawick and Langholm is more than a physical barrier! More anon.

The task of the Depot was of course to man the seven Battalions of The Regiment with trained soldiers. The 1st Battalion had just taken part in the Dunkirk evacuation as part of General Montgomery's 3rd Infantry Division, the 2nd Battalion had been in India for years and would shortly play a gallant part in the Burma campaign. The 4th and 5th Battalions had just taken part in the 2nd British Expeditionary Force, known irreverently to the Jocks as "The Cook's Tour", had been evacuated from Cherbourg, losing most of their transport but not their weapons, and were now stationed with the rest of the 52nd (Lowland) Division in East Lothian. The 6th and 7th Battalions were in the 15th Scottish Division "somewhere in East Anglia". The 7th were later to become an airborne Battalion and were to play a prominent part in the Battle of Arnhem. The 9th was a Holding Battalion, composed mainly of older soldiers, and they were employed on home defence duties.

The barracks itself was only geared to accommodate little more than a company or so, and a well-built militia hutted camp had been quickly erected to the north of the town on the cliffs at Magdalene Fields, adjacent to the ranges. It was like returning to school again. We were courteously welcomed by Colonel Anderson, the C.O., and allocated duties with the training platoons. The N.C.O.s did the majority of the instructional duties and the new boys spent most of their time finding their feet and getting to know people. Some of the training proved that we still had a long way to go. A wireless class was practising in groups on the square. "Hullo l. Hullo l. How do you hear me? How do you hear me?" droned the operators over and over again, until finally from the other end of the square came the exasperated bellow "Ah cannae hear ye, but ah can effing see ye."

Fortunately, there was a more active role for the subalterns. A German submarine had recently landed a spy at Spey Bay in Banffshire so anti-submarine patrols had to be mounted all round the coasts. Each night we set off on motor cycles to site six man look-outs all along the cliffs by Marshall Meadows Bay. It was a most improbable place for a landing but we felt we were doing something positive for the war. It was summertime and a delightful experience - but tiring. Without a reasonable amount of sleep, efficiency drops fairly rapidly, a lesson soldiers are constantly re-learning.

There was insufficient accommodation in camp, so the novices were billeted in the Avenue Hotel hard by the Scots Gate. The manageress was very strict; we had to be in by 11 o'clock. We complied dutifully, but as our bedroom window led straight out on to the famous Berwick walls, we went straight out again.

We were itching to get away to our Battalions, particularly as the Captain in charge of us was the one officer who, over a long period of years, I found to be quite impossible. He was a regular officer, English, ambitious beyond his abilities, totally humourless and he spoke to the men as though they were dirt. No names, no pack drill. I was overjoyed to be posted to the 4th (Border) Battalion, our local T.A. Battalion in the Eastern Borders - no doubt due, once again, to You Know Who.

Not many officers of the British Army can have reported for their first duty at Fushiebridge Station, a minuscule stop on the Waverley line just south of Dalkeith. There I was deposited with a kit bag and a rugger bag, and there to greet me was a smiling Borderer with the best cap badge in the Army and a one-ton truck. Our destination was Preston Hall, Pathhead, the home of the Callender family, where the Battalion was under canvas. I knew several of the officers and was given a grand welcome, though I thought the C.O. a bit gruff: "Thank God you're here

- it's taken a helluva lot of correspondence to get you". This was Lt Col "Chokra" Kelly, quite a character. After the war he stood as a Labour candidate for Parliament and lost, so he settled for growing heathers in beautiful Moniaive. It was Chokra and his wife who first gave me the idea that I might, if worthy, stay in the regular Army. In a T.A. Battalion, regular soldiers were usually referred to as "bloody regulars", in a fairly friendly way. About six months later Chokra and his lady invited me out to dinner at the Red Lion Hotel in Stirling and it dawned on me that the Army was really very civilised.

But I digress. The 4th Battalion was a remarkable institution. It had a fine reputation in the First War in France, Gallipoli, and Palestine and it had kept going against the odds in between the wars, starved of cash and often ridiculed. There was unstinting support from the three Lords Lieutenant, The Earl of Home (father of Sir Alec), Chairman of the T.A. Association, the Duke of Buccleuch, its Honorary Colonel, and Major Scott Plummer. Colonel "Pondo" Jackson of Glen Douglas, Jedburgh, and Lt Col Malcolm Thorburn of Melrose, were towers of strength, but the real dynamo behind the 4th was the unique Jack Hankey, the regular Adjutant from Darnick who, for a generation, was "Mr KOSB" in the Borders. He galvanised the duplication of the Battalion in the winter of 1938/9, assisted by the Master of Napier who subsequently commanded the 6th Battalion as Lord Napier and Ettrick. Jack knew practically every soldier in both the 4th and the 6th by name and where they came from. It was he who organised the huge 1939 camp at Dreghorn in Edinburgh where the Regiment had marched proudly down Princes Street as Freemen to mark the 250th anniversary of their foundation past their Colonel-in-Chief, H.R.H. the Duchess of Gloucester. The Duchess, now Princess Alice, is still our Colonel-in-Chief after 54 years, a record second only to Queen Elizabeth The Queen Mother as Colonel-in-Chief of The Black Watch.

The essence of the 4th Battalion was that they were all volunteers and they came from fine Border stock, honed on centuries of Border warfare on the marches and hard work as farmers or millworkers. They were the salt of the earth and deserved the best of officers, which they had.

It would interrupt the flow of my narrative to mention them all here but I have set down their names in an appendix. Five years is a long time for a group of people to live and work together in close proximity and we all became very close friends. The Mess was always a very happy place and we were to discover to our dismay that this was not always so in other Regiments and Battalions. The only time I was conscious of dodging the C.O. was when he was looking for a bridge partner.

Every soldier should consider his unit *the best*. We had every reason to believe that this was so.

I was posted to 'B' Company - the Hawick company, and thought I'd joined the Foreign Legion. I couldn't understand a word they were saying! "Yow and mei" for "you and me" etc, but it didn't take long to get the hang of it. They say that the best commands in the Army are a Platoon, a Battalion and a Division. I was fortunate to have command of a platoon, with interruptions, for the next 4 years and was privileged to know upwards of a 100 Borderers better than their mothers knew them.

One of the most unwelcome of an officer's duties in war-time was the censorship of the soldiers' mail. I suppose it was necessary for security, but I found it degrading and embarrassing. It really is the ultimate loss of freedom when a chap can't pour out his heart to his wife, sweetheart or mother without a nosey Platoon Commander reading every word of it. If the system had one saving grace it was that it built up a certain trust between officers and men because officers never, never discussed the contents of censored letters between each other. However, after all these years perhaps I could be permitted to pass on this gem:

> 4th KOSB
> Somewhere in Scotland
> Dear Mother,
> It's a buger. I was pised again last night.
> Please send £5 and the *Christian Herald*.
> Your loving son
> > Jock

One of the well tried methods of getting to know the troops was, of course, through the medium of sport where officers and soldiers could always meet on an equal footing. Most of my platoon played rugby or were sympathetic to it, so that was easy, but soccer is the soldiers' real game (and it so much easier to organise under wartime conditions). I would dearly have loved to have had a knowledge of soccer, sufficient at least to referee a match intelligently. Another essential qualification for a Platoon Commander would be the ability to sit down and play the piano at a Company "Smoker". Budding Field Marshals take note.

A subaltern's duties were very many and varied. There was no Roman Catholic officer in the Battalion so the Orderly Officer had to march the R.C.s to church. When we reached the chapel "wee Mid", Sgt Middlemiss (who was cruelly killed by a German Reigel mine which he was defusing) chuckled to me, knowing full well I was a son of the manse: "Come on in, Sir, and I'll show you the ropes". So began my ecumenical life. Church parades were compulsory in those days - they didn't do anyone any harm and probably did some a lot of good, though the preparations and inspections were overdone. We had a fine Pipe Band under Pipe Major Jimmy Bunyan - with whom I was often privileged to play - and his son, Davie, and his grandson, Drew, the best piper of the lot. The Military Band was the former Galashiels Silver Band who joined up to a man under the baton of Mr Amos. The pipers by tradition wore the Buccleuch tartan and the Battalion made a brave sight as they swung up the A68 to Cranston Church, where our Padre, Ronnie Selby Wright, the Prince of Padres and later the Radio Padre, gave us something to think about and shook a few consciences.

The first interruption to the command of a platoon was a 155 Brigade Young Officers course. The 7th/9th (The Dandy Ninth) Bn The Royal Scots were at Archerfield House, Dirleton, and the 5th (Dumfries and Galloway) Bn of the KOSB at Gosford so we met daily in Aberlady. The course consisted of minor tactics, map-reading and some basic intelligence work, all in the idyllic surroundings of Luffness golf course. We flew for the first time (in a Lysander from MacMerry), met the Brigadier, "Whistling Tom" Grainger-Stewart, and learned to drink gin and tonic in the Golf Inn Aberlady.

Flying was still in its infancy and the Lysander was the first Army/Air co-operation plane, an awkward looking job with one engine and swept back wings. We approached this monster with trepidation and were fed in two at a time, but it wasn't just a joy ride. We had maps and had to spot defensive positions. The problem was I was so scared I sat rigid in case any movement would topple the plane.

The rugger season had started again. It was no push-over getting into the 4th Bn side which was composed of top players from all the Border XV's - rank meant nothing. Throughout the war, even in Germany, we were always able to get together a good side and the only team who could beat us was our own 6th Bn whom we met five times, losing the series in the last match in Schleswig-Holstein - due entirely to their excessive hospitality the night before the match! I could also immodestly add that I had a broken collar bone and had to run the line.

We did a lot of route marches and got to know the back roads of the Lothians well. Light Infantry marching was in vogue, which meant walking 100 paces and then running l00. In the middle of one of these runs, the C.O. would appear from nowhere and shout "Gas!" and the march back to camp had to be completed in respirators. Back at the Guard Room, the piper would break into the regimental march *All the Blue Bonnets are over the Border*, heads would lift high and we'd fall out, laughing and ready for aromatic foot inspection.

A real delight was our initiation to Officers Mess Guest Nights with their superb mixture of tradition, beautiful silver, good fare, fine fellowship, hospitality - and hilarity. After the Pipe Major had played the obligatory pibroch and the three or four pipers had played a couple of sets, followed by toasts to "Our Colonel-in-Chief" and the guests, it was the custom for Donald and Colin Hogg to play round the table. I was invited to join them, and this custom persisted for the next four years, to uproarious applause.

Our winter quarters in 1941/42 were at Alloa in Clackmannanshire, with its friendly folk and delicious ales. Battalion HQ was in the Town Hall and the companies were spread around various halls throughout the town and nearby Sauchie. Chokra had two fetishes; one was fresh air in the barrack rooms and the other was the standard of the mens' food. Two incidents illustrate his eccentricity. In a barrack room he asked the Room Corporal why the window was not open. "It's fixed, shut, Sir" he replied. "I'll damn soon fix it" quoth the C.O. and smashed his walking stick through the pane. Breakfast was always a dreadful meal in the Battalion dining hall and poor Tam Beattie from Selkirk, the Cook Sergeant, had a terrible job to compete with poor rations, inadequate equipment and inexperienced cooks. One morning Chokra was first in the queue, banging his mess tins on the counter and demanding: "Breakfast is late; the men can't work without breakfast". He then went round every table asking for complaints. Everyone complained that the bacon was too fat, so he got up on a table, banged for silence, got down on his knees and in a loud voice prayed: "O, Lord, send us a lean pig". Such events brightened the day and gave us a good laugh.

An Infantry Platoon Commander has the responsibility for the lives of approximately 35 men. First, see that they are happy - fed, housed, clothed with reasonable leisure facilities when possible. Next, they must be trained for war which is an all embracing subject and requires a great deal of preparation and enthusiasm on the officer's part, particularly if he has to keep up the momentum for three long years.

For Platoon training to be effective the minimum requirement would be about 24 men on any working day, 3 sections of 7 and a small Platoon HQ. But assembling 24 men becomes problem No.1. Many agencies are at work against you. First the Sergeant Majors, Regimental and Company, will steal your Platoon Sergeant for Battalion or Company Orderly Sergeant and two or three of your best men for some wretched Guard of Honour. Then there will be two or three skivers on sick parade (the sick, the lame, and the lazy). One or two may be on compassionate (or passionate?) leave, and the doctor will suddenly decide that your company is due for re-vaccination or something which will knock them silly for 24 hours. The obstacles are enormous and it is a real test of determination to overcome them. For a lazy Platoon Commander, they are of course heaven sent!

Once out of barracks you are your own man and away from the demands of routine and the bugle call. In 1941 training aids were in very short supply. There wasn't much ammunition about and we didn't do nearly enough range work. Stripping the Bren down to its component parts becomes boring after a time - and we could all do it blindfold. We did a lot of route marches and small tactical exercises in attack and defence, never withdrawal now. There were very few restrictions on the use of land but we were sensible about crops and parties of soldiers went to the join the land army at harvest time for food supplies were vital to the nation.

The Ochil Hills were nearby. To my dismay the C.O. sent for me. "Coutts, I want you to put on a demonstration on camouflage - the whole Battalion will be there." I didn't know a damn' thing about camouflage, but in the Army there's a pamphlet on everything and I was soon a self-styled expert on Shape, Shine and Shadow. The problem was where to get a place from which 800 men could see and hear. Luckily I found an ideal spot in the hills just behind the village of Menstrie where the Battalion could sit on the hillside and view the "actors" in a field far below. Lugging the batteries for the amplifiers up the hill was the hardest part of it. Soon I was blinding 'em with science.

A Platoon is of course only a cog in a much bigger machine consisting of companies, Battalions and Brigades, all comprising a Division. We had to train at every level, and the higher the level the more the fog of war descended. The first Divisional exercise for me was down in Fife, 52 Div against the Poles as "enemy". They were fierce opponents: the poor devils had so much to fight for. It was a bitter winter, and I will always associate the village of Kingskettle with sentry duty in arctic conditions at 3 o'clock in the morning.

We spent a lot of time in TCVs (Troop Carrying Vehicles)

52nd (Lowland) Divisional Battle School. C.O. Lt Col Jack Lambert RSF (bare-headed). Jack was a professional actor.

practising a phase of war known as 'Advance to Contact'. The Platoon Commander, with map, had the privilege of sitting comfortably beside the driver - but heaven help him if the C.O. found him asleep!

The next interruption to my Platoon life was a course at the GHQ Battle School at Humbleton Camp in Barnard Castle, County Durham. Some bright T.A. officers had persuaded the War Office that our Infantry training needed a revolution as our out-of-date tactics could not complete with the Blitzkreig techniques of the opposition. Everything was brought up to date, taught as a drill and done at the double.

From the time that we paraded in the morning until we flopped into bed (when there wasn't a night scheme) it was double, double, toil and trouble all the time. By this stage in the war the Canadians were with us and they kept us laughing. One of the new fieldcraft movements was the Leopard Crawl. There was snow on the ground and as we inched forward on our knees and elbows a Canuck voice was heard to say "Gee, this is good for the copulation muscles". The Chief Instructor was a brilliant Jew, Lt Col Lionel Wigram. His tactical lectures were fascinating. He was later taunted with being only a theoretician and he took himself off to fight behind enemy lines in Italy, losing his life unnecessarily. Our instructors were the delightful Major Ian Buchanan of the Liverpool Scottish and Captain Charles Burtt, one of my previous officers in the 2nd Bn London Scottish. We battled non-stop over the moors of North Yorkshire, fully equipped for war as a Rifle Platoon and carrying full scales of ammunition, grenades, entrenching tools etc. Competition was keen to avoid being detailed for the hideously heavy Boyes anti-tank rifle. It was a two man load, firing a .5 inch bullet, and with a kick like a mule, it could just penetrate the armour of a light tank. A lot of live ammunition was used by friend and "foe" alike and, sadly, people got killed. But we really felt we were getting somewhere.

To my dismay I was asked at the end of the course to stay on as an instructor in Ian's Platoon so I had to go through the whole performance twice more, but this time without rifle and equipment. One of my students was Chan Blair, later Lt-General Sir Chandos Blair, GOC-in-C Scottish Command, who had just won a fine MC for escaping from Germany to Switzerland. We very nearly wrote each other off by siting a wretched little 2-inch mortar under a tree without noticing that a spindly dead branch was sticking out. The bomb went off in the tree, scattering shrapnel all around us. Unbelievably, we escaped and could only roar with laughter.

It was three months before I got back to the Battalion, with Jock Borthwick my batman, to discover them in Aviemore for the Division had been declared a Mountain Division, presumably as a threat to German-occupied Norway. We had felt somewhat aggrieved that the Highland Division, so wickedly mauled at St Valery, had been preferred for service in North Africa, where they performed brilliantly as usual. This was something of a compensation. It was a fascinating role and has been fully recorded by George Blake in his book *Mountain and Flood*. We were issued with rucksacks, anoraks, string vests, skis and all sorts of new and strange equipment. Adam Wyllie, the QM, and John Tully his "RQ", were doing their nut. We took to the hills, and our only transport were mules provided by Indian Pack Transport Companies. The "Johnnies" as the Jocks called the muleteers were very popular and they had an amazing knack with these stubborn brutes. Loading up before dawn was absolute bedlam as some of the mokes, usually carrying ammunition boxes, were guaranteed to kick the traces and run amok. We swore that "Johnnie" could sleep on his feet, leading one mule and holding on to the tail of the one in front.

The Battalion was under canvas on a delightful site by Coylum Bridge on the Rothiemurchus estate. I had been a temporary Captain while on instructional duties at Barnard Castle. When the back pay came through my friends in the Subalterns' Union got to hear about it and blew the lot on a grand night out at the Lynwilg Hotel.

That was a memorable summer of '42, doing what many people in peace-time would consider a splendid holiday. (On reflection I doubt if I would want to carry a 90lb rucksack including a 3-inch mortar bomb up Ben Macdhui for fun). Not so most of the Jocks, who were not impressed and continually

The Anti-Tank Platoon, 4th KOSB, North Berwick 1943

wondered when we were to get into action.

Before the summer was out, I was appointed to command a new Platoon - the Anti-Tank Platoon in Support Company. I was allowed to pick my own NCOs to the fury of the Rifle Company Commanders and we became a very close community for the next 3 years - Sgts Smith, Douglas, McEwan, McNaughton, Richardson and later Scott. We went to Strichen in Aberdeenshire to learn the job from the City of Glasgow Yeomanry who were the Divisional Anti-Tank Regiment and to take over their 2-pounder guns. They were getting 6-pounders, which some months later we took over from them when they got 17-pounders. The 2-pounder was a beautiful little gun, made pre-war to the highest standards - the breech and firing mechanism were things of beauty, but it had a violent muzzle blast which I'm sure has left a lot of ex-servicemen deaf in their old age. It didn't take us long to get the hang of things, including the tactics - you have to learn fast in war - and our Gunner friends were complimentary, feeling, I think, that their precious pieces were in reliable hands. A new vocabulary was opening up in which the buzz words were enfilade and defilade. I never really did discover the difference. The secret of anti-tank tactics was to site your gun so that it could hit the tank side-on where its armour is most vulnerable. The tank v. anti-tank battle escalated continually during the war with the defence (anti-tank), being static, usually holding the whip hand. Now the battle is being fought with guided rocketry.

We returned to Buckie to select our "Gunners" mainly from the Pipe Band and the Rugger team! They did us proud - 51 strong, including our own mechanics from the newly-formed Royal Electrical and Mechanical Engineers, and Carden Lloyd tractors which were a brute to drive with rod steering, but they got us all the way to eastern Germany.

The next move left lasting impressions, for we invaded the tiny village of Maud in Aberdeenshire's Buchan. Its only significance was the weekly auction mart and the fact that it was the railway junction where the train from Aberdeen split into two for Fraserburgh ("The Broch") and Peterhead. We had two companies there - about man for man with the civilian population - and the rest of the Battalion were at Brucklay Castle. What wonderful people they were! They couldn't do enough for us. One of the real characters of the village was "Ma" Smith who gave the farmers their mid-day meal on mart days. In addition, she found time to run a canteen for the boys and to feed the officers. We just handed over our rations and she made far more use of them than any Army cooks. As so often happens, this saint of a woman had an idle, useless husband. He was ailing and the doctor advised him to go and dig the garden and get a good reek of the soil. Ma took him to the garden with the spade and Jim promptly growled: "You dig and I'll sniff". Another personality-to-be in the village was Jack Webster, then a 10-year old schoolboy and now the

Her Royal Highness, The Duchess of Gloucester, Colonel-in-Chief, with the Officers of the 4th (Border) Battalion KOSB at Brucklay Castle, March 1943.
Standing *(L to R): Allan Hill (M.O.), Allan Sherriff, Jock Elliot, Charles Phillips, Ebbe Roede, Dick Ross, Viney Scott, Frank Coutts, Charles Marrow, John Henderson, Ally Ross, Bob Bearpark, Tommy Gray, Adam Wyllie, Frank Findlay (Padre)*
Seated: *Jock Milne Home, Allan Innes, Jim Bennett, Harcourt Rae, Major-General E.N. Broadbent (Colonel of the Regiment), Lt Col W.A.H. Maxwell (Commanding), Her Royal Highness, Horace Davidson, Colonel The Duke of Buccleuch, Donald Hogg, Andrew Stewart, John Henson, Colin Hogg.*

illustrious journalist and TV man. He fell completely under the spell of the Anti-Tank Platoon, and particularly Sgt Jock Gray who was also Pipe Band Sergeant. When we came to leave Maud after many happy months, we marched to Blackdog Ranges in Aberdeen. Jack fell in with us and marched to the first halt in 50 minutes. When we fell in again, I had to say sternly to Jack: "Now you'll have to go home, son". I've never seen a sadder laddie.

During the years 1942 and 1943 the Division trained continuously in mountain warfare and we were seldom off the hills. Unfortunately they were poor years for snow and the specialised ski companies had to make do with heather. General Sir Neil Ritchie, back from North Africa, was our dynamic GOC. Woe betide anyone who was found inside any sort of building on an exercise; we had to learn to live rough and never to use maps greater than $1/_4$ inch to the mile. When it came to the real thing we used buildings constantly and the map scales were enormous! But he was right. He tested the Division out on the two longest exercises ever held in Britain - Goliath I and II, each of three weeks duration. The aim of these exercises was to test 52 Div in its role as a mountain division and the scenario was clearly designed to simulate Norway as closely as possible. For the troops the main test was physical endurance. For the "boffins" at Div HQ there were obviously valuable lessons to be learned in logistics - how to maintain a force of 20,000 men and its vehicles, equipment and ammunition up a single track road before the days of helicopters. The first exercise took the Division right down the Caledonian Canal and up the mountains on both sides of it, then round the corner into Speyside. The second was in Perthshire, finishing on the Forth. There is hardly a corner of the North East of Scotland that doesn't bring back the memory of some exercise activity, grave or gay.

The Commanding Officer of the 4th was now Bobby Maxwell, a jolly extrovert, who liked to see the Jocks comfortable. He loved his shooting or a night out at the greyhounds with Harold Lawrie, and he was very much hoping to be invited to shoot on the Royal Estates at Balmoral. After an exercise which finished at Mar Lodge he told his "O" (Orders) Group "Make certain this place is left spotlessly tidy - we mustn't offend the Monarch". Bobby had served during the lean inter-war years and had been a subaltern for 17 years. During his time in command we were stationed in the Aberdeen area - at Hayton Camp, Aberdeen, the Glen O' Dye Sanatorium in Banchory and latterly Stonehaven. We had a lot of fun playing Rugby in Aberdeen against the Grammar School F.P., University and The Wanderers. Chris Melville, Black Watch, who was our 2nd-in-command and a pre-war Scottish Internationalist and I used to go off to Edinburgh to play representative Rugby for the Army and Scottish Services against England. The Anti-Tank Platoon also spent three very hard weeks training at the Scottish Command Anti-Tank School at North Berwick and we fired regularly at Barry Buddon. I spent long hours in the lighthouse trying to ensure that we didn't hit any fishing boats.

There were some tremendous characters in the 4th Battalion. Nearly everyone had a nickname. The Regimental Sergeant Major was Andrew Beattie from Hawick. He was tiny so he became "Nap" for Napoleon (and a lot of other names too). We had two Norwegian officers, principally as ski instructors. One was called Gdendemsjø, which was impossible to pronounce - so the Jocks just called him "Jimmy Sna'". The other Ebbe Roede, was a first-class Platoon Commander and could swear in the language of the Gorbals with the best of them. Then we had two Canadians, Don Urquhart and Phil Carruthers, who gave sterling service in action. Don was right out of the movies. When battle was joined he became the security guard to the commanding officer, Chris Melville, with Tam Beattie, the cook sergeant, armed to the teeth, in close support. Don was festooned with pistols, grenades and other armaments and he was quite liable to fire shots in the air just to make his point.

If you were looking for the archetypal Borderer it would have to be CSM Jock McTeer, in peace-time the postie from Earlston. One day he was Acting RSM. With pride, he stood with his pace stick at the front of Battalion Headquarters and shouted "Duty Bugler!" The cry went through the camp: "Duty Bugler!" Eventually, wee Kerr arrives, panting. "Sir?" Jock McTeer: (with pipe

Horse play at Banchory 1943. Major General Hakewell-Smith (Sir Hak) with the Sergeants Mess v Officers Mess VII at the Battalion Seven-a-side competition.
L to R: RSM Andrew Beattie, Jimmy Brown, John Tully (RQMS), Jock McTeer ("Bugler, have you got a match?"), Frankie Pook, CSM Fitzpatrick, Bob Bearpark (Groucho), Bobby Maxwell (CO), 'Pipey' (Jimmy Bunyan), GOC, Ally Ross, Jimmy Sna', Harry Cartner, Mark Wells, Allan Hill (M.O.), the cat is reckoned to be 'the meenister', Frank Findlay.

in his mouth) "Bugler, have you got a match?"

Ally Ross's Pioneer Platoon were especially popular - not just because of their social graces, but because they could fix things. Their operational role was to work with explosives and mines. Training on Deeside, they shattered all the windows in the Farquharson ancestral home at Invercauld. In their "Mr Fix-it" role, they were known as "Wimpey's" and were only just dissuaded from painting their trucks yellow which was the trade colour of that firm at the time.

The Allied Forces were now building up and eager to open the Second Front in Europe - under strong pressure from the embattled Russians who were nobly holding the Germans at bay. In the spring of 1944 the whole Division was put through the Combined Operations course at Inveraray, learning how to use assault landing craft and the like on Loch Fyne with live ammunition. There is a certain beach in Argyll where I wouldn't advise anyone to go swimming now-a-days! It must be hotching with duds. In one of the huts in the grounds of Inveraray Castle, Allan Hill, the M.O., was giving the officers their up-to-date jags. "Come and catch me" I taunted Allan and he ran round the room with his syringe poised. Eventually he caught me under a bed. I paid for my foolhardiness. While the Bn was carrying out their tank-cooperation at Langholm and Hoddam, I landed up in Bangour Hospital where (on D-Day!) they removed a pint and a half of pus from my arm.

Fortunately, and to my intense relief, the Battalion had not gone overseas in my short absence, and it looked as though the threat to invade Norway was now only pretence. We were now to be an airborne Division! There is a limit to the length of time a soldier can be prepared for war without actually going into action. "Wolf, wolf" can be taken too far, and in June 1944 the Lowland Division was mighty near that limit. The change of role to airborne was a godsend. We knew damned well that we hadn't got enough troops to invade Norway and this was our chance - probably the last - to get into the war.

First, we put on a huge decoy exercise to convince the Germans that 52 Div was a Corps just about to invade Norway. I'm told that it succeeded. Then we shed most of our mountain gear and sped South to be near the airfields. From the moment that "Monty" broke out of the Normandy beachhead we were to be in support, as air-landed troops, of the airborne operation which was laid on for every obstacle between Normandy and Arnhem. It was a frustrating time for the planners. Chris Melville who had now taken over as C.O. was staff-trained and very good at it. We were now on a Jeep-transport basis and practised continually getting them, and the guns, in and out of Dakotas and Wako gliders which were built like match boxes. Thank goodness we didn't have to go war in them.

After weeks of planning came Arnhem. We were to follow the 1st Airborne Division and land at Deelen airfield once it had been taken. As all the world knows from *A Bridge Too Far* that they never got there. We had the sad task of welcoming back the survivors at Woodhall Spa and other bases in Lincolnshire.

Now at last we were needed in France as an ordinary, well-trained, Infantry Division. One Brigade (157) was already there at the sharp end in Holland, where the Arnhem operation had ground to a halt. The 4th Bn embarked on the *Lady of Mann* at Southampton on the 16th of October. The Embarkation officer was Arthur Nelson KOSB from Melrose; he had seen the Battalion off to France in 1940. This time we wouldn't be back so soon.

Chapter Six
Five More Rivers to Cross
The Scheldt, The Maas, The Rhine, The Weser & The Elbe
(1944-1945)

We shall crack about on the plains of North Germany.
General Montgomery

We landed at Ostend with some difficulty - unopposed, except by sunken shipping - quite close to the front line because the Germans were still fighting a fierce rearguard action in the Breskens pocket on the south bank of the Scheldt. The whole Canadian Corps and most of the 2nd Army's artillery were engaged against them - a very sanguinary affair. We moved in behind them to two peaceful Belgian villages called Vive St Eloi and Vive St Bavon. In the continental fashion the whole battalion was billeted in civilian houses; no argument, the gendarme knocked at the door and pushed in soldiers till the poor house-holder cried halt. We were the first Allied troops they had seen and they treated us as liberators. Indeed, they have done so ever since. Parties of Old Comrades return there regularly and receive a tremendous welcome.

The No.1 priority in the Allied plan at this point was to free the port of Antwerp. The whole of Eisenhower's force was still being maintained across the beaches in Normandy, where the Germans were by no means defeated and were digging in for a winter campaign, supported by Hitler's latest secret weapon, the V bombs, which we wistfully watched heading towards the UK to our nearest and dearest. The Allies had to have a major port well forward - and it had to be Antwerp with its outstanding port facilities. But it was a long way from the sea up the estuary of the Scheldt which was thick with mines and totally dominated by Breskens on the south bank and Flushing on the island of Walcheren, on the north bank, both strongly held by the Germans.

Before launching the reader into battle, it will probably make things easier for the layman if we take a simple look at how an Army is organised in the field. The basic unit of Infantry "at the sharp end" is the Platoon, armed with rifles and machine guns; there are three of these in a Company (100 men), six companies in a Battalion (800 men - four Rifle Companies, a Support Weapons Company and an Administrative Company); three Battalions in a Brigade and three Brigades in a Division (about 20,000). Above that one reaches the dizzy heights of a Corps which commands a flexible number of Divisions. Army Headquarters - in our case was the 2nd Army under General Dempsey, with 21st Army Group under Monty in overall command.

This is an over-simplification and does not take sufficient note of the vital part played by the Royal Artillery, Engineers, Signals and the various administrative corps without which the fighting element of a Division cannot exist. As soon as Breskens had been cleared by the Canadians, the 52nd Lowland Division - the Mountain Division! - was to make a three-pronged attack on Walcheren : 157 Brigade (Glasgow Highlanders and HLI) from the East via Bergen Op Zoom; 156 Brigade (Royal Scots Fusiliers and Cameronians and HLI) across the Scheldt from Terneuzen to the sea dyke between Hoedenskerke and Molenberg in South Beveland directed on Middelburg; 155 Brigade (Royal Scots and KOSB) across the Scheldt from Breskens to Flushing; the Commandos and Royal Marines strongly supported by the Royal Navy making a major assault from the north at West Kapelle.

We had only a few days to prepare for such a major operation. We had made such friends with the good people of St Eloi that the CO asked them if we could use the village as our "firm base" while we were on the continent. They agreed and we left in their safe keeping The Colours, the Officers Mess silver and several inessential boxes of stores. Otherwise, these treasures would have bumped around the rear areas, from battle to battle, taking up precious space in the back of a truck. The Battalion crossed the Dutch frontier at Kleit and entered the utterly devastated area of Breskens. The town was a smashed heap of bricks and matchwood, reeking with the sickly smell of burning and of bodies buried beneath the rubble. The roads had been obliterated. We quickly became accustomed to this sort of scene. The minute the Canadians had cleared the south bank of the estuary, the mine sweepers came in and made ready for our crossing - and a good job they did. Behind them came the armada of assault landing craft, each under the command of a brave Royal Marine.

D-Day for Flushing was dawn on the 1st of November 1944. Nearly the whole battalion attended a service of communion conducted by our Padre, Frank Findlay, later of St Serf's, Goldenacre, in a bombed-out biscuit factory. Those of us who attended kirk regularly were slightly surprised at the sudden upsurge in enthusiasm. Fear can be a great spur to the faith! The attack on Walcheren had been worked out weeks beforehand by specialists from the Royal Navy, The Canadian Army, the British Special Services and the Royal Air Force at a Combined HQ in Bruges. After D-Day in Normandy it was quite the biggest Combined Operation to confront the enemy during World War II. The famous dykes were breached in the first week of October by brilliant precision bombing by the RAF so that the island was completely flooded at high tide. Only the towns and roads on high dykes were above ground. Between the 11th and 31st of October Bomber Command softened up the defences with 4871 tons of bombs delivered in 941 sorties. In addition, during the last three days of October 654 Spitfire sorties and 150 Typhoons were launched against gun positions, Ack-Ack guns and radar sites.

The German defenders were mainly from the 70th Infantry Division, a low-category outfit. Some of the men had internal disorders, having returned from the Eastern front. But there were some particularly tough remnants of the 64th Division, just

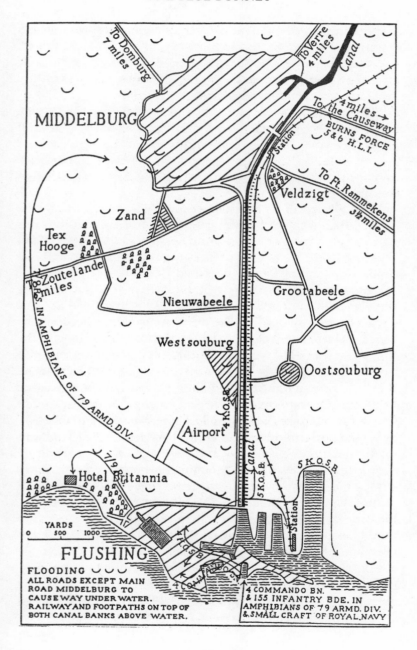

returned from Russia, and the Fortress Gunners were fit and highly competent, backed up by nearly 500 guns of all calibres. All in all, they were a power to be reckoned with, and in this sort of battle all the advantages lie with the defence, aided by stormy seas, mined beaches and boobytraps galore.

The deciding factor, as in all battles, would be morale. One thing was sure. The morale of the Jocks in the 52nd (Lowland) Division was sky-high. We were fit and trained to the nth degree, sick of Hitler and all he stood for, and rarin' to go, to finish the war and get back to Civvy Street. The Boche were on a hiding to nothing.

4 KOSB were in the lead followed by the Dandy Ninth and the 5th KOSB. It was a reasonably calm night at sea but up above all hell was let loose. A massive artillery barrage was homed in on Flushing and the beach defences right up to H-hour. Our thoughts were not for the wretched Germans but for the unfortunate civilians; we were relieved later to find that most of them had concentrated on Middelberg, which we had decided not to bomb anyway because of its architectural beauty. The Germans were not thought to have any tanks in Flushing so the eager Anti-Tank Platoon left their heavy equipment behind and assisted in the assault by forming up the assault craft, helping the RSM with ammunition re-supply and guarding prisoners of war.

The first troop ashore at the very narrow Uncle beach (only about 150 yards wide, and well guarded) was commanded by Alastair Thorburn from Melrose who had left the 4th Bn to join the Commandos. Our 'A' and 'C' Companies were right behind them, with Charles Marrow sounding his hunting horn. Three days of bitter fighting began. Street fighting or FIBUA (Fighting in Built-Up Areas) as it is now called is a notoriously difficult Infantry operation. No sooner had the 4th Battalion passed through the Commandos than they were met by a hail of fire from the main crossroads in the town which was defended by a huge pill-box, code-named "Dover". Meantime, in the surrounding streets, the Borderers were winkling the enemy out house by house, Platoons and companies slowly advanced. As one man or a small group dashed from door to door, they would be covered by fire from another group. The official Divisional History *Mountain and Flood* (p104) described it well: "slinking along the walls of buildings, crawling over roofs as occasion demanded, occasionally (perhaps wriggling, even wading) through the carefully-tended back gardens of Dutch civilians". Often it was necessary to "mousehole" from one house to the next i.e. bash down the wall.

Back on Uncle beach I felt "buckshee" and very concerned for the boys up there, just a few streets away, but I was exhilarated to be in action at last. We had waited so long. Soon the first casualties and POWs began to trickle back to the beachhead. Lance Corporal Willie Brown, brother of "Pye" (Arthur) the Melrose full-back who was in the 6th Bn and a near neighbour at the manse, was the first man to be killed and Jim Bennet, my Company Commander in Support Company, was gravely wounded in the spine. Snipers were a menace, particularly from the top of the cranes in the shipyard. They were finally winkled out by our mountain gunners with their 4.5-inch howitzers which alone had the necessary elevation to reach them - and even then the guns had to be dismantled and re-assembled on the top of a factory.

A Royal Scots Company, under Hugh Rose who won an immediate DSO, put in a superb attack waist deep in water on the Britannia Hotel which turned out to be the German Headquarters. The astonishing feature of this attack was that the entire approach - at 3 am - was through 3 feet of flood water. Imagine The Royals staggering forward waist deep in water - which was running at 5 knots - laden down with machine guns and wireless sets; all encumbered with "Mae West" lifebelts. The attack went in at 0415, at which point "a state of mad chaos prevailed within the Hotel". There was much hand-to-hand fighting, where revolvers were of more use than rifles. Before long the Hotel Britannia was ours - along with the Garrison Commander, Colonel Reinhardt. The Germans lost 50 killed and 600 prisoners between 3 am and breakfast time.

The next phase was for the 5th KOSB under the command of the redoubtable Lt Col "Willow" Turner to push through us, take a vital bridge over the canal (Jim Henderson's Company) and the suburbs. Viney Scott's Mortar Platoon was having a field day with red hot barrels and he was in high spirits when I visited his firing positions in the Martello Tower, surrounded by German equipment and the debris of war. We relieved him of his POWs and marched them back to the beach. "For you the war is over." Stories of the Germans' appalling behaviour in the concentration camps were beginning to trickle through and it might have been tempting for the Jocks to abuse the POWs, but they were such a miserable bunch one could only despise them for being so easily led. A year or two back the Battalion had escorted a bunch of Afrika Corps POWs to their ships on the Clyde en route for Canada; they were an arrogant lot and so different from these cowering, dispirited members of the Herrenvolk.

The Division was gradually closing in on Middelburg, the capital. 156 and 157 Brigades had had a vile time sloshing through South Beveland against heavy opposition. Soon they were to breach the formidable obstacle of the Sloedam, the "cut" between Beveland and Walcheren, and join up with 155 Brigade. Meantime, 4 KOSB were required to advance up the broad canal from Flushing to Middelburg. The banks were only about 20 yards wide and studded with the horrible Shoe mines which under pressure would blow a man's foot off. D Coy (Harcourt Rae) advanced up the left bank, and B Coy (Colin Hogg) up the right. They made reasonable progress, stopping to lift mines, which was the work of The Sappers (Royal Engineers) and Ally Ross's Pioneer Platoon. About halfway up they were held up by heavy fire from pill-boxes defending Middelburg. By this time our General, Hakewell-Smith, ("Sir Hak" to all, though he hadn't yet been knighted) was in touch with the Germans by phone, trying to persuade them to surrender. They were stubborn - but "Hak" had a trick up his sleeve. He launched the Royal Scots in Buffaloes, floating troop carriers, to do a left-flanking attack on Middelburg through the floods. That was too much for the Boche and they put up the white flag of surrender. It was 8th November, seven days since the assault. The 4th Battalion casualties were 3 killed and 65 wounded, many of them to return later in the campaign - a merciful baptism of fire and a tribute to the leadership at every level.

A few days were spent back in Flushing, sussing out Germans in hiding and collaborators. We felt sad to have ruined this busy port and caused so many civilian casualties (36 killed and 175 wounded) but the good burgers of Flushing were eternally grateful to us. We return regularly every year for a service at the 52 Div memorial at Uncle beach and the Burgomeister and many others from Flushing and Vive St Eloi come annually to Hawick for the reunion of the 4 KOSB Old Comrades Association, which has been brilliantly organised for 45 years by Gid Lumsden of the Signal Platoon.

The Battalion returned again across the Scheldt, now being frantically cleared of mines right up to Antwerp, and married up with the Rear Party, transport and heavy equipment in Kleit. A moving service of thanksgiving was held when the CO read out the names of the fallen and the wounded. After a few days of rest and reorganisation the caravanserie set off again in TCVs (Troop Carrying Vehicles), through Antwerp (via the tunnel which was a novelty) and north to Berendrecht. The front line in Holland, after Arnhem, was very untidy. There were still a considerable number of Boche west of the Maas and the British and Canadian Armies had been busy either capturing them or driving them back over the river. Orders for the next phase were not long in coming - but not before one or two bright sparks managed a night out in Antwerp. A party with Chris Melville is always one to be remembered; this one in Antwerp, with one of his wild brothers in the Camerons, riding shotgun on the back of an Antwerp tram, was evidently extra special!

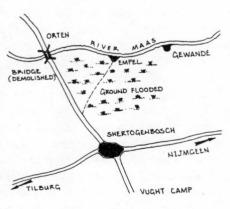

Vught Camp outside 'sHertogenbosch was the next destination, an eerie place which had recently been used by the Germans as a concentration camp. I didn't have a chance to see round the place myself, but one of our officers, Peter White, did. This is an extract from his unpublished book *With the Jocks*, the diary of an Infantry Platoon Commander:

"We walked as in a daze from one monstrous site to another. Here were chambers where people were gassed to death, then for experimental variety where they were locked in and steamed to death. A guard was reported to have said: "You can tell when they are dead when the screaming stops". Near this was a vivisection room where people were trussed on marble operating tables thoughtfully provided with grooves to drain off the blood. Six-inch iron spikes formed a carpet with a possible use we shuddered to think about. Then there were the more orthodox tortures of thumb-screws, racks for stretching and solitary confinement cells and other horrors we could only guess the use of. Some of the confinement cells were small brick structures the size of dog kennels in which the victim was doubled up to fit in. Outside stood a gibbet with a well worn noose. Beside the gibbet stood a crematorium...."

Peter was a South African who had joined our Army voluntarily, despite strong pacifist leanings. Diaries were strictly *verboten*, but Peter kept his on scraps of paper and sent them home to his father. I recently sent the diaries to the Military History lecturer at the Royal Military Academy Sandhurst and he described them as the best record he had seen of a front-line Platoon Commander in war. Peter's Platoon was 37 strong when he took over in Flushing. By the time we reached Bremen, only four of the original Platoon remained and yet our casualties were not high by First War standards. Although quiet and reserved Peter himself was a most gallant officer. After the war he became a professional artist and picture-restorer.

From this base the 4th Bn had to take over from The Lake Superior Regiment a huge stretch of the Maas in front of 'sHertogenbosch. The River Maas is nearly 300 metres wide at this point and a considerable defensive obstacle, so a 4-mile front was a tall order for an "ordinary" Infantry Battalion equipped only with the inadequate 18 wireless set. (The Canadians were a motorised Bn and had the much stronger 19 and 22 sets). The Germans dominated the area from a town called Orten on the east bank and a huge fort with the Foreign Legion-type name of Creveceur. A fifth, composite, Rifle Company was formed from the two strong Mortar and Anti Tank Platoons so Viney and I were teamed up as usual.

Our riverine defences were concentrated in two tiny hamlets on the raised banks of the river, Empel and Gewande. (There's a motorway running through Empel now!) Any daytime movement at all was punished by heavy mortar fire, the underfoot conditions were appalling and, to make matters worse, some nasty collaborators were on the loose cutting signal cables, giving John Henderson our conscientious Signal Officer all sorts of headaches. To give the Jerries their due they crossed the river a good deal more than we did, and one of their patrols killed dear Willie Lees from Selkirk, a superb Sergeant and a fine centre threequarter. Several Germans were killed and prisoners taken, giving valuable information after skilful interrogation by German-speaking Intelligence officers.

If street-fighting is the most difficult infantry operation then patrolling is the most dangerous, and requires the most guts. When two armies confront each other they must "dominate the battlefield," know what the other fellow is up to. There are three types of patrol: Recce - to get information, Fighting - to inflict casualties, and Standing - to look and listen. We were involved in all three on the lonely freezing banks of the River Maas in November and December 1944. It requires a lot of courage to be brave in the still of the night when a Verey light goes up and you stand rigid, pretending to look like a bush. Give me a full frontal assault behind the Divisional Artillery any day rather than a night patrol in No Man's Land.

We were convinced that the Germans were using canal barges in the middle of the river as observation posts so the Anti-Tank

Platoon came into its own at last and set about sinking them -
unorthodox, successful and satisfying, and, surprisingly, bringing no response which probably signified: "You're wasting your
ammo - Heil Hitler!"

On another occasion it was different. Peter White again:
"On this particular trip forward to Empel, Frank Coutts
and I had to get the guns ready for firing early in the
morning.... We had previously located the target on an
earlier afternoon with the aid of the sniper section and
their telescope situated in the attic of the house. We were
up there a considerable time peering through a hole in the
tiles. Unfortunately, soon after we had spotted some
enemy movement on the opposite bank over the swirling
muddy waters of the River Maas, they must have seen
some movement of ours. Five mortar bombs straddled our
hide-out with amazing accuracy, one landing with a crash
of tiles and clouds of dust right on the attic roof. Nobody
was hit but we all made a dash for the ladder. Frank's
massive frame shook the attic as he thundered down the
flimsy ladder and he had nearly reached the bottom when
he yelled out "Christ!" in pain as he was stunned by a
heavy crack on the head. A sniper's voice from above
remarked: "You couldn't be righter, Sir. Christ it is". The
heavy vibration had dislodged a painted plaster effigy, so
common in this Catholic part of Holland..."

This thoroughly unpleasant defensive battle lasted for nearly
a month. On St Andrew's Night, 30th November, we gave the
Hun in Orten an absolute pasting - everything from Viney's
Mortars up to the Divisional Artillery, as a signal of our
indignation at being denied our customary St Andrew's Night
celebrations in the Battalion.

Shortly after, we had a visit from the great "Monty" himself.
About 100 officers from the Brigade were assembled in a hall
behind the line and he spoke to us for about half-an-hour. I didn't
meet him until many years later (Chap IX). On this occasion he
didn't impress us younger officers. Of course he had done a
marvellous job and his confidence (arrogance?) was inspiring,

but he dismissed our Walcheren losses as trifling. This hurt; they were our chums. Looking ahead he said he had "a little job for you to do". Ominous.

Once the Great Man had spoken things of course began to happen. We handed over the line to The Canadians again, moved back to Vught, and then drove half the length of Holland to cross the second of our five rivers, the Maas, by Bailey Bridge at Maastricht. God bless Mr Bailey, we'd never have won the war without him!

The Division was now in General Sir Brian Horrocks' ("Jorrocks") famous 30th Corps along with the Guards Armoured Division, the 7th Armoured Division ("The Desert Rats") and the 43rd (Wessex) Division. They had punched over the Maas and were now holding a rather uneasy line between the German frontier near Geilenkirchen and the Dutch town of Roermond. Monty's "little job of work" was to be an armoured/ infantry thrust up to the River Roer behind Heinsberg - apparently a necessary preliminary to our advance to the Rhine. This operation, under the code-name of "Shears" was planned for 16th December, but the ground was too wet for the tanks and it was postponed.

Meantime, we had to go into the line for nearly a month to relieve the 43rd (Wessex) and The Guards. Once again it was a very extended front, through several German villages - Kreuzrath, Birgden and Waldenrath. The opposition - 15th Panzergrenadier Division - were just a few hundred yards away and life had developed very much into trench warfare 1914-18 style. Well, that's being unfair to the Old Contemptibles. At least we were based mainly in buildings in small villages where, in daylight, we could observe the enemy with ease and enjoy some of the comforts of life. The snag was that there were only 6 hours of daylight, so that for 18 hours we had to man slit trenches round the perimeter of the houses and farms. Two hours "on" and four "off" was the normal "stag" (sentry duty), but constant alarms such as mortar and shell fire, the rip of a German "Spandau" machine gun and the interminable crackle of the wireless set meant that there was precious little sleep for anyone. The weather was atrocious and a great deal of the time we had to "stand to" for 24 hours at a time. The Anti-Tank guns were well forward and we could hear the rumble of the German self-propelled guns, but they never appeared. We celebrated Christmas in the line. The Germans sang carols ("Stille Nacht" etc) but we weren't tempted into fraternisation as in the First War. We were sick of them and gave them a good stonk from the Artillery. They went on singing - I guess they were fu'. Enter, in this operation, a notorious 4 KOSB character called "Pinkie". He was the German horse who, with Teutonic regularity, brought up the Heines' rations at exactly the same time every night; clippety-clop, clippety-clop, in the still frosty moonlight. Now, most Borderers are horse-lovers but war is total and eventually we had to do something about it. Poor Pinkie got an artillery shoot all to himself - no more clippety-clop. About the same time wee Tam Murray of the Anti-Tank Platoon obliged the Gunners by disposing of a windmill which was being used as an Observation Post.

To show that they were still very much in the war, the Boche put in a strong attack on the 5th KOSB to our left in two villages called Vintelen and Kievelburg. We could do little to help as it was a very foggy morning and we were being continuously shelled anyway. But the Doon-Hamers ("Ah'm gaein' doon hame tae Dumfries") needed no help. They saw them off with 30 Germans killed and 100 taken prisoner.

The intention was that we should now come out of the line for New Year. We did - relieved by the Fusil-Jocks - but I think we'd rather have stayed because the Germans had just launched the Ardennes offensive immediately to the south of us and alarms and excursions were very much the order of the day and night. The weather cleared to reveal some fascinating air battles before that dangerous episode of the war - Hitler's last fling in the West - was concluded so successfully by the Americans. Then back into the line again at Tripsrath and Hocheide Woods, just north of Geilenkirchen - another dose of "stand-to" at dusk and "stand-down" at dawn when the rum ration came round. What nectar! It went right down to your boots and back again.

At Hocheide some of our chaps at Bn HQ, mainly pipers, batmen and regimental policemen, were laying a minefield with the Sappers. Something went wrong and 2500 anti-tank mines went off instantaneously; 17 Borderers and 30 Sappers perished without trace - a humbling example of the futility of war. Winter had now arrived with a vengeance and we pulled out of Geilenkirchen in a blizzard. This was the kind of weather Monty had wanted for his "little job" - now code-named "Blackcock" and under command of our old General, Neil Ritchie and XII Corps. It was our first experience of armoured warfare and the Jocks' eyes boggled at the array of tanks, Kangaroos (armoured troop carriers), Flails (for mine clearance), Flamethrowers and the like - all camouflaged white (and we looked a bit stupid when the thaw came in).

The 7th Armoured, principally The Queens Regiment, took the brunt by breaking through at Susteren. The gallant Sappers had to build a Bailey under fire over and over again. The 4th Battalion poured across it in quick time in our lengthy armoured column and swung deep in behind the enemy's lines directed on Koningsbosche which housed a German battalion. A sharp action took place and the enemy withdrew, but we were constantly reminded that we were now within range of the infamous Siegfried line and its heavy guns, which hampered our advance the whole time. The Germans were particularly skilled with their self-propelled 88mm guns which prowled ahead of us constantly in hull-down positions, far more powerful than our puny 6-pounders. At dusk on 20th January one of them hit Viney Scott when he and I were returning from an "O" Group. He died in the Regimental Aid Post shortly after in Allan Hill's hands. The Mortar Platoon were shattered, and so were all of us; a bright light had gone out.

That night we pressed on to Waldfeucht (which the Jocks not unnaturally called by another name) where the 5th Bn had been hard at it and had knocked out two Tiger tanks. From Waldfeucht was planned the *coup de grace* of Operation "Blackcock" - the capture of Heinsberg. The Royal Scots and our B and C Coys were to encircle the town after which A and C Coys would sweep through. It worked well, supported as ever by superb artillery fire and by the newly thought-up 'Monty's Moonlight', searchlights directed up the line of advance, a great help for night operations and an aid to bad map readers!

A German Army doctor came into our lines complaining bitterly that no one had bothered to tell him that they were withdrawing. He said the German troops were very dispirited. They had all gone down to the "kellers" (cellars) until the sentry

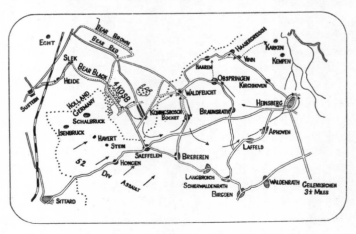

The ground over which Operation "Blackcock" was fought.

came down and said: "OK boys, you can come up now; the Tommies are here". The "doc" was very helpful with casualties of both sides - one of the few fine traditions of war. But the Germans were not being so friendly to the north of the town. B Coy had run into a packet of trouble, Jock Elliot had been killed, Colin Hogg badly wounded and the Company saved only by the incredible bravery of L/Cpl Alec Veitch who, with one leg shattered, was operating the company wireless set and bringing down an artillery smoke screen which enabled the company to move to a better position. This calculated courage very properly earned Veitch the Distinguished Conduct Medal. He lives happily in Musselburgh today - with never a complaint about his "pin leg" which must have caused him a lifetime of pain.

The aims of "Blackcock" had been achieved. 52 Div was the first British Division to operate on German soil and General Ritchie complimented the 4th Bn by saying: "The capture of Koningsbosche was the turning point of the operation". We returned to Waldfeucht to lick our wounds. Alan Innes took over command of B Coy and I became his 2nd-in-command, handing over my treasured Anti-Tank Platoon to Jimmy Wannop after three memorable years. We hadn't knocked out any tanks, but we'd worked like beavers and been a very happy team.

The winter of 1944-45 dragged on. Monty wouldn't strike for the Rhine until the weather and the balance of forces were right, so we soldiered on in appalling conditions of cold and mud, first on the Roer and then on the Maas, further north near a place called Gunn. This time, although the Hun was still the No.1 enemy the River Maas was a close second as the Germans had blown the dams on the River Roer and it was a raging torrent, overflowing its banks into our positions as they had intended. After an acutely uncomfortable and hazardous 10 days we were relieved by an American battalion. The two forward companies were able to get back through the flood waters only with the aid of our old friend from our mountain warfare days, the "Weasel", a light tracked vehicle made for snow that could also swim.

Something was cookin'. The Allied guns were thundering at the Siegfried Line over the river and the air force had joined in.

The battle for the Rhineland, the highly-defended stretch of territory between the Maas and the Rhine, had started. There followed, all old soldiers agree, some of the fiercest fighting of the Second World War. 52 Div crossed rivers at Mook and Gennep, courtesy of Mr Bailey, and were on the right flank of the advance with the Highland Division on our left. Our old friends the 52nd Division Recce Regiment under the redoubtable Jack Hankey were in the lead. They had been formed from the scrapings of the Division early on in the war and Jack had of course welded them into a first class fighting unit. When they were held up at a place called Afferden the foot sloggers had to swing left-flanking into Afferden Woods where the Jerries gave us an absolute pasting. Every time we tried to advance forward of the wood we were pushed back by intense 88mm fire. They were even using solid shot, one of which got Tommy Gray on the very foot which subsequently kicked the goal that won the Calcutta Cup for Scotland in 1950.

The place which was holding us up was a sinister fort called Kasteel Blijenbleek. Even in peace time it gives you the creeps. It was surrounded by a huge moat and could only be approached by a narrow causeway. This was the objective of "The Sweepers", Donald Hogg's C Coy, which he commanded for the whole war and very properly won the MC. They tried mighty hard and suffered 40 casualties but it was too big a task for an Infantry Company. Eventually it had to be reduced by rocket-firing Typhoons and medium bombers. During a lull in the fighting Allan Hill MC, the MO, with Pte McBeth MM invoked the Geneva Convention and calmly walked across to the German lines to arrange for the evacuation of wounded. Allan said he had been fired on once and had an interesting chat with the German MO. Returning to C Coy "he lit his pipe and walked back to Bn HQ". A cool customer, now living in Kilmelford.

All this time my Company (B) was in the forward edge of Afferden wood waiting to advance. To say that it was excessively unpleasant would be the understatement of the year. The ground was absolutely sodden (February) and we could only dig down about a foot before reaching water. I shared a scrape with our genial Company Sergeant Major, Jimmy Hutton, the Hawick butcher. Every time another shell or mortar bomb went off near us he would say with deep feeling: "You realise that this scrape in the ground is not affording us any protection whatsoever?" To which the only reply could be, quoting Bruce Bairnsfather: "If you knows of a better 'ole, go to it".

The most extraordinary things can happen in war. In the middle of this battle five RASC lorries suddenly appeared in the front line, loaded to the hilt with petrol and ammunition. The Jerries loaded up with tracer and had an absolute field day. The other Divisions to our left were having just as rough a time at Goch and Kleve, but the enemy were taking a pounding and gradually they began to "give". News came through, too, that the Americans were on the move in the south. The Germans slowly eased away from us towards the Rhine, but it was a long, hard slog. The media called the German opposition "of nuisance value only", an expression which infuriated us as we still had to fight our way forward dealing with demolitions, blown bridges and booby traps - where people get hurt. By 4th March we had made contact with the Americans at Kevelaer and by the 7th we were within sight of the Rhine on the high ground above Alpen and Xanten. Here we relieved the 53rd Welsh Division ready for the operation which was to eliminate the Germans in their last stand west of the Rhine, "The Wesel Pocket".

For once this battle was fought not on a broad front. There were so many troops - British, Canadian and American - that we felt that we were being "squeezed" into the battle. The KOSB objective was the main north-west railway line and a farm called Haus Loo which was easily identified as it stood on a small knoll surrounded by distinctive trees. The railway was supposed to have been our Start Line and already secure, but of course it wasn't and it took A and C Coys all morning to capture it. Now it was the turn of B Coy. We lay for a long time on the railway embankment with machine gun fire zipping overhead. The casualties were building up; morale is not improved when the mournful cry "Stretcher bearers!" is passed down the line. This was right out of the movies (Errol Flynn style) - "over the top".

90 Borderers were crouching there watching the two of us, Major Alan Innes, the Company Commander and Captain Frank Coutts his No 2, waiting for the right moment to say "Go". At this juncture join the writer in doffing your hat to the Scottish Soldier - lying there, tired, frightened, soaked, hungry, far from home.

"Let's go!"

And they crossed that railway line to a man. It was about 1000 yards to Haus Loo, and the Gunners' wireless set, usually so reliable, had a bullet through it and was "on the blink". The Spandaus were sweeping the ground and it was only a question of time before we would have to go to ground. Suddenly, the Gunners' radio came to life again and, not for the first time, we blessed Walter Ross, the battery commander of 186 Field Regiment. They put down a beautiful smoke screen to enable us to cover the remaining ground to our objective which, fortunately, was only lightly held. We dug in at once in sandy soil and were in a position to deal with a lot of Jerries retreating on both sides of us. It became a little like a shooting gallery, with cries of "I got him" and "No you didn't, I did". For the next 48 hours the Boche, obviously having decided that the Wesel Pocket was no longer tenable, let loose all their remaining ammunition from the other side of the Rhine. The battalion suffered 81 casualties in that battle against opposition which the BBC apparently thought was "of nuisance value only".

During the entire war the inadequacy of the Infantry signal equipment was a major failing. At Platoon level we had the wretched 88 set which could communicate for about half a mile under "parade ground" conditions. In battle it was useless. On the second day of our pounding at Haus Loo - it was a Saturday afternoon in early March - I kept shouting to Jock Borthwick in another trench: "Are you through to Coy HQ?" No reply. Concerned that he had been hit, I went over to his trench and posed the same question. With a beatific smile, he replied: "Scotland's leading 1-0 at Hampden, Sir!"

Once the guns at Wesel fell silent, everything to do with the preparations for the Rhine crossing were pure pleasure. We moved into a charming undamaged village called Marienbaum, just north of Xanten and about three miles back from the river. B Coy lived in bungalows in real beds - with duvets! - sorry General Ritchie.

The work was congenial too - rounding up stray Germans and a lot of stray animals, acting as the stage hands for the remarkable array of "props" which were arriving prior to the crossing of the Rhine - bridges, boats, artificial fog, every gimmick new to warfare - and then welcoming the Black Watch (Mick Baker-Baker) who were to pass through us and be first across. We also had a visit from Mr Churchill on the day when he made his shortest ever speech: "I have peed in the Rhine!" The great day came - 24th March 1945, the crossing of The Rhine, River No 3. A terrific barrage went on all night as the forward troops crossed the river. The next morning at 10 am precisely we witnessed an amazing sight - the biggest airborne expedition ever mounted went right overhead. It went on for an hour and the sky was black with planes.

Our job at the crossing was the protection of the remarkable Sappers who built two colossal pontoon bridges on our front in 24 hours, often under fire. As soon as they were complete we were their first customers, followed by two armoured divisions. The Battalion was in good form - "Smyg" (Allan Innes) was giving his hunting horn "big licks". "Smyg" was his Officers' Mess nickname because of his supposed likeness to Admiral Smygly-Ritz, the Hungarian leader.

There was a good deal of euphoria and it was quite unjusti-fied. We were in for a long slog and the war still had another six weeks to run. Over the river, 155 Brigade came under command of the 7th Armoured Division who, as Monty had bid them, were bent on "cracking about the plains of Northern Germany". Now tanks are fine when they are charging across open country, but the minute they come to a wood with a bazooka team in it they scream like mad for the Infantry. That's just what happened here. The armour rushed away from us, doing a great job, until they came to the Dortmund-Ems canal which they crossed - brilliantly.

Mind you, they were lucky - but luck plays a large part in war.

While our colleagues in 156 and 157 Brigades were battling for the town of Rheine[1], the tanks of 7th Armoured Division rushed round the town and "bounced" an intact bridge over the canal just south of Reisenbeck. They poured across, only to be confronted by a body of fanatical German officer cadets and NCOs from a training school in Hanover. With the Third Reich crumbling round them these young lads were fully prepared to die for the Fatherland. Many of them did. This nasty little bunch were well situated on the wooded heights of the Teutoburgerwald and they brought the famous Desert Rats to a grinding halt. "Send for The Footsloggers". As soon as we in 155 Brigade had "debussed" from our trucks in Reisenbeck we were subjected to a fierce and sustained "stonk" from air-burst shelling which is quite the most unpleasant experience known to man - apart, maybe, from the 'Moaning Minnies', rockets which came at you moaning and whining; though their bark was very much worse than their bite. Once over the canal, we were met by an amazing sight - the best part of two armoured divisions crammed into a few fields about a mile long, all held up by a group of fanatical young Nazis.

It took 155 Infantry Brigade 3 days (3-5 April 45) to prise that little lot out of the Teutoburgerwald. The Royal Scots and HLI were first into the woods, and had a thoroughly unpleasant time. As we passed through them, one of the HLI Platoon Commanders (a school chum) said to me: "This is one hell of a place, Frank. We've been driven off here once already. We've been counter-attacked all day, and I expect you'll be counter-attacked all night. Good luck - and goodbye!"

More officially, the Divisional History put it this way: "It was

---

[1] There was a superb rumour (probably true) within the Division that the town of Rheine was in fact "captured" by the Divisional Mobile Laundry and Bath Unit. Due to a "little fancy map-reading" the MLBU did by devious side roads enter Rheine without opposition and finding an undestroyed railway bridge set up shop ready to serve showers according to regulations. When one of the leading Platoons arrived, holding close to the wall in single file, imagine their astonishment when they were offered a shower and clean change of underwear!

then the turn of the 4th Bn King's Own Scottish Borderers to come over the ridge and attack Ibbenburen frontally across the fields. It was a gallant attack over some 2000 yards of open ground, but it received a painful check in its later stages. The enemy had a well-concealed position, expertly manned, on the western edge of the town, and a company of the Scottish Borderers, caught on a forward slope, suffered rather heavily".

I've never found it so hard to get the boys moving. After five years of war and six months of combat they were whacked. Once or twice I had to say emphatically: "Hey, we're going that-a-way" when they were heading in the opposite direction. After a thoroughly dogged 24 hours advancing field by field we got to the outskirts of Ibbenburen. We took 51 casualties in 4 KOSB in that little battle. The war was far from over. When the 53rd (Welsh) Division passed through us the town was clear.

We pushed on to river No 4 - the Weser - with Horace Davidson in command, Chris Melville having been transferred to Divisional HQ as Chief of Staff. The next few weeks are very blurred in my memory. Perhaps it is just as well that memory fades because we saw some incredible sights. The saddest for me was turning over a dead Cameronian lying in the middle of a field and discovering to my horror that it was a school friend. I'm afraid we became quite numbed and oblivious to horror - towns and villages razed to the ground by bombing and shell-fire, whole populations on the move, a nation literally ground into the dust - the detritus of war. My lasting impression is exhaustion and lack of sleep. There was always something to be done, right round the clock; even when the opportunity for sleep arose, it wouldn't come.

From Ibbenburen we chased after the tanks, sometimes in lorries, sometimes on foot. We fought sharp actions at Einste, Sudweyne, Eilsdorf, Rethem and Wahlsrode. At Sudweyne, the truck in front of me took a direct hit from a medium shell, killing 2 and wounding 6. One had to admire the Hun, he was still fighting well. I suppose we would have done the same if our homeland had been invaded. At Rethem they defended so well that they held up the whole advance for 24 hours. From the 4th

Bn history: "For this attack, B Company were again used with a squadron of "Skins" (Inniskillings) supporting the attack from outside the wood, and a fairly good concentration from the artillery on the known enemy position. This attack was entirely successful and some 15 dead were found on the enemy positions - no casualties being suffered by B Coy. The attack for some reason seemed to go like a demonstration in peace time, and it was rather difficult on this lovely spring morning to realise that this was the real thing, and not just another exercise". Peter White reminded me that when we arrived on the objective our rifles were steaming from over-use. There was no shortage of ammunition. At this stage of the war we were determined to avoid casualties - on our side anyway.

By this time the 7th Armoured had crossed the Weser at Nienberg, and we chased after them, to learn that the next objective was Hamburg and the Elbe via Luneburg heath, the

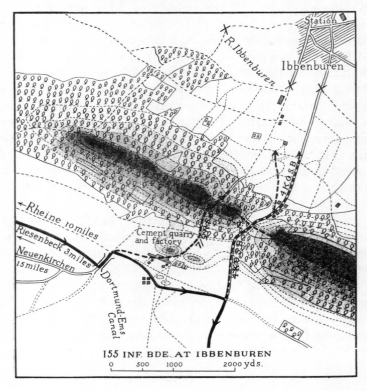

155 INF. BDE. AT IBBENBUREN

0   500   1000   2000 yds.

Salisbury Plain of Germany. The "Fatherland" was crumbling, and we now began to face problems almost more daunting than the German Army. Streams of DPs (Displaced Persons) had released themselves from captivity and were looting wine shops, causing no end of mayhem. The ones who had been compulsorily working on farms invariably strung the farmer up on a gate before they left, rather a gruesome sight as we drove along. Then we were advised that we had to move post haste to Fallingbostel to release 20,000 POWs from Stalags XIB and 357. About 7000 of them were British. The camps consisted of long wooden huts, row on row, surrounded by huge barbed-wire fences and watch towers. A wave of cheering POWs surrounded our Jeeps, carriers and trucks and it was a real struggle to achieve any kind of order.

Unbelievably, the first men we met inside the gate were our own two Jocks who had been taken at Koningsbosche. There were also a goodly number of the 7th KOSB from Arnhem; their RSM had been an inspiration in keeping order in the British lines. It is on occasions like these that the traditional values of soldiering come to the surface. Despite acute shortages of food and clothing the British contingent had managed to maintain a level of smartness and alertness in their dress and bearing. They were organised and under control of their leaders. Discipline among the other nationalities had snapped. They were wandering around in gangs with ragged clothing and unkempt appearance and many of them just "sugared off" and roamed the country-side. One felt proud to be British. We had a great night with Robin White from Melrose who had been a prisoner since 1940 at St Valery and was looking fine after his five years ordeal.

The situation was getting a bit out of hand. There was a war on, and we couldn't get bogged down with DPs and POWs, however urgent their needs so we left them to the Lines of Communication organisations and pushed off to Soltau which was being taken by The Royal Scots. Then on, on, with the armour to take Schneverdingen plus 200 prisoners and a fine cache of champagne buried in a peat bog. About this time in the war the problem of looting became evident. It occurs in all victorious armies. It may be all very well to "borrow" a blanket or two from a ruined house, but after a time whole suites of furniture could be seen in the back of 3-ton trucks. This was not on and Monty's HQ issued very stern orders - although it has to be said that the avarice of certain Generals was only exceeded by that of the "civvies" in Military Government. In this case, we were not looting champagne - it was a prize of war! We drank sparingly and stashed the rest away for the victory celebrations, which couldn't be far off now.

That was the end of our flirtation with armoured warfare and it was back to basics - 155 Brigade was recalled to the Weser at Verden for the final attack by 52 Div - on Bremen. The Boche were still not giving in easily. The Division had to edge its way northwards down the river taking village after village, strongly opposed by 88's and our pet hate, "Moaning Minnies". The last village before Bremen was ours - Uphusen - the last bit of real nastiness before the end. The Boche had somehow or other got some 16" naval guns trained on to us; they made an enormous crater but fortunately didn't achieve any direct hits. We had good support from a troop of the Royal Scots Greys, commanded by a Callender from Preston Hall, and some flame-throwers which put the last of the Germans to rout, followed by B Coy with fixed bayonets, in good voice.

That night "Bomber" Harris gave Bremen the full treatment - a thousand bomber raid - and 4 KOSB were in the front seat of the stalls. It was an awesome sight. At midnight we got our orders for the next day: "The objective is Bremen". "What? *All* of it?" "Well, most of it".

Praise be, the Germans had had enough and we advanced up deserted, shattered streets. B Coy was the first into the central square by the railway station and we cautiously made our way down into the air raid shelters - what a stench! There were about 1500 soldiers and civilians all huddled together, cowed and defeated. That took some sorting out. "Alles soldaten *raus* (out)". My Toronto German came into its own.

We set up shop in what remained of a hotel. Jock Gray got his pipes out, and we had a double rum ration - to take the smell away. The next day was spent rounding up hundreds of German

Army prisoners, piling arms on the square and marching them off in batches of 50, with 2 Jocks as escort, to the POW cages. The RSM had a field day. An SS Police Battalion marched from the Town Hall to surrender with some elan, their CO handing over his ceremonial dagger to the astonished Horace Davidson. We were glad to get out of Bremen. The German Army was still in strength in the area between Bremen and Hamburg. We moved

The centre of Bremen

there to take over from 43 Div, and it was there, on a blasted heath, on the 7th of May 1945 that we heard that the Germans had surrendered to Monty. As the Bn History recorded: "It seemed difficult to believe. No more mortar bombs, no more 88's, no more spandaus. The CO immediately called in all Company Commanders and the Padre held a short service in the Command Post. Donald Hogg then proposed the health of the King and the CO. Everybody was very subdued and felt suddenly very, very tired".

My own feelings were muddled through lack of sleep. We couldn't really believe that we were still alive. I certainly didn't expect to come through in one piece. Next, undoubtedly, was a feeling of sadness and remembrance of the 413 members of the Battalion who had either been killed or wounded - that was about one out of every two who stepped ashore at Ostend with the British Liberation Army. I couldn't help thinking also of brother Ben who had been so grievously wounded in North Africa and then torpedoed on the way home. Revenge is not a very Christian motive, but it was human and I think justified. It was a great privilege to have been a member of such a superb unit and I was very proud of the way our well-trained Borderers had stuck to their task through thick and thin.

The next day General "Hak" kindly passed on a copy of the letter he had received from "Jorrocks" of 30 Corps: it concluded "... I am certain that there is no better fighting Division in the British Army than the 52nd Lowland Division. I should like to congratulate all ranks on writing another glorious page in Scottish history".

There was still work to be done. The 4th Bn were moved back north of Bremen to a town with the splendid Teutonic name of Osterholz-Scharmbeck. Jock Beattie of Selkirk, who had been commissioned from Sergeant with the Bn, was dubbed "The Duke of Osterholz-Scharmbeck" for his nickname was already "The Duke". We were well received by the inhabitants many of whom came from East Germany and had fled from the Russians - our next problem. Although we were rather hoping for a move to Norway, it was not to be, and we were moved down into the American zone to Magdeburg and shortly after crossed our fifth and last river, The Elbe. We moved deep into what became Eastern Germany to Letzlingen and Oebisfelde-Kaltendorf - another splendid dukedom for somebody! Here we came face-to-face with "The Russian Problem". The German civilians were terrified of them. "Fraternisation" with the Germans was forbidden, but some of the German girls flung themselves at the Jocks in the hope of getting away. No hope. Here, the Hawick contingent carried out the only Common Riding ceremony to have been held on German soil with Pte Jimmy Reid of B Coy as the cornet. The German civvies were even more mystified than the rest of the battalion.

Little did we realise that we were at the centre of a political storm - the division of post-war Germany. We were not all that far from Berlin and, for sure, Churchill wanted to keep us there. But he lost that argument and after a few weeks we bumped our way back over appalling roads and innumerable bridges - to Belgium (Moorsel near Aalst), once more to stand by for an airborne move, this time to Palestine. Bearing in mind our previous experience of airborne ops, with more than a dozen cancelled after much planning, we were becoming a little sceptical and were not at all surprised when this one too was cancelled. Instead, some of our most recently joined Jocks went as reinforcements to the 3rd Division which included the 1st Bn KOSB. Peter White went with them.

The war is (nearly) over. Minden Day 1945, Alost. Support Company for the cup. L to R: F.H.C., Jock Milne Home, Harcourt Rae, Harry Shirley (6 HLI), Jock Beattie, StoorRichardson, Jimmy Douglas ('Doods').

Just when we were sitting back and getting ready to enjoy ourselves we were warned to get ready to move to the Far East. The Japanese war was still going strong. Then came The Bomb at Hiroshima and Nagasaki. I doubt if you'll find one man in 4th KOSB who supports the CND. We gave three cheers for the Yanks and another three for the Forgotten Army who had suffered so long.

Serious celebrations were now the order of the day. The local lovelies were extremely friendly and the delights of Brussels were only a tram ride away. More healthily, the Belgian channel resorts were opening up to give everyone a holiday weekend in an official leave centre. We made our own amusements too. Minden Day, the 1st of August, has always been a regimental holiday in the KOSB in honour of the Battle of Minden in 1759 (on that occasion we fought with the Germans against the French: what a crazy world it is). In 1945 we celebrated Minden in style (and drank the rest of the Letzlingen champagne): the Minden Rose parade in the morning, a well-organised regimental athletics meeting in the afternoon and an Officers' Ball in the opera house in Ghent in the evening. The Pipe Band was kept busy, and often left us to play with the Divisional Massed Bands all over Europe. Led by our own Drum Major Bruce Lindsay they were a magnificent spectacle.

The war was over.

Chapter Seven
Knocking Off The Rough Edges
(1946-1952)

It's a way we have in the Ba-Baas
And a rule that we play to;
For the Rugby game we do not train,
But we play it with a will
It's a way we have in the Ba-Baas -
And a jolly good way too!
Barbarians RFC theme song
rendered by the Alickadoos after each try.

After six years of war everyone was naturally keen to get home, but the world was a very troubled place and there was still work to be done. Germany was in chaos and no one could be sure of Uncle Joe Stalin's intentions in the East. 52nd Division was moved back to form part of the Occupation Forces (as they had in the First War) - back to that notable ridge which runs north and south through Westphalia, the Teutoburgerwald, with HQ in the pleasant country town of Halle near Bielefeld.

The demobilisation system was fair and efficiently run on the principle of "first in, first out". Those with low demob numbers began to trickle home, after tearful demob parties. One of the first to go, and well-deserved, was the CO, Horace Davidson, who was eventually replaced by Jack Hankey when his dear Recce Regiment had been disbanded.

"Decisions, decisions, always decisions" (as Andy Capp said when Florrie was clinging from the cliff-top and the cry of

"They're open" came floating down from the pub). I was still a PC in the Metropolitan Police with 8 years service (most of it in Army uniform) - but I was also by now a Temporary Major in the KOSB commanding Support Coy at Kunsebeck. The Army were very keen to recruit Regular officers to replace war casualties, and Jack Hankey worked hard on me. To be fair to the Police I went back to London for an interview with an Assistant Commissioner who made it quite plain that commissioned service in the Army would win me no favours in the Police. Decision taken quick. The Regular Army Commissions Board, similar to the war-time War Office Selection Boards (WOSBies) had now become a well-tried system for selecting leaders. It was a forbidding 3-day experience. One was under very close scrutiny the whole time during practical tests, essay, lecturette and the all-important interview with the Commandant, a Major General who, inevitably, was an old chum of Jack Hankey's in India. Sighs of relief all round - about 50% passed. I was now a Regular officer - with seniority dated back to my 21st birthday. I must say I have always found the War Office to be fair employers.

The next year was a little unreal. We certainly lived the high life. Drink was ridiculously cheap. Donald Hogg's Coy was in Steinhagen where they made appalling gin, selling at five bob a bottle! Most of the work was again concerned with Displaced Persons who had a big camp near us. One of my Corporals decided to marry a very nice Russian girl, and we laid on a wedding with all the trappings including a coach and horses. At the church door the Russian Liaison team from Bad Oyenhausen arrived and arrested her. She was never seen again. The Cold War was closing in.

We did quite a lot of training and played a lot of highly competitive inter-Coy sport. There were some excellent Rugby matches: the three Scottish Divisions, 15, 51 and 52, took on a Scottish Command side at Hanover before a huge crowd and we had a riotous weekend in the Harz Mountains with "The Flying Scotsman" (Ian Smith, named after the famous railway engine) as the chief entertainer. Between 1924 and 1933 he was capped as a wing three-quarter 32 times for Scotland and scored 24 tries in internationals, exactly twice the number of his nearest rival. By a strange coincidence, he was *also* a Smith - Arthur (A. R.), another charming gentleman, who scored 12 tries in the lean 1950's. We also had two excellent games - British Army of the Rhine v the redoubtable Kiwis, the New Zealand Army side from Italy, captained by Charlie Saxton. They were splendid ambassadors for their country and well worthy of the Silver Fern, the All Blacks jersey. That led to selection for two of the so-called Victory Internationals in 1946. These were unofficial; no international caps were awarded, but they were played before packed houses because everyone was delighted to resume peace-time activities. We were just glad to be alive and playing rugby.

There were six matches in the series - England and Wales (twice each), Ireland and the New Zealand Army. I missed four of them due to a broken collar bone in Germany. I had been selected for the Kiwi game in January at Murrayfield, and ten days before the match we had an inter-battalion match against the 5th Bn KOSB. If I had called off because of international duty I would have been considered 'snooty'. The inevitable happened. A huge forward from Jedburgh (who really should have been in the 4th Battalion!) floored me in the line-out and the damage was done. He apologises to me every year at the Jed Sevens!

I was fit by the end of March and ran on to the sacred turf of Murrayfield, wearing the coveted blue jersey and the thistle, against the Welsh on the 30th March 1946. Harry Simson, the legendary Secretary of the SRU was very sparing with the jerseys - two players who had played pre-war, Ian Henderson and Donny Innes, were told: "You've got your jerseys already!" Nowadays they very properly get a jersey for every match, sponsored of course. The thrill of running on to Murrayfield is unique and something to be remembered forever. Wales had a fine team with Haydyn Tanner as captain, Billy Cleaver, the great Bleddwyn Williams, Jackie Matthews in the backs and a pack of forwards to put the fear of God into anyone. Yet there was never the open violence which we see in rugby these days. Sure, the odd punch was thrown, but it was a matter of honour that it should not be seen by the referee.

We won 13-11 and were back again three weeks later against the Auld Enemy, England. They had won the first of the series at Twickenham 12-8, thanks to a last minute drop goal by Jack Heaton, their captain. We had sweet revenge and took them to the cleaners to the tune of 27-0. It was a slightly hollow victory in that England lost their scrum-half injured, and in those days there were no replacements. The Scottish side was beginning to shape up for the full internationals in 1947 with Keith Geddes (in yellow gloves!) at full-back, Charlie Drummond, Russell Bruce and Billy Munro in the backs and Douglas Elliot at the beginning of his outstanding career in the pack. I had teamed up with Gordon Watt of Edinburgh Academicals in the second row of the scrum. It was a most comfortable pack and we were always able to supply our speedy backs with plenty of ball.

I also played with Gordon Watt in the Army XV, and in one inter-service match at Twickenham we had a real problem. Before the game I had to present the Army players to the King, H.M. George VI. Gordon had a full set of false teeth, and protested: "I can't possibly speak to the King without my teeth

SCOTLAND v. ENGLAND
PLAYED AT MURRAYFIELD, 13TH APRIL 1946
SCOTTISH FIFTEEN

A. W. Black W. B. MacLennan R. Aitken A. G. M. Watt F. H. Coutts T. G. H. Jackson I. J. M. Lumsden G. G. Lyall Referee—N. H. Lambert
(Edinburgh University) (Watsonians) (London Scottish) (Academicals-Wanderers) (Melrose) (Cheltenham and Army) (Watsonians) (Gala) (Ireland)
W. H. Munro I. C. Henderson K. I. Geddes D. W. Deas, Capt. C. R. Bruce J. H. Orr W. I. D. Elliot
(Glasgow H.S.F.P. and Army) (Academicals-Wanderers) (London Scottish) (Heriot's F.P.) (Glasgow Academicals and Army) (Heriot's F.P.) (Academicals-Wanderers)

in". We speedily improvised. After His Majesty had passed Gordon, his 'snappers' were wrapped in a handkerchief and passed down the line to the waiting touch judge!

As post-war Germany began to take shape under the Military Government and the Marshall Plan (massive economic aid from the USA) force levels could be reduced and 52nd Division was disbanded. We had a splendid farewell parade on the football stadium (every German village has one) and "Sir Hak" came down to review us and wish us well.

Fortunately I was spared the last rites of packing up and handing in kit. Jack Hankey seemed to know everyone who was anyone and he was determined that his officers all got good postings. I really should have gone to the 1st Bn KOSB in Palestine, but Jack Hankey knew that I was in the running for a Scottish Rugger cap and he wouldn't let me go. I was posted as an instructor to the British Military Mission in Denmark, with the faithful Cpl Arthur Marshall as batman/driver and our own Jeep, which in the next year clocked up a phenomenal total of kilometres.

It was a sad day to leave 4th KOSB, but I needed a change and I had to think seriously about my newly-chosen career. There were a few rough edges to be knocked off. I had been in close proximity with soldiers for six years and my language was apt to be a little erratic. Mother said that I spoke with a sing-song Border accent - and what's wrong with that?

We received a great welcome from the 7th Regiment of the Danish Army in Fredericia (Jutland) and I formed lasting friendships with Axel Lohmann-Kragh, the Adjutant, who was an Olympic fencer, Aanders von Buchwald, a real aristocrat, and Neills Winter, a pure playboy. They had had a miserable war, they were all regular officers and determined to re-establish the pride and efficiency of their Army. It was an uphill struggle. National Service was only eight months, and you can't do much in that time. Those selected as Kornets (Corporals with officer potential) had to do a year - so there wasn't much enthusiasm for promotion! I supervised the support weapons training and soon mastered the words of command in Danish. Later I took Danish lessons in Copenhagen with Benny Engelsen, who came more than once to see us in Scotland: although I was a Class V interpreter, I wasn't much credit to her. The language barrier may have made life difficult with the Rank and File, but not so with the girls of Fredericia and Vejle, who were terrific, with lovely names like Inge Lise.

Dad came over for a much-needed holiday after a difficult war on the home front and stayed at a wee pub at Middelfart on Fyn (over the Lille Belt), birthplace of Hans Christian Andersen. He came with us to Oxbøl near Esbjerg to see the anti-tank guns firing and partake of a typical Danish Officers luncheon with far too much aquavit!

It soon became clear that the Danish Army were not enamoured of our British support weapons. They were rough and ready and had none of the finish and finesse of the Swedish weapons (Huskwana) which they had used pre-war. I was re-deployed to the Danish School of Infantry in Copenhagen and Axel went to command their PT School. There I was under-employed but consulted quite a bit on tactics, planning and umpiring exercises, with and without troops. For a few months, our base was the lovely Kronstadt Castle, at Elsinore, whence we could take day trips to Sweden.

I gave of my best, but my thoughts, I have to say, were very much on rugby. I was able to play occasionally in Germany - there was no team in Copenhagen - and I trained like mad on my own, but it's not the same as the real thing. Eventually I went across for the Scottish Trial (at Netherdale), played very badly, and was lucky to be reserve against France at Colombes on 1 January 47, the first full post-war international and the first since 1931 when relations with the French Rugby Union were suspended.

Harry Simson, with a twinkle in his eye created a superb "first" at the Trial. The selection committee, wishing to be bang up-to-date had decreed that the height, weight and personal statistics of all players were to be recorded, so Harry produced an old-fashioned coin-operated weighing machine. As we all stepped forward nervously to be weighed Harry enquired: "Well, where's your penny?" I honestly think he meant it.

We were beaten 8-3 in Paris in a lack-lustre performance. George Cawkwell, a New Zealander at Oxford University[1], took "my" place with Wattie in the second-row, and was sunk without trace thereafter. The incomparable Cyril Gadney of England was referee. Guy Basquet, Jean Prat and "Soro and Moga" (they were always coupled like "bacon and eggs") were members of a superb French pack and they have remained life-long friends as members of the French Rugby Union. I had the privilege of playing our team on to the field with the pipes at the old Colombes Stadium as I did again 30 years later in Tokyo, as President.

Many stories have been told at Rugby dinners about that first peace-time international, most of them true and most concerning the ebullient Charlie Drummond, one of Scottish rugby's greatest characters. The night life of Paris was getting back to normal, and the night before the match (something that would horrify the modern coaches) a few of the brighter sparks visited an "exhibeetion" where naked ladies performed unbelievable antics. The re-telling of the tale to the goggle-eyed Harry and the selectors was even more amusing than the original. A visit to the Follies Bergeres after the match-dinner in the Eiffel Tower was compulsory for all those who were still upright. At least two were "coupit". I returned to Copenhagen, deflated - but at least revelling in the luxury of the first post-war wagon-lit between Paris and Copenhagen. The only passenger.

The sequel has also been told at rugby dinners. I was up in the north of Jutland on the ranges when I was called to the telephone. An excited Welshman in the Movement Control office of the Mission in Copenhagen said; "*The Daily Telegraph* says you're picked to play for Scotland against Wales on Saturday; I've booked you on the plane from Kastrup to Prestwick on Thursday". The official post-card from the SRU Secretary, with a penny stamp on board, arrived a fortnight later; it took a good

---

[1]He was shown in the official progamme as being from *Cambridge*, which must have made him a Francophobe for life!

British Army v French Armed Forces
*Ken Wilson to Frank Coutts: "Now don't drop it Frank". Coming up
fast, Paddy Valentine (Hawick and Scotland) - Colombes Stadium,
Paris 1947 - watched by Field Marshal Montgomery. Paris Match:
"La seconde ligne Neale-Goutts (sic) ne mit souvent en valeur, et ce
dernier n'a rien perdu de son coup de botte magistral"*

deal longer to extract the £32 for the air fare - a year to be exact.

The winter of 1947 was brutal with every game subject to
cancellation up to the last minute. It was long before the days of
the electric blanket and the ground staff at Murrayfield did a
great job with straw and braziers to enable the games to be
played. "Then and now" comparisons abound. Now, the teams
assemble on Wednesday (!) to prepare. (One recalls how Jimmy
Ireland asked his boss for Saturday morning off so that he could
play for Scotland in the afternoon and the response was: "What,
the *whole* morning!"). Then, we crept out of the dressing rooms
at Goldenacre late on Friday afternoon with precious little idea
of what we were about. The fact that we had three different
captains that season - Keith Geddes, Billy Munro and Russell
Bruce - did not indicate a great deal of confidence on the part of
the management. The forwards unanimously elected Wallace
Deas to be leader of the pack as we were training at his ground!

Next day, my first international against Wales was something
of a let-down after the flamboyance of the 1946 side. Bleddwyn

100

Williams seemed to mesmerise our backs. The official history records: "In arctic conditions Scotland held their own up to half-time and then faded badly especially during the last quarter". There had been practically no club rugby due to the weather and we undoubtedly lacked peak fitness. We were beaten 22-8. Once again the Welsh forwards were immense; it was a lasting privilege to have locked horns with the likes of Bill Tamplin and Rees Stephens. Post-match dinners at the "N.B." Hotel resumed - always in black tie, a tradition which remains. The confrontations of the day were forgotten and lasting friendships forged.

The Scots-Irish match is always the most enjoyable of the season. Unlike England, Wales and France we can genuinely say that we don't care who wins provided it's a good game. We knock hell out of each other but it's all good fun. 24 February 1947 was no exception. It was "even-Steven" all the way until their scrum-half, Ernie Strathdee, sneaked round the corner of a scrum and passed to Barney Mullan who scored the only try of the match. Barney, a horse-dealer, during a Barbarians tour sang clean songs all the way from Penarth to Swansea because there was a lady in the bus, and dirty songs all the way back. There was another Mullen in the Irish side, Carl, a surgeon who later captained the British Lions. After an Army game in Dublin he took me straight to hospital and pierced my ear, thus preventing a disfiguring "cauliflower" for the rest of my life. Such is the comradeship of the rugby field.

If the Welsh and Irish matches had been a disappointment the English match on 15 March 1947 was a disaster. The country was still under feet of snow. The East and West coast railway lines were totally blocked, but we left Waverley eventually and crept down through the Borders to Carlisle. We reached London 20 hours later, totally exhausted, four to a side in a 3rd class compartment. Harry Simson sat with his soft hat on throughout and his walking-stick between his legs. David McLean (exams) and Micky Stele-Bodger (Dick Vet College) playing for England didn't arrive till the Saturday morning. The official history: "The match was played on a hard pitch in bitterly cold weather which deteriorated into a blizzard of snow in the second half". Douglas

Did it go over Haydn?
Barbarians 19, Newport 3.
Rodney Parade, 8th April
1947. The Times: A
magnificent match. (It did
go over, plus two others).

Elliot was hirpling throughout the match, Graeme Jackson limped off and it was the final straw when Charlie Drummond broke his collar bone. We did well to hold them to 5-24. The famous Calcutta Cup was on display again at the dinner, the first time for eight years.

Fortunately, this was not my only outing on the Twickenham turf. I enjoyed many good wins there for Army and London Counties over the next few years and in 1949 got to the final of the Twickenham Sevens with London Scottish. An article in the programme for the 1990 Army-Navy match was over-generous: "And that brings us to Frank Coutts, who also played in the 1947 match. He was to be another inspiring leader at a time of outstanding results, scoring in almost every one of his Inter-Service games. In his closing 1950 season the Army retained the championship without their line being crossed in either match."

To win an international cap was of course enormously

satisfying, but rugby offers a more unique honour - selection for the Barbarians. Founded in 1890, the "Ba-Baas" are not to be confused with the British Lions. They aim their selection towards good rugby players who are known to play open, friendly rugby. They invariably include one uncapped player. I was lucky enough to be selected eight times for the Barbarians between 1946 and 1948. The Easter weekend based on the Esplanade Hotel at Penarth with matches in Penarth (Fri), Cardiff (Sat), Swansea (Mon) and Newport (Tues) was for me the very pinnacle of rugby enjoyment. It wasn't namby-pamby either; in '46 I lost one front tooth in Cardiff on the Saturday and another in Swansea on the Monday!

Meantime, the training teams in Denmark were withdrawn and we went as instructors to Rhine Army Schools. My boss at the School of Infantry was the formidable Colonel Joe Kendrew, formerly Captain of the English Rugby team and later Governor of Western Australia. He kindly sent me home on a course to enable me to finish the season by playing against Ireland and England, and the first of three seasons for the Barbarians. While I was in UK the Military Secretary's Branch of the War Office posted me to be the Army instructor at the Royal Naval College, Greenwich. I crept back to BAOR to collect my kit and got the biggest "rocket" of my Army career from Colonel Joe who, quite wrongly but understandably, thought I had gone behind his back to the War Office.

The two years at Greenwich were a real educational and civilising experience. The Junior Officers War Course had recently been set up to give young Sub-Lieutenants a brush-up after their initial sea time. They certainly picked the right man to run it - the extraordinary Wally Hammond - not the cricketer, but a magnificent all round sportsman, Navy caps at rugby, cricket and squash over and over again; he would certainly have been an English rugger cap had it not been for the war. Round him he built an inter-service team who could almost certainly answer a Sub-Lieutenant's question on any Service matter. The 2nd-in-command, a "Salt Horse" $2^1/_2$ (Gen Duties Lt Cdr), a "Pusser" (Administrative Branch), a "Plumber" (Engineer), lots of

"Schoolies" (Education Officers), a "Gerook" (Royal Marine - subsequently Commandant-General Royal Marines), a "Pongo" (Soldier), and a "Fliegieman" (RAF Pilot).

The "Subbies" were a lively bunch, all disappointed to have missed out on the war, but planning a peace-time naval career - many of them were sons of naval officers. They did a lot of naval tactical work and staff duties, on which I had to "mug up", quite a lot of school (and certainly too much naval history, however well it was taught by the brilliant but soporific Prof Lewis), inter-service work and some very interesting lectures from politicians, trade unionists and industrialists - a very broad and stimulating spectrum. There were also some very interesting visits. For example, we went to London Docks to watch a ship unloading frozen beef from Argentina. I have never seen such uncongenial work and will never criticise a striking stevedore or "dockyard matey" again. We also did sea time on the Naval Gunnery ship at Whale Island, Portsmouth. It's no disgrace to be sea-sick; after all, it's only emulating Lord Nelson.

The Naval College was naturally run to naval routine - we slept in "cabins", visited the "heads", went "ashore". The Mess was The Wardroom, the Sub-Lieuts pigged it in the Gunroom and we all dined in state in the illustrious Painted Hall. I will never forget the thrill of entering that lovely Wren building for a Guest Night with the Marine Band playing "Roast Beef of Old England". There was a fine team of WRNS (different sort of Wren) to care for us. The Commander was none too sure when I asked his permission for the girls to partner the Sub-Lieuts at my Scottish Country Dancing class. With some misgivings he relented and, with strict rules in force, it was a huge success.

It was in the chapel at Greenwich that, on the 24th of July 1948, I married Morag Fullerton, a fellow Glaswegian. The chapel still had some tarpaulins on it from war-time bombing, but St Columba's, Pont Street, was even worse, it was flattened. It was a "fix". Mutual friends living at Morag's home in Bramley, Surrey, Kenneth and Ruth Jackson, told each of us separately that the other was "lonely in London". Ha-ha. We met at Piccadilly Circus (Eros must have been busy that night) and went to the Bernard Shaw play *You Never Can Tell*. You can say that again! The Bishop of Southwark put a bit of a damper on the proceedings by refusing to give permission for my father to marry us, despite the fact that he had christened Morag in Glasgow. (We were born 4 days apart and about 4 blocks away, but didn't meet for 29 years). He generously consented to allow Dad to read a lesson. Jimmy Fullerton gave us a splendid wedding. The guests came down from Westminster Bridge by launch - and kept me waiting 20 minutes at the altar, in

Hersell. Black eye courtesy Harlequins, not Morag.

borrowed breeks which were going to split any minute. The reception in the Painted Hall was an uplifting experience after so much war-time austerity; indeed, rationing and belt-tightening was even worse after the war than during it. The London Scottish contingent, led by George Horsburgh, gave me a rough passage on leaving by lifting the back wheels of Pa Fullerton's car off the ground for what seemed like ages.

Alastair Thorburn was best man and Alison Heady, brother Pip's fiancee (he was in Uganda) was bridesmaid. When Alastair and I went to open up the office safe for the ring, orders of service, bridesmaids' prezzies etc, the safe key was not in its usual secret place. We suspected a leg-pull. All those "in the know" were at Lord's for the Navy-RAF cricket match. Try phoning Lord's - it's impossible. With one hour to go we found a splendid chap in Maze Hill with an oxy-acetyline blower who calmly took the back off the safe. Flames poured out - but the only effect was that the hymn sheets had a rather distinguished, singed edge. After note for the present occupant of Room 33 at the RNC - "have a look at your office safe - the back is held together with sellotape".

We had a memorable honeymoon in Utne, a charming village

on the Hardangerfjord in Norway. We had previously spent the weekend of the wedding on the Thames, because the good ship *Venus*, didn't leave from Newcastle for Bergen till the Wednesday, so we sneaked back to London and went to one of the Sweet and Low shows (Hermione Gingold). We couldn't understand the giggles behind us in the stalls - the entire George St Clair Murray family from Edinburgh, having been at the wedding, were sitting behind us! It was worth it. They took us out to supper at the Savoy - with Hermione. Norway was magic. Each night we stood with the other hotel guests from many countries and sang the Norwegian national anthem as the flag was lowered - a demonstration of loyalty from which we could learn.

On our return to Newcastle Morag's Uncle Leo and Aunt Elise said: "How are you going to get to Edinburgh?" We didn't realise that all the bridges in Berwickshire had been washed away by flash floods. We went round by Carlisle and spent some time harvesting with the Jacksons, as promised, for they were now farmers in Glenalmond.

Back at work, we moved into a flat at Dartmouth Grove, Blackheath, the first of 29 houses in our married life. Who would marry a Serviceman? (And there were mice in the kitchen cupboard).

The icing on the wedding cake was that there was a letter waiting for me at RNC to say that, to my great surprise, I had passed the Staff College entrance exam and had been granted a vacancy on the 1949 course. It was another of the benefits of the RNC that I had ideal conditions for studying; I didn't make full use of them and I know that I didn't pass the Military Law exam. There must have been a Borderer or a rugger fan, or both, tucked away in the selection team somewhere.

The year at the Staff College has to be the best year in an Army officer's life. No Orderly Officers, no responsibilities except for oneself and family, no sudden moves, twelve months in one home, guaranteed for a year - provided one worked hard enough. There were no quarters, but Granny Fullerton had been hard at work, and we moved into a very pleasant lower flat in Upper Gordon Road, within easy bicycling distance of the College. No cars in these days and the rent ran away with exactly 50% of one's income. Brigadier Freddie Graham ("Old Black and White") so-called because one side of his moustache was white and the other was black and famous for his subsequent "Save The Argylls" campaign was Deputy Commandant and he was waging war against the Camberley landlords who were fleecing the Army. His efforts led to significant improvements in later years.

The only Saturday on which we worked at Camberley was the first one - and that had to be the day I was captaining the Army XV against Oxford University at Oxford. I confidently expected to be sent down when I asked my Divisional Colonel for permission to be absent. He roared with laughter: "Of course you must go; I don't want to face the wrath of 'Poo' Hobbs". General Hobbs was the Chairman of Army Rugby.

The policy during the first term was to drive the students into the ground, to humiliate them. Many of the students had filled staff appointments and considered themselves "high fliers". There was a deliberate attempt to bring us down to earth. Every piece of written work came back covered in red ink and one's spirits sank lower and lower, but it was a relief to find that everyone had received the same treatment. The instructors were a grand bunch, many of them reaching the highest ranks in the Army. General Dudley Ward, an ex-ranker, was Commandant, and he endeared himself to us all, especially when he joined the Scottish Country Dance class though he was not much of a performer. The professional qualification granted at the end of

the staff course was "PSC" (Passed Staff College). We Scots decided to institute our own diploma - "PHD" (Passed Highland Dancing). General Dudley's PHD was conferred with due decorum. Lieutenant Colonels' Pat Hunter Gordon of The Sappers (whose wife invented *Paddipads* the first disposable nappy and rightly became rich on them) and Douglas Drysdale of the Royal Marines were

particularly helpful.

Succeeding terms dealt with the different phases of war and we roamed the Surrey and Berkshire countryside in tactical exercises without troops. It was surprising to find that there was always a good pub nearby at lunch time.

Saturdays meant rugby at Richmond where I had the good fortune to be captaining London Scottish, and on Wednesday it was either the College team or the County of Kent, for whom I became eligible at Greenwich. They actually invited me, a Scot, to be their captain. We had mixed fortunes, but a lot of fun.

Morag, surprise, surprise, was expecting, and on the 4th of May she gave birth to Fiona in the Cambridge Military Hospital at Aldershot. Poor Morag had a very hard time, and I was called in urgently from Exercise Odiham, fearing the worst. Typically, the Commandant rushed me to the hospital in his staff car, the human face of the Army. Barbara Gordon, the Ward Sister who later went on to become head of the QA's (Queen Alexandra's Royal Army Nursing Corps), was a tower of strength as was Grace Richmond, Morag's cousin, whose husband Walter (Cameronians, Scottish Rifles) was on the same course. After a lengthy stay in hospital, during which Dad came down and baptised Fiona, Morag returned to Camberley with a splendid daughter who has been a great credit to us. She was a model baby.

As the Staff course developed it became more and more interesting. We went to Normandy for a battlefield tour with commentary from the real live participants in each battle. We lived rough in the Lycee Malberbe and were very strapped for cash. When Walter and I got back to our wives we were both carrying exactly the same miserable ornament, a tiny brass jeely pan; it was all we could afford.

We visited the other Services and watched all the annual demonstrations put on by each of the arms and services in turn, with shoals of Military Attaches gorgeously attired in attendance. In the Royal Army Medical Corps demonstration, Doug Smith, a Rugby chum from Aberdeen days and now an Army doctor, put on such a realistic performance in an active service operating theatre that several of the Military Attaches withdrew hurriedly, fingering their handkerchiefs. Doug had rather over-done the red ink.

Towards the end of the year we awaited our postings with trepidation. About half would go to Grade II postings as Acting Majors, the remainder to Grade III as Captains. To my great joy I was posted to HQ Scottish Command in Edinburgh Castle as General Staff Officer II (TA and Cadets), right up my street; the joy was tempered only by disappointment for others.

Although it was five years after the war, Scottish Command was still Big Business. The Headquarters had numerous offices in North Bridge and other parts of the town as well as The Castle. Compulsory National Service (2 years plus four on the reserve) was in full swing and would remain so until 1961, an indication of the effect which the Cold War had on Britain and the withdrawal from Empire. Infantry Training Centres and all the Regimental Depots were churning out recruits, the two TA Divisions, 52nd (Lowland) and 51st (Highland) had been reactivated. There was a new "toy", 264 Scottish Beach Brigade in Glasgow, which had always played second fiddle to Edinburgh as a military centre, retaining all the skills of amphibious warfare gained during the war, and there was a TA Armoured Brigade. Worse was to come. When Maryhill Barracks, a grim place, were finally abandoned nothing was planned or built to replace it - a disastrous decision which has left Glasgow without a military presence of any kind, and a housing scheme of dubious worth. As a consequence its recruiting potential has never been properly realised.

The job of the GSO II (TA and Cadets) was to implement the General's policy for the training of the Territorial Army and Cadets in Scotland. I got no hand-over; Richard Hanson (KOSB), my predecessor, had 'flu so I was dropped in at the deep end. From Day 1 my "In" tray was piled high with files and it was still that way in the early evening, so that some had to go home, much to Morag's disgust. The GOC-in-C was Lt General Sir Gordon MacMillan, a marvellous person to work for. One of his sons, Sir John, is GOC today. The two TA Divisions in Glasgow and Perth did most of the detail. The General liked to go round all the TA

Associations, a peculiarly British organisation, for the local administration of part-time soldiers, airmen and cadets. There was one in every county in those days and now there are only two, in Glasgow and Dundee. The General was good enough to take me with him in the remarkable "Old Grey Mare", a grey Rolls Royce which had been gifted by an old lady to General "Bulgy" Thorne, the war-time GOC-in-C. I learned so much from him for we had long distances to travel. We met all the Lords Lieutenant and senior TA officers, serving and retired, many of whom I had known in the war.

A 15-day annual camp was the principal training medium for the TA and it fell to the GII (TA) to organise these. They all had to be staffed by the regular army - a most unpopular assignment, as it meant separation from the family during the school holidays - the bane of the Serviceman's life. There was much competition for the camps in England - the Jocks like to get away from Mum to commit their misdemeanours - but most years units had to put up with the well-known Stobs (near Hawick), Barry Buddon (by Carnoustie) and Cultybraggan (Comrie), although there were many other sites for specialist units. In 1951 a part of the Z Reserve - war-time officers and soldiers - was called up and units went to camp immensely strong. We had to open a new camp at Dallachy, a disused war-time airfield near Fochabers that housed a whole Brigade.

Large quantities of vehicles and stores had to come from central UK Depots and it was my job to draw up enormous lists of these, column by column. The typing pool dreaded my approach. The Royal Ordnance Corps were superb and everything miraculously arrived by rail and on time.

At this time we lived at 17 Durham Road, Portobello, a nice part of the world, much favoured by Glaswegians in the old days for holidays. I travelled by train to Waverley from Portobello station (4d return) and enjoyed the steep hill up to The Castle via Ramsay Lane. It was a marvellous place to work, and it hadn't yet become the tourist trap it is today. The skirl of the pipes was never far away, for the great Pipe Major Willie Ross ran the Army Piping School a few blocks away. But it was an eerie place at night for the Duty Officer who slept in a dungeon where the wind made banshee noises all night. There wasn't much sleep anyway because the Korean War was at its height and there were many emergencies. One night Barney Henderson's (KOSB) father rang to say that they had had the dreaded telegram to say that their son had been "seriously wounded". How serious was it? Thanks to vastly improved Signal services I was able to put their minds at rest by 6 o'clock in the morning.

The Cadets side of the business was more difficult. They had always been the poor relation and under-funded, due to a stupid undercurrent of accusations of militarism, which continues today. The schools with Officers Training Corps, soon to be called Combined Cadet Forces to cater very properly for naval and air force sub-units, were still in good heart, although one or two succumbed to pacifist school boards. It was the Army Cadet Force in the cities, towns and villages which was struggling. Their uniforms were desperately unattractive, equipment was outmoded and inadequate and the leadership, in many cases, suspect. The only way we could compete with the splendid Boys' Brigade and the Boy Scouts was to offer a good youth organisation with a military flavour. We banged away at the War Office and ran a lot of courses, but the Cadets remained a very low priority despite some dedicated men at the top. I remember taking Brigadier ap Rhys Pryce, the Director of Cadets at the War Office up to Crail to visit cadets in camp. From the time I met him off the sleeper, breakfasted him in the Castle and drove him to Crail by road he talked Cadet shop the entire journey. He had never been in Scotland before, had never seen the Forth Bridge, and yet he never even looked out of the window as we crossed on the ferry! He certainly was doing his best for the cadets.

Occasionally the War Office could be quite maddening in its "Englishness". Once they insisted that a Permanent Staff Instructor living in Lerwick, Shetland, should occupy a married quarter in Aberdeen. According to this sage in the Ministry the PSI could then "nip across to work on the ferry"! Because Orkney and Shetland are so far north there is no room for them on the War Office maps so they stick them as inserts in the North Sea just off

111

Aberdeen.

No mention of Scottish Command would be complete without The Edinburgh Military Tattoo which was then in its infancy. That great character - lovable, maddening - Lieutenant Colonel Alastair Maclean of Pennycross (don't ever get the Pennycross wrong) was on the staff of the Headquarters as Assistant Adjutant General and it was he who lifted the Tattoo from being a side-show in Princes Street Gardens to the famous international spectacle which it is today. As soon as the TA camps were over everyone in the Headquarters was involved in some way. I started as "dogsbody" to Alastair and, over the years, became his assistant and commentator in several Tattoos during the 50's. They were much more amateur in those days - although there were far more troops involved than today - and, I would venture to say, much more fun! There were problems galore, but everyone enjoyed being part of a theatrical show once a year. One night when the Admiral was taking the salute the audience gasped when the Senior Drum Major came out of the Castle and over the drawbridge staggering all over the place, completely fu'. We had to endure this staggering performance right down the esplanade and up again. To his eternal credit he never dropped his mace. Alastair, Bob Happer, Douglas Spratt (lights) and I were really busy on the phone. While the bands were counter-marching at the top of the esplanade, the lights were directed elsewhere, the Military Police emerged unseen from the Castle and when the lights came on again the "Drummie" wasn't there. He was in durance vile. Considering the number of troops involved there were very few dramas of that kind. The Lord Provost always gave us a thundering good party at the end and attended himself. Nothing so chummy as that now-a-days; it's all very professional.

Another memorable Tattoo occasion was the night when Sir Thomas Beecham came with the London Philharmonic Orchestra to play Handel's Music for the Royal Fireworks, complete with real live fireworks and the 25 pounders of the Saluting Battery from Mills Mount high on the Castle ramparts. At the afternoon rehearsal Beecham said to the Artillery officer: "Now your cue to fire the guns is the only time I will raise my baton in the air and point it right at you up on the ramparts". Unfortunately, he didn't give the poor Gunner time to walk back up to his post. When it came to the "moment critique" the guns did not roar out. Sir Thomas dropped his baton and put his hand up to his ear. The orchestra hooted with laughter. Everything went fine on the night.

It was great being back in Scotland again - and there was occasional time off. We were able to visit my folks who had recently moved in retiral from St Fillans to Wester Balgedie, near Kinross. In the rugby season it was Glasgow Academicals at New Anniesland. Melrose had little need of me. Under Charlie Drummond they had one of their best teams ever. I felt that I owed something back to The Alma Mater - and there were more trains to Glasgow than Melrose. Hamish Dawson, the Accies captain, was very patient with me for my sedentary appointment was not very conducive to athleticism.

The two years flew by. On the 30th of December 1951 Sheena was born in the "Simpson", a much easier arrival for Morag this time. Sheena was a rebel from the start - but what a stimulating and rewarding life she has carved out for herself, a great gel. This time the christening was in the tiny St Margaret's Chapel high in the Castle, a privilege reserved only for the children of those actually serving in The Castle. It only holds 16 people - which certainly cuts down on the cost of the christening party.

I hated trumping Morag's ace, but I had to tell her at her bedside that The Queen was going to make me an MBE in two days time. I would like to think that the rough edges had been knocked off.

Chapter Eight
The Cold War
(1952-1959)

Take up the White Man's burden,
and reap his old reward:
The blame of those ye better,
The hate of those ye guard.
Rudyard Kipling

The British Army staff system, unlike those of most other armies, ensures that staff officers return to regimental duty in between staff appointments. A staff officer has a lot of power - he is acting in the name of his commander - so it does him good to be brought down to earth again at the receiving end. In my case the earth was Korea which was a perfect example of the Cold War. In 1945 the country was split into two by the 38th parallel. North Korea espoused the communist cause and was eventually supported in the war by the Chinese; South Korea espoused democracy of a kind and was strongly supported by the Americans and other United nations allies. In 1950 the North Koreans surged over the 38th parallel and very nearly reached Pusan in the south. For years the battle raged north and south and back again. As ever, air power was to be the crucial factor. The 1st Battalion KOSB were part of the Commonwealth Division in Korea from April 1951 until August 1952, and on Guy Fawkes Day 1951 they fought a memorable battle at Kowang San near the Imjin River, killing over 1000 Chinese for the loss of 7 Borderers.

Private Bill Speakman, a regular soldier, won the Victoria Cross and 2nd Lieutenant Willie Purves from Kelso, a National Service officer aged 19, won the Distinguished Service Order. He is now head of the Hong Kong and Shanghai Bank.

In preparation for regimental duty we moved to a stable flat in Gifford and acquired a bone-shaker of a car, so that Morag would have some mobility.

To my great surprise I received a charming letter from General "Tiger" Miles, the Colonel of the KOSB, saying that the 1st Bn did not require me; they were overstrength in officers and anyway they were returning to Hong Kong and the UK. I was required at the Depot in Berwick and later at the 5th (Dumfries and Galloway) Battalion in Dumfries. This came as something of a shock. I had been away from the Regiment for six years and the 1st Bn would be entitled to say "Who is this guy who goes around playing rugby and doing cushy staff jobs in the U.K."? However I've always been a great believer in "Dae as yer tellt"; it always pays off.

In my Scottish Command role I went to Berwick and the Borders as often as I decently could without too much bias. I knew most of the Regular officers and always attended the Regimental weekend in August when we played cricket against the Eton Ramblers and golf at Goswick. The first one was pretty agonising for Morag, but everyone was very kind, particularly Nancy Turner. I am the world's worst cricketer and was only selected simply because I was available. My main roles were to drop catches on the boundary and act as runner for Ross Logan, who had lost a foot in the war with the 8th Royal Scots. He was a very fine all round sportsman, one of the toughest scrum halves ever to play for Scotland, and he was belting the ball all over the ground. As his runner I was hurtling up and down the wicket when a senior KOSB lady leant over to Morag and said: "I say, your husband really is in top form today". Thank you, Ross.

The training of the National Service intake was a fascinating experience. It really was a case of *Duke's son, cook's son* so far as the call-up was concerned. They didn't all come from the Borders and we had our fair share of tough nuts from the

Lowlands of Scotland (quoth he, protecting his native Glasgow). The delightful Terry Coverdale was in command. I had the training company (back to my substantive rank of Captain) with war-experienced Barney Henderson and Sandy Rundle as lively subalterns. The great RSM "Fister" Walls MC ruled the square - and nearly everything and everyone else. We were back in the old barracks again, and Magdalene Fields was deserted, soon to be turned into a holiday camp, as it is now. Among the NCO instructors were several who were to make their name in the Regiment: John "Paddy" White, George Smythe, Tom Kirkhope (who had won his MM with the 4th at Ibbenburen) and Bill Dover, still serving at Berwick. The area of the barracks was ideal for basic training - weapon training on the ancient walls of Berwick, a good little range on the cliffs, sports on "The Stanks" and, best of all, tactical training at Scremerston sand dunes with a plunge into the sea afterwards and a route march back to Berwick. Happy days. These young men only had 12 weeks training - not long enough - but they passed out proudly, went home for a few days leave and then went off to their battalions - mainly 1 KOSB - all over the world. They were the men who fought the Cold War and the aftermath of Empire, and Britain should be very proud of them.

I lived in the Mess during the week and travelled back to Gifford to be with baby Sheena and the family at the weekend - by train to East Linton where I kept "The Camel", an enormous bike gifted to me by Pip after he left Jesus College, Cambridge, and still labelled J 517. Then back to East Linton at some unearthly hour on Monday morning.

This was only a six-months assignment. I handed over to Edward Atkinson and departed for Dumfries to be Adjutant of the 5th Battalion, at Nunfield House. Married quarters were being built in the grounds, but they weren't ready and we moved into an extraordinary "hiring" in a converted church at the tiny village of Haugh of Urr between Dalbeattie and Castle Douglas, known principally as the home of a Regimental family, the Herries of Spottes, and also Andrew Biggar and his bulls. We had about nine months of rural charm there, travelling into work

National Service squad marches past the Mayor of Berwick upon Tweed. David Crake and Sergeant J. P. White

with "J.B." (Marshall), the Quartermaster, who came from Castle Douglas, but were very glad to move into the sparkling new quarters at Nunfield, courtesy of the T.A. Association at a good fat rent.

The 5th Battalion had been set up again after the war by a very special KOSB Godfather, Lt Col "Father" Batchelor, former regular officer and well known breeder of Galloway cattle. He had commanded the 5th Battalion with distinction towards the end of the war when Willow Turner went to command the 1st. Now a new team was in position. The C.O. was the bold Walter Ross, farmer from Bridge of Dee, (who as a gunner had saved our lives at Haus Loo), now an Infantry Officer, the 2nd-in-command was "Teedo" Stephen, Aberdonian and headmaster at Wigtown. In charge of the companies were: A Coy Tommy Bell, postmaster at Lockerbie, (with Bill Friell, postmaster at Langholm); B Coy George Moodie, the organist, from Stranraer; C Coy Gordon Grieve, estate agent from Gatehouse of Fleet; D Coy at Sanquhar and Kirkconnel Wyllie Irving, a Dumfries solicitor, and George Thomson, chartered surveyor and Aberdonian and another gunner who had seen the light commanded HQ Coy in Dumfries. Iain Drape at Whithorn and Ken Biggar in Dalbeattie were special chums. They were a great team and worked very hard.

Part-time National Servicemen with 5 KOSB,
Kirkcudbright

There was a permanent staff of three officers, RSM and ten Warrant Officers and Sergeants scattered over 17 Drill halls or TA Centres, and a few civilian staff, catering for a battalion nearly 1000 strong (about 25% TA, and 75% reservists). This was my first experience as Adjutant and I was lucky to have a superb Chief Clerk in Archie Lawson, a wonderful Borderer who understood the mysteries of acquittance rolls &c. I wasn't completely stupid; I had taken the precaution of going on a pay course with the Royal Army Pay Corps - the best course I ever attended - for several officers had come to grief over financial matters while with the T.A.

The character of the soldiers in Dumfries and Galloway was very different from those I had been used to in the eastern Border counties. The pace of life was slower west of Dumfries; indeed it was positively soporific - something to do with the climate no doubt.

Private McDowall from "west of the Cree" was the Commanding Officers despatch rider. On an exercise near Kirkcudbright he was asked - at 3 am - to take a message to one of the companies at Brighouse Bay. He delivered it to the irate occupant of a local estate. When challenged about this he expostulated: "I was told to tak' it to the Big Hoose, Sir". Luckily the irate gentleman was the Commanding Officer's brother-in-law.

We fought constant paper wars with authority about shortages of money, transport and equipment. Every letter began: "Due to the scattered nature of this Battalion...". There were courses at HQ every weekend and drill nights somewhere every night. Even on "days off" mid-week T.A. officers dropped in to talk "shop" and they were such a delightful crowd that you just had to drop your spade and get them a drink.

The Pipes and Drums under Pipe Major Jimmy Brown were my pride and joy. It was agonising waiting for them to turn up after work, but we nearly always managed the basic eight pipers and three or four drummers. Except once - the Castle Douglas show - a prestigious event. I had to change into piper's kit and play in the band, a great thrill, but nearly a disaster because all the farmers stood me piper's drams and I was hardly capable of performing my main function of driving Pipey Broon home to Auldgirth.

A special event in 1953 was the Coronation of Her Majesty Queen Elizabeth II. We trained up a Colour Party for the parade in London. None of them had any previous experience, and nor had I. Back in Dumfries we celebrated in style by firing a "feu de joie" from the historic Devorgilla Bridge over the Nith. Other ceremonial occasions were the Freedoms of Selkirk in the 4th Bn area, and Dumfries and Stranraer in the 5th. We also went to Ballykinlar in Northern Ireland to see the 1st Battalion receive new Colours.

The Doonhamers were super people and we made a lot of friends. Fiona went to Miss Trotter's school in Maxwellton and we worshipped with the Battalion Padre, Neilson Peterkin, later of Broom, Newton Mearns. Come the Riding of the Marches, 'Guid Nychburris Day', Tony Cran, now the Adjutant, and I played an official part, and I fell off my horse galloping up the Nith, causing grave damage to the Town Seal. Luckily it was a facsimile. I got an occasional game of rugger for Dumfries and particularly enjoyed a fiery tussle with Hector Monro at Langholm - later Member of Parliament for Dumfries and President of the Scottish Rugby Union.

Camp in 1953 was at Stobs - pretty awful - then in 1954 the whole Division was selected to go to Salisbury Plain for a full Divisional exercise, complete with all our reservists, something which had never been tried in peace-time before. It was a mammoth task. P.S.I.s went round isolated farmhouses picking up Jocks - luckily it was a good bit before harvest - and taking them to one of several troop trains, starting in Stranraer and stopping off at every station on the way. Only 2 soldiers out of the Battalion failed to show up - Walter Ross was so angry that he had them court-martialled - a unique occurrence in the T.A. The whole exercise was voted a complete success and proved to the Russians that we meant business. The 4th Battalion, there as the motorised Battalion of the Armoured Brigade, ran a spectacular Guest Night after which we played Seven-a-side rugger on a concrete floor with much blood spattered on stiff white dress shirts.

But my time was up. The War Office wanted their pound of staff-trained flesh. "Would I like to go as in instructor to the WRAC Staff College?" "What? Teaching women?" "No, not WRAC - *Iraqi* Staff College. You'll be a local Lt Col" (Morag used to chat up an Iraqi officer at Staff College. He was a student in my Division and stood on the touch line, complaining that he was putting on weight. He said he rode a lot at home. Morag said: "Why don't you borrow the Colonel's horse; it's eating its head off in the stables". No, it wasn't that kind of riding - he *rowed* a lot on the Tigris). So, we had to pack up again and label the ever-increasing packing cases "Baghdad, via Beirut and the Nairn Desert Bus". The packing cases intrigued me. Before I was married my only possessions were a rugger bag and a bedding roll. By the time the second child had arrived we were up to about 30 enormous boxes. After interviews at the Iraqi Embassy in London, which did not inspire confidence, the Iraquis regretted that they now wanted an Armoured Corps instructor and not an Infantryman. (It looks, in 1991, as though he fell down on his job).

I was now to go to Trieste as D.A.A.& Q.M.G. to 24 Infantry Brigade. These ridiculous initials stand for Deputy Assistant Adjutant and Quartermaster General - the chief administrative officer of a Brigade of about 8000 souls, including families. Re-label boxes and send them to Trieste, only to be told that peace had broken out in Trieste and the Brigade was returning to Barnard Castle. What again? Some decent chap spotted the boxes somewhere down the line in Germany and returned them.

After farewell parties in Dumfries (A Trieste, très Triste", said witty Walter in his speech), over the Border to "Barnie" and a load of work as O.C. Advance Party. 24 Brigade had been formed in Italy by General "Boy" Browning and carried the shoulder flash of his own coat of arms, the Phoenix rising. They were now to be a fly-anywhere, anytime Brigade, linked to the Yorkshire group of airfields. We had two marvellous Brigadiers - both in the Devonshire Regiment - Hugh Borrodaile and Paul Gleadell. The Brigade Major was a fellow Scot, "Choo" Maclagan of The Seaforth Highlanders. Two Scots in charge of all these Sassenachs! They put up with us well and came in droves to the Scottish Country Dancing class. You are bound to ask why he was called "Choo". At Sandhurst, a far from sharp Sergeant Instructor had bawled at him: "Wake up, sir, that Chinese officer cadet in the rear rank".

Apart from the Glorious Gloucesters, not long back from their epic battle in Korea, we had entirely North country Battalions - The Loyals (North Lancashire), the South Lancashires, the Border Regiment from Carlisle, The Durham Light Infantry, and

14 Field Regiment RA. The Brigade was spread all round the town of Barnard Castle in four fairly uncomfortable camps - grim in the cold weather - Startforth, Stainton, Barford and Humbleton. The biggest problem on the D/Q's plate was married quarters. Although we had a very large estate centrally at Stainton Grove, a fair sized village, there were never enough to go round and there were always large waiting lists. They were allocated on a points system - but there were so many grey areas; for example, a case which could be described as compassionate would take precedence over many non-moaners. I'm afraid I took the whole thing into my own hands and acted as the sole arbiter. Having a Scots bonnet helped; the distraught wives thought it looked "kind of cute". I had an excellent Staff Captain, John Burkmar, to look after the "A" side, Courts of Inquiry, Courts-Martial etc, and Dickie Bird, the GSO III kept us all happy by drawing outrageous cartoons and running the Bde HQ Rugby team.

The real job was to get the Brigade ready for operations abroad, anywhere, anytime. From the start we took over a sheaf of operation orders catering for emergencies all over the ever-decreasing Empire. We exercised frequently in getting to the airfields, mainly Dishforth, but rarely took off, and we had our own Flight of Prestwick Pioneers which could land and take off from the rugger field at the back of HQ.

Our relations with the town were excellent. We were good for "biz" of course, but an invasion of so many troops could have caused all sorts of problems. I can't remember a single punch-up taking place and we ensured that we kept them in the know about our doings, within the bounds of security. "Jones, the Press", an amusing Welshman, came to the office every week to get copy for the local rag.

One of the things which kept the soldiers reasonably happy was that they could often get home at weekends. The trains still ran over the Pennines from Darlington through "Barnie" to the west. The worst job I had to do in the Army, bar none, was at Barnard Castle Station. It was Thursday of Easter weekend and the entire Brigade was going on leave in special trains. There had been very serious flooding on the east coast, leave was cancelled and the whole Brigade was required for relief work. The D/Q had to go to the station and, with only a hand megaphone, tell the boys "All leave is cancelled for operational reasons - go back to your barracks". I thought I would be lynched. The British soldier is an amazing chap. British Rail were none too pleased with me, though.

We had dreaded going to "Barnie" but it turned out to be a delightful posting. The countryside is quite lovely, Fiona went to the Army school and learned a few words she hadn't heard at Miss Trotter's, shortly to be joined by Sheena, whilst I carved out a most satisfying garden out of what had been a field at 3 Wellington Road. We made a whole lot of new friends in English Regiments, and on Sundays we piled into a jeep to hear Tom Nicol preaching in the Scots kirk at Catterick. He knew to finish his sermon when Sheena's thumb dropped out of her mouth in deep slumber. The Army Air Corps kindly flew me to Edinburgh to carry out my duties at the Tattoo.

Eventually, the balloon went up. Suez. The Brig and I flew off to Cyprus via Malta, a very rough ride, to make arrangements for the Brigade to move into the Famagusta area to fill the place of those who were going on to Jordan. It soon became obvious that things were going wrong. As we were just hanging about, Brigadier Paul, who was a great sport, suggested that we go up to Kyrenia and see The Dragon Aunt and Jimmy Murray, her second husband, who had settled there for good. With our Military Police escort to protect us from EOKA, we had a great day out.

The Suez operation was kyboshed by the Americans and we came creeping home. But I was off again - back to 1 KOSB in Malaya - and this time they wanted me in a hurry, so I flew out and Morag and the kids went round the Cape - six weeks on the *Dunera*. Even by air the trip took four days with night stops at Brindisi and Karachi. I was delighted to be greeted by one of our Glosters from Barnie - in a greatcoat at 2am - some of them had been moved to The Gulf. At Karachi there was a ramshackle transit camp run by a Mrs Miniwalla; the Jocks wouldn't post their postcards there because they said she licked the stamps off!

After a night in Nee Soon transit camp in Singapore, (scene of *The Virgin Soldiers*) and an issue of rifles, we were heaped on board the back of a truck and over the causeway to Malaya. With two brothers in the Colonial Service - Wally as Chief Secretary in Kenya and Philip a District officer in Uganda - I was naturally very interested in Colonial organisation. This was before the "wind of change", but there were plenty of critics about, particularly in America. After our disastrous showing against the Japanese in 1941, the British did well to re-establish the rule of law in Singapore and Malaya, and I was very impressed by the infrastructure - hospitals, schools, roads, bridges - they were all there and working. The much maligned P.W.D. (Public Works Department) can take the credit for a great deal of sound construction around the world. But were the people oppressed? If they were, which I very much doubt, their oppression certainly compared very favourably with other states in the Far East with the rubber estates and tin mines, lynch-pin of a prosperous country, all being efficiently run. All this the Communists wanted to overturn, and they had been worming away for years - even during the Japanese occupation. Chin Peng (OBE!) was their leader. He fought long and hard from inside the jungle, and he had many ruthless supporters.

Spencer Chapman's book, *The Jungle is Neutral*, is required reading on the Malayan Emergency. When I arrived in 1956 the back of the emergency had been broken thanks to the persistent efforts of successive British and Gurkha battalions and a staunch Police Force with British Officers. But the real heroes and heroines were the rubber planters and their wives. Their bungalows were very isolated, they had all been shot up, and they only had special constables to guard them.

1 KOSB were part of a Gurkha Brigade in 17th Division, looking after a huge slice of Johore State. Battalion HQ was in the busy little town of Batu Pahat on the west coast. This coastal strip had been declared "white", reasonably free of terrorists, and this enabled us to operate from a secure base. Tactical Headquarters was at Yong Peng on the main north-south road, as sleazy and nasty a place as you will find in the whole country.

When General Templer visited Yong Peng he gave them an absolute tongue-lashing . (I passed through a year or two back, and cashed a cheque in the local bank - it still felt evil). Colin Stonor's C Company was also in a tented base there, next to the Police Station, on the edge of the town. A Company under Jock Scott was about 10 miles down the road at Ayer Hitam, and B Company (Cyril Wilson-Clarke and later Alan Smyth) was at Nyor on the railway north of Kluang and D Company (Alastair Thorburn) was out on its own, farther up the railway at Paloh. I was to take over from Alastair but he was in no particular hurry as he had just become engaged to Ann in Singapore .

I arrived in Paloh on New Years Eve 1956, eager for the fray, only to be told that we were going out to a party! In accordance with tradition the Battalion had been stood down for New Year, our duties being taken over by the Rhodesian African Rifles north of us at Labis. In the Paloh area there were 19 rubber estates, surrounded by jungle - and 17 of them were managed by Scots. We repaired, with a piper, to Freddie Thom's beautiful bungalow on a hill at Bukit Paloh and brought in the New Year in fine style.

Our main job was to bring confidence back to the "kampongs" (villages) and to protect the rubber tappers when they were out doing their job. The CTs had been bullying them and forcing them to hand over money and food. It was a huge task - we had over 50 square miles of rubber and jungle, spreading from the rubber edge eastwards over the whole country. But confidence was beginning to creep back. Templer's food denial plan was brilliant. Every kampong was wired in - and isolated families forced to come into the kampong - with police on the gates. The tappers were only allowed to take out enough food and drink for their mid-day "makan" (meal). There were very few active gangs left in the Paloh area, but a lot of sympathisers. Once the British Government had announced that Malaya was to be granted independence - and they had fixed a date, 1st August 1957 - there was nothing left for them to fight for.

We worked hand in glove with the police. Our Police Sub-Division under Inspector Bill Barnes was in Paloh, a seedy little place. We should have been alongside him but there was no accommodation so we were in a tented camp at Kim Swa on the Kempas Estate (Bill Anderson), near another railway halt, Beradin. We were able to use the railway quite a lot for operations, and it was really handy for going on leave.

The work was very arduous and I lost 3 stones in 1957. It varied between rubber patrols, wire patrols round the kampongs (it was an offence for the wire not to be properly maintained), night ambushes, and deep jungle patrols, based on Special Branch information which was usually wildly inaccurate. The usual scenario would be that the Operations Officer from HQ would tell us that groups of terrorists would be uplifting food from such-and-such a kampong in two or three nights time. An ambush party of about six to twelve with an officer or sergeant in command would be briefed and rehearsed. They would creep into position at dusk, probably after a long, silent and devious approach march. There they would lie for 12 hours, being eaten alive by mosquitos and listening with apprehension to every

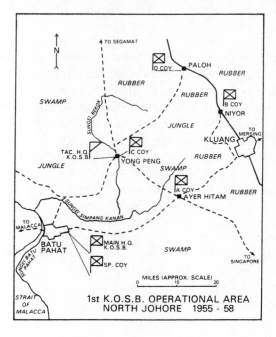

1st K.O.S.B. OPERATIONAL AREA
NORTH JOHORE 1955 - 58

cracked twig and rubber nut. Come the dawn, the doleful message would be passed to HQ: "59 Alpha. November Tango Romeo (Nothing To Report)".

There was a total curfew and no movement outside wired villages was permitted between dusk and dawn. Some of the trickiest ambushes were on the main road. A car with blazing headlights would come booming up the narrow Yong Peng to Paloh road. To fire or not to fire? You only had seconds in which to decide. More than likely it was some drunken planter taking a chance and we didn't want another accidental death on our hands.

The jungle could be very lovely with its high canopy, and exotic fauna and flora, and sometimes with reasonable tracks, but mostly it was cruel with progress only possible by bashing one's way through. Keeping direction was extremely difficult, and compass and map reading skills had to be of a high standard. Each platoon had an Iban from Borneo or Sarawak attached who could "read" the jungle intimately, dissect the sights, sounds and smells, and say if anyone had passed that way. They were thoroughly spoiled by the Jocks. At Coy HQ we had a Chinese Liaison Officer, Foo Wah Koon, a well-educated young man who didn't like the jungle much - but he eventually learned our ways, including some nasty expressions which he had never heard at his English lessons. The mosquitoes were a pest and the leeches even more so; it was a courtesy to remove them from your "mucker" (chum) by using a cigarette end or a dab of salt. They gorged themselves on our rich Scottish blood.

Setting up base camp was an art form. One or two men made a "basha". A groundsheet over a pole was the basic ingredient remembering that it often rained heavily around stand-to (dusk) - but many variations including vine hammocks were in vogue. As movement in the jungle was virtually impossible after dark, it was a long night, although with sentries posted, one felt reasonably secure. We carried rucksacks and far too much kit, including a "parang" (machete) that was essential for slashing the undergrowth and an SLR (self-loading rifle) which never left one's hands. Feeding was left very much to the individual and his "mucker". We were still on the excellent war-time compo rations and a chap could take more or less what he liked, but it had to last for up to 7 days at time before an air-drop or re-supply at the jungle edge. If he was stupid enough to take tins, then that was

up to him. Cooking was singly or in pairs on small hexamine cookers. Most "went native" with rice and additives, which were very satisfying and so much lighter.

The new Belgian 7.62mm self-loading rifle was the main personal weapon. It was heavy but accurate and it was a major advantage in this type of warfare not to have to re-load a bolt action rifle. The war-time sten had been improved and a type of shotgun known as the 'pump gun' was popular.

Operationally, 'shoot to kill' was the watchword, for these were desperate men (and women; the last terrorist the KOSB disposed of in Johore was known as the *Pineapple Pin-Up*). The trouble was identifying them. They weren't necessarily going to pay you the compliment of wearing a red star on their jungle hats. More often than not they were dressed exactly like the rubber tappers, but if they were carrying weapons that was good enough. It was imperative to shoot quickly and accurately and we practised our drills with live ammunition over and over again.

When it happened in earnest it was all over very quickly. Platoon Commander Ian Christie: "I fired six shots with my carbine at the CT. Cpl Martin fired a full magazine of his Owen gun at the movement in the ferns. We pulled back the under-growth, and two bodies were lying there, twitching."

In two and a half years in the jungle the battalion only had twenty two contacts with terrorists, killing eight and wounding others. It was a very frustrating campaign.

Back in base camp at Kim Swa we made our own amusements on the few nights back in camp. We had our own skiffle group with "Elvis" Graham from Ecclefechan, and at Company Smok-ers in the tented dining hall, aided by the potent Tiger or Anchor beer, most people put on a turn. The boys were allowed one weekend a month in Singapore. Usually they came back with grotesque tattoos around their bodies. Willie Thyne bet me a fiver he would go back to the UK with our cherished 17 Gurkha Div tattooed on his upper arm. He paid up.

Once a month the Army Kinema Corporation put on a film in the open air, demanding exorbitant wages for coming to the sharp end. On occasional Sundays the Padre, Douglas Scrimgeour, later to be Moderator of the United Free Church of Scotland, made no such demands for taking a homely church service. It was completely voluntary and there was a 90% attendance (someone had to guard the perimeter). The comradeship engendered living under these conditions was very intense. Although the National Servicemen hung calendars in their tents and struck off every day, they felt a real loss when the moment came. I remember saying goodbye to an outstanding National Service corporal in a jungle base camp, going 'out' with his escort to the jungle-edge. We shook hands: "Goodbye, Cpl Stillie. We shall miss you. Good luck and thank you." His eyes filled with tears: "I don't want to go, Sir".

Some people would like to see the return of universal National Service. It would certainly be good for the backbone of the nation, but it would be a political hot potato that no party would handle. In any event, the army is now so pared to the bone that we haven't enough instructors to train our own regulars, let alone half the male population of Britain.

D Coy was a great team. David Legg was the second in

command, from a Regimental family, harum-scarum, more interested in preserving the wildlife than killing terrorists -'charm the birds off the trees', the Jocks said - three super Platoon Commanders, all different but complementary. John Aitkin from Hawick, a qualified Chartered Accountant doing his National Service late, now a Regimental trustee, Willie Thyne from The Yair on the Tweed, debonair, very popular, and Tom Butson, a regular New Zealander, attached for a year, a splendid Kiwi - the rugby arguments were long and fierce. The Company Sergeant Major was John 'the Doc' Docherty, a superb anchorman, and Wee Fraser, the Colour Sergeant, who should have been a Gordon. Two of the sergeants were in a class of their own as leaders of men - Pat Devenney MM (Korea) and 'Harryrya' Harrigan BEM. For the whole of the 1957, D Coy traversed the Paloh district assiduously, wearing out dozens of pairs of jungle boots.

Every now and then Higher Authority would think up operations which took us farther afield. Once, the whole company was air-lifted into a piece of jungle near Malacca which was reputed to be hotching with terrorists. RSM Ron Maddison MBE came with us and also a bold journalist from Annan, who had been a great supporter through the years. On another never-to-be-

Lam Lee Ambush. Sgt Harrigan won the beard growing competition

forgotten occasion, I took 12 hand picked Borderers into a horrid, soaking wet piece of jungle behind Lam Lee kampong for a 17 day ambush. The CT's were bound to turn up; it was a regular meeting place - tell that to the Marines. Of course they didn't appear; it was a bitter disappointment. We weren't allowed to wash or shave because the CT's could smell the soap. Harrigan was the clear winner of the beard growing competition.

When Morag arrived in the trooper, D Coy were miles away in the jungle west of Labis in an area which had not been surveyed. The maps were white and devoid of detail, but did show the rivers quite well. Signals, my old bug-bear, had improved enormously. We now had the Australian 510 set, light and efficient when properly used with a high aerial. This was achieved by throwing a bobbin as high as possible into the trees. David McConnel, the Commanding Officer, Hugh Gilles the 2IC or Andrew Myrtle, the Adjutant, would come on the blower every night at the same time. The whole Battalion in turn gave their sitrep (situation report). This night David came on and ordered me back to Singapore to meet the family. I protested: "How can I? I'm halfway to Thailand!" "Do as I say" crackled David firmly over the air, "I'm not prepared to face Morag's wrath if you're not there!"

Taking two escorts, who could ill be spared, I handed over to David Legg and trudged back through the 'ulu' (jungle) for a day and a half. We had a blissful reunion at the dockside, the girls looking marvellous in their tropical kit. We stayed in a guest house for a couple of nights and then moved into a nice quarter at Selarang Barracks, Changi, near the infamous prison. There they came under the benevolent wing of the regimental family and the kids went to Selarang Primary.

There was great excitement in August when Merdeka (Freedom - Independence) Day came round. The Duke of Gloucester represented The Crown in Kuala Lumpur at the Merdeka Day celebrations, while we contrived mini-ceremonial parades in our Company bases. In the afternoon, the boys played the locals at football in Paloh.

Down at Batu Pahat, we were honoured by a visit from our

Colonel-in-Chief H.R.H. The Duchess of Gloucester who had of course accompanied her husband to K.L.. It was a memorable visit. The Duchess's charm and constant interest in her fellow Borderers raised morale sky-high. After she flew off at the minuscule airstrip, to the skirl of the pipes, we repaired to the Sergeants Mess for an uproarious barbecue round the swimming pool. A lot of people took the plunge, accidentally or intentionally. It was fine to meet up with officers and sergeants from other Coys, as we were miles apart and rarely met except at occasional 'O' (Orders) groups at Yong Peng. One day I was going down to an O Group in an armoured car through a rather sinister five mile strip of jungle when I had a strong feeling that something was wrong. When I dismounted at C Coy, CSM Cowan said to me, stiff upper lip, holding a telegram in his hand: "Bit o' bad news, Sir. Your old Dad's dead". A great man - and so far away.

Merdeka didn't mean the end of the Emergency and it took another year to wind it up. The tappers were very Bolshie. They firmly imagined that Merdeka meant they would never have to work again, and the Estate Managers had a lot of trouble. We intensified our activities - rubber patrols by day, night ambushes by night - a hopeless situation with diminishing efficiency. By now the Impossible Officer had taken over command, and he drove us relentlessly. The whole battalion was patrolling in rubber and jungle round Yong Peng, when he ordered Colin Stonor and myself to meet him at a certain bridge. "Ah," we thought, "a dram or at least a nice cup of tea!" He drove up in a cloud of mud, gave out staccato orders in a high-pitched voice and disappeared as quickly as he came. Unbelievable.

At the back end of the year, the monsoons came with a vengeance and we patrolled in terrible conditions, wet through day and night. In late December 1957 Edward Atkinson came up to relieve me for Christmas leave. We still laugh about that historic rendezvous. When we shook hands the water was literally up to our waists. He had to put his fags in his breast pocket, wrapped in cellophane. We just couldn't get shaved because the razor blades were all rusted.

I was feeling far from well, and only just got back to Selarang (what a rotten Father Christmas), then on to hospital at RAF Changi and finally to the British Military Hospital Singapore. The next few days are pretty hazy, but I could tell that the medics were somewhat puzzled. They sent a blood sample back to London. By the time the answer came back I was just beginning to feel better! I had leptospirosis - nearly always fatal - the result of a rat bite in the jungle. It was complicated by a slipped disc, and the fact that Morag now arrived in another ward to have her thyroid gland operated on. A sorry pair. Bill and Ann Jardine of Applegirth nobly took the girls for which we were eternally grateful. Fortunately this tale of woe had a happy ending. Barbara Gordon was now the Matron of the B.M.H. and she arranged for us to go on the casevac plane to the military hospital in the Cameron Highlands for recuperation leave. Authority was somewhat perplexed to have a man and wife at the same time. We were firmly allocated to separate wards and said goodnight gratefully - but chastely.

The Battalion was now back at Selarang for re-training with one or two companies at a time up in Johore on operations. Robin Oatts dealt with the last two CT's to be killed during the Emergency. It was a well prepared ambush, based on Special Branch information, just north of Johore Bahru. The Regimental history: "The leading CT came on, reached the ambush position, began to peer through the bushes, and saw the ambush. Captain Oatts fired one shot, killing him at a range of six feet." The remainder surrendered.

We were kept pretty busy but the delights of the RAF Officers' Club and visits to Singapore were a great joy. Morag had a most congenial job at the Tanglin Club, teaching swimming, and we went back to the Camerons, a delightful spot, for a family holiday; by courtesy of that wonderful person Miss Griffith-Jones, the Headmistress of Tanglin School and heroine of the Japanese occupation. During the war the Japs had assembled all the European women in Singapore and inhumanely marched them under the scorching sun the 17 miles out to Changi. When they got to the prison gates 'Griff', who had been in command throughout, shouted to her group: "Now, heads up girls, swing your arms - and we'll go in singing Rule Britannia!"

It was not a very happy time in the barracks. There was an unnecessary amount of 'bull' and an unnecessary inter-company competition which proved most divisive. The Jocks were restless and wanted to be home. They had been happier in the jungle. One inspiring occasion was a joint Beating of Retreat on the square at Selarang by the bands of the 23rd regiment of Foot (The Royal Welsh Fusiliers), the 24th (The South Wales Borderers) and the 25th (the KOSB). Colin Stonor's company furnished the guard for Her Majesty's Birthday Parade on the padang in Singapore.

News came through that the battalion was to move to Berlin, staging for a time at Milton Bridge Camp near Penicuik. In due course, we embarked on the troopship *Dilwara* of the British India Line, on one of her last voyages. These were great occasions, not experienced by the present day army. With the Pipe Band of the 5th Royal Malay Regiment (affiliated to the KOSB) and the streamers from the ship to shore gradually parting, it was a very emotional scene. Most people in war-time have grim memories of *troopers* but in peace-time they were a great joy. True, the Jocks had pretty uncomfortable accommodation, but everyone fed well and had a lot of fun. It was quite a job to keep the chaps amused and out of trouble. I was Training Officer for the whole ship and had to show a good deal of inventiveness. We ran an NCO's Cadre, the officers had to study, we fired off balloons at the back of the ship, played fierce deck hockey, did a lot of PT and generally kept everyone busy - especially the children who had their own school. Everyone got a good tan after the pallor engendered by the jungle.

Movement by troopship was so much mare civilised than rushing about the world in aeroplanes. It gave everyone a psychological break after a hard tour overseas. But, of course, it was not cost effective so they had to go. Nowadays the Ministry of Defence is only happy when a chap finishes a job one day and starts the next at the far ends of the Earth: thoroughly unsettling.

Shortly after we left Singapore, it was announced that the whole of Malaysia had been declared 'white', and the Padre nearly fainted when told he had been Mentioned in Despatches.

AVERAGE DAILY CERTIFIED SALE EXCEEDS 3,000

The Straits Times

Malaya's National Newspaper

FASHIONABLE CREATIONS IN
FINE JEWELLERY
By
S. P. H. de SILVA LTD.
45 HIGH ST & AIRPORT
SINGAPORE
A. STATION ROAD—IPOH
ASSOCIATE COMPANY
S. P. H. de SILVA (K.L.) LTD
HONG KONG

Estd. 1845. SINGAPORE, THURSDAY, AUGUST 28, 1958 ✶ 15 CENTS

Red stronghold is broken and telegram is sent to Templer

NORTH JOHORE GOES WHITE

Seven million leaflets to tell of big surrender

KUALA LUMPUR, Wed.-A big operation—code-named St. Helena—will be lunched tomorrow to tell the remaining Reds in th Malayan jungle about the surrender of Hor Lung, the No. 2 man in the terrorist organisation, and 160 other bandits.

About seven million leaflets in Chinese will be air-dropped from Royal Air Foce Valetta aircraft and

Bristol freighters in "black areas" throughout the country.

This campaign follows yesterday's announcement by the Prime Minister, Tengku Abdul Rahman, of the big surrender.

Operation St. Helena will be completed on Aug. 31, Merdeka anniversary day.

Another victory in the Cold War. The Commies had a long run for their money.

Berlin really deserves a chapter to itself. It was a fantastic posting. This was the first of three tours the 1st Bn KOSB spent there during the Allied occupation. I was delighted to get away from Milton Bridge in January 1958 - it was so cold the Jocks were burning their furniture for fuel. I was O.C. Advance Party, then A Company, with Paddy White as my CSM, and President of the Officers' Mess. We were allowed to go by car and stopped in Amsterdam with Van Heels, Munster with the Nicols and a transit hotel in Hanover. Driving through the Russian zone was quite a performance. Under the four power agreement for the occupation of Berlin the Russians were obliged to give us free access by rail and road, but they made it as difficult as possible. At Marienborn, the autobahn junction with West Germany, there was tension in the air. Everyone had to be thoroughly checked and briefed by the British Military Police - then through No Man's Land to the Russian Military Police in a cold, sparse office with pictures of Lenin and Stalin on the wall. The Russians were so suspicious that travellers had to complete the journey within a small bracket of time - if one took any longer we had obviously been spying, if one took shorter we had been speeding! No one was allowed to stop anywhere on the route. Of course, Sheena had to stop to spend a penny! From the agitation in the

135

rest of the party you would think that the Third World War was about to start.

During our time in Berlin I had to take my turn as O.C. Military train. Each night a train pulled out of Berlin for the west. Often there would be no-one in it, but it had to go because it was part of the agreement and the routes to the west had to be kept open. We invariably shuffled up all the passports and forms to make it more difficult for the Russian Movement Officers. Childish, but they were the ones who were being bureaucratic and difficult.

We moved into a pokey little quarter in Hardyweg, but this disappointment was far outweighed by the joy of having the Scotters and Broughies of the Border Regiment at Barnard Castle as neighbours. One of the great compensations in Army life is meeting up with old chums.

1 KOSB and 1 Border were in neighbouring barracks in Spandau and the Royal Scots were down at Montgomery barracks on the Havel Lake. The duties in Berlin were so regulated that it is the only station I have known where a Company Commander could write a training programme for a month and see it through without alteration. Good soldiering. The duties were planned months ahead and didn't change - border patrols in Landrovers up by the Eiskeller, a bit dodgy, guards on Spandau prison where old man Hess and Co were still languishing (as they did for many more years), exercises in the Grunewald - a huge area of Berlin is given over to woods - range work at Ruhleben and a lot of ceremonial. The annual Queen's Birthday Parade on the Maifield at the Olympic Stadium was the big day in the British calendar abroad. 1958 was no exception and I was honoured to command the centre guard which had the privilege of calling the whole Brigade to attention! A Coy had an impressive right marker, Sergeant Bill Speakman VC, all seven feet of him. Afterwards we rubbed shoulders with all the Allies in the Brigadier's house by the Havel (his wife was M.M.K. of the Indian novels *Shadow of the Moon* etc). The Russians were very cagey, and we were briefed to talk only about the weather and sport. The social life was hectic, but one had to keep it up because

it was part of the job. Every night we were involved - either home or away.

Visits to East Berlin were obligatory; after all, Berlin was being occupied by all four allies and we had a right to be there. It was a really depressing place - and that was a few years before The Wall. The most popular venue was the opera. We took Granny (my mother) there and she loved it. We were obliged to wear uniforms in the East. Someone in the row behind whispered loudly in German: "That's a Polish officer". Surely a compliment.

The War Office was on the prowl again. They had given me a good run at Regimental - nearly three years. An excited voice from the Military Secretary's Branch said: "You are to be a GII in the Training Branch of the War Office". He spoke as though it were the Holy Grail. I was not impressed. I wanted to stay in Germany because the work was far more interesting and most of the Army was there, but also for the selfish but understandable reason that our cars, bought in the UK, were tax free, and if we moved back to the UK within a stipulated time we had to re-pay the tax. He persisted: "But it's a very important job - you have *two* offices - one in Berkeley Square and one in Whitehall." "That makes it doubly unattractive" I replied. He relented and came back with a dreary job at Rheindahlen, the HQ of BAOR. I knew, but couldn't say it, that I was in the zone for promotion and a command of some sort, but doubted whether I was really in with a chance. I couldn't command 1 KOSB. Roddy Robertson-McLeod had just taken over from the Impossible Officer, and both Alastair and Colin Stonor were much better qualified than I was when the time came. A few days later - out of the blue, I think someone tragically had died - I was suddenly posted as Commanding Officer of the Infantry Junior Leaders Battalion in Plymouth.

I paid my car tax with good grace and moved to Plymouth, sadly saying farewell, temporarily, to that wonderful community of people, the 1st Battalion, The King's Own Scottish Borderers.

Chapter Nine
Going Places
(1959-1965)

In my entire service I have never visited a better
unit that The Infantry Junior Leaders Battalion.
Lt General Sir William F. R. Turner
GOC-in-C Scottish Command and
Colonel, The King's Own Scottish Borderers.

Apart from bandboys and drummers, the Army had been slow to realise the Jesuit maxim of "catch 'em young". By the early 1950's things were changing and planning for the all-regular, volunteer Army included a junior unit for each Arm and Service. Mistakes had been made. "Insufficient attention has been given to the selection process" which was a polite way to saying that the recruiters had taken on any old roughs from the back streets who wanted to join the Army. Trouble followed, certainly so far as the Infantry was concerned, a boy was killed in a bullying incident and a major enquiry was set up. This produced *The Taylor Report* which was "The Bible" for all the very successful junior units now established all over the country.

By August 1959, The Infantry Junior Leaders' Battalion at Crownhill Barracks in Plymouth was in tip-top shape under the inspired leadership of Lt Col Christopher Man, of the Middlesex Regiment, a legend in his time as one of the heroes of the fall of Hong Kong and subsequent brutal imprisonment by The Japs. His wife, Topsy, a Scot, was part of the legend. Chris was

Adjutant at the fall of Hong Kong and they were married just before the Japs invaded. After fighting most gallantly, Chris was captured and Topsy interned. Chris was shipped off to a POW camp in Japan and Topsy was sure he had been torpedoed on the way. Shortly after VJ Day they walked into each other in Colombo, so emaciated that they could hardly recognise each other. Chris went on to become a Major-General - and retired to Scotland to help the Duke of Atholl to create his caravan park.

Sometimes "hand-overs" in the Army can be tricky. Perhaps it was because Chris was a vicar's son - but we hit it off from the word go. Chris and Topsy even moved out of the stately residence, The Red House, and moved into a caravan so that we could move in.

The first few days one felt exactly like a new boy at school. You could almost hear the buzz: "Seen the new CO? Wot's 'e like? Cor, a ruddy Scotsman". On being called "Colonel" in the Officers Mess the inclination was to turn round and see where the Colonel was! The staff came from every one of the 64 Infantry Regiments of the Line. It sounds pompous to say it but they were "hand-picked". *The Taylor Report* strengthened our hand enormously; "duds" were simply RTU. The Second-in-Command and all six Company Commanders were senior to me, had been passed over for promotion and had gallant war records. They could not have been more loyal and we were soon heading in the right direction.

The boys enlisted at the age of 15, which was then the school leaving age, and left at about $17^1/_2$, giving us about seven terms in which to turn out a potential Infantry leader. (The school leaving age is now 16, and that makes it much harder). On arrival, the junior went for the first term into "Z" Coy, where they were "wet-nursed" and gently but firmly taught the fundamentals of soldiering - "good order and military discipline". Of course, there was homesickness and tears, but 80% knuckled down happily and the other 20% exercised their right and "bought themselves out" (£50) - probably just as well, though sometimes it was the parent who was applying the pressure and not the boy. They fed like gannets, and sometimes their Mums could hardly recognise them when they came in droves to the Passing Out Parade at the end of each term.

After the first term, their training in the four Companies was roughly 50% military and 50% education - week about, a full week of each at a time. This was a sound move. Rather than dash from the classroom to the square and back again, which would

have been very distracting, both sets of instructors knew that they had their charges individual attention for a full week. The Royal Army Education Corps was in the process of becoming an all-officer Corps, an elitist policy of which we did not approve. We had the last RAEC Sergeant in the Army - Sgt "Wheels" Cartwright, so called because he ran the Cycling Club. All the educational work was geared to Army use, and one can honestly say that they enjoyed it - probably after fairly indifferent teaching standards back home. There was virtually no "free" time, the evenings were spent in compulsory hobbies, and the boys flopped into bed, tired out.

Military training followed the standard pattern for the Infantry. "Methods of Instruction" started in the Army and by now had reached a very high standard. "Adventure training" played an important part in developing the boy's character. Dartmoor was an ideal locale for canoeing, abseiling, rock climbing, caving (in my opinion a hideous and dangerous pastime - but then I kept getting stuck!) - anything to make a chap say: "Gosh, I never thought I could do that". Danger had to be an element - and we spent many a sleepless night worrying about "missing" parties, on land and sea. The only fatality to a Junior was, ridiculously, when a boy's Go-Kart went over the edge of the square - in spite of crash helmet, straw bales, every possible precaution. We lost three officers - one from natural causes, one road smash, and one abseiling - tragically, the head of the Adventure Training wing.

With all the Infantry Regiments represented there was of course intense rivalry between them. This was to be encouraged, and Companies were formed, more or less, by groupings of the different Brigades, but this was not absolute. The boy was first and foremost an Infantryman and wore only the IJLB badge. He could plaster his bedside locker with Regimental propaganda, but on parade every boy was dressed the same.

This policy came very much to the fore during my first term. The only Brigade not represented at the IJLB was The Brigade of Guards, who had always trained their own Juniors at Pirbright. We had a Guards RSM and one or two Sergeant Instructors - but no Juniors. One day the Major-General of the Guards Brigade said he would like to visit us. We shook at the knees. In The Guards "The Major-General" is God. Well, Major-General George Burns, as he then was before he was festooned with honours, came down and gave us the once-over. He was utterly charming, seemed totally convinced by what we were doing, but insisted that if the Guards were to join in with us they must be in their own Company. We came to a compromise. We insisted that they join "Z" Coy and be indoctrinated the same as everyone else, thereafter they could join a Guards Company. The Guards Coy was formed and undoubtedly helped to raise standards all round, though the other boys called them "Woodentops". General Burns came down to take the Passing Out Parade - the last at Plymouth. Even in a static unit, we seemed doomed to have to move. The whole caravansarie - 850 boys, 200 staff and 500 or so families - upped and moved to Park Hall Camp at Oswestry in Shropshire, quite close to the Welsh border. (Crownhill Barracks is now a roundabout on the Plymouth ring road).

Park Hall had been a Royal Artillery Training Brigade and they were none too pleased to be handing over to the Infantry.

Due to the contraction of the Army and the impending demise of National Service they were all moving to Woolwich. One Regiment (Barney Brooke-Fox) remained for a bit and we hit it off well.

In many ways Oswestry was a better location than Plymouth. We had the whole sweep of the Welsh mountains and seaboard for training and, geographically, we were nearer the centre of the UK. The Scots and North Country Regiments had always complained that Plymouth was "out on a limb" and prevented visits which were so important to The Recruiters. Within the Infantry itself, it would be true to say that there was a certain amount of prejudice against the Junior entry. I asked the Director of Infantry for 30 minutes at the annual Infantry Conference in Warminster to put this straight. I didn't speak; I made the boys do the speaking in a "playlet", which was the "in" form of instruction at that time. They were brilliant and the battle was won. From that day on, Colonels of Regiments, Commanding Officers, Regimental Secretaries and Recruiters arrived in droves.

The aim was continually to improve the quality of the termly intakes. The people we had to get at were pacifist Headmasters, Youth Employment Officers and parents. We tried to concentrate them on one day a week, but every visitor whenever he or she came got "the full treatment" - a briefing from me with wall-charts and lots of question and answer, followed by a talk from Jock Howie, the Headmaster. They would then split up in groups and tour the Battalion at work with carte blanche to talk to boys, particularly from their own home areas. The final discussion was always lively - and very encouraging. One day we had the Lord Mayor of Cardiff who had been encouraged to do so by his Education Committee who had recently visited. Peter Excell, the 2nd in command, was in The Welch Regiment, and he soon had The Lord Mayor wildly enthusiastic. "Come to lunch in the Town Hall - just name your day." With one voice Peter and I said; "No problem; we'll come on the day of the Welsh-Scots match at the Arms Park". We did and Scotland won 5-3 in 1962.

We had two superb Chaplains, one after the other - Walter Evans of the Church of Wales, and Gerry Murphy of the Church of Ireland, an Irish Rugby International full-back. They had a golden opportunity to influence hundreds of young men at a very formative time of their lives, and they certainly took that opportunity. Sunday service was not always compulsory, but Wednesday morning - for 10 minutes only - always was, rifles and all. One Sunday Gerry said in his lovely Irish lilt: "I'm always getting complaints that the order of service is always the same - it's so boring - so this week we're going to start with the Benediction and work backwards"! On Wednesdays the officers had to take their turn at a 3-minute homily. When the RSM's turn came, he thought for a moment and then said: "Very good, Padre - but only if I can take my pace-stick with me into the pulpit". He was RSM "Dusty" Smith of the Coldstream Guards, the finest soldier in the British Army - except perhaps "Fister" Walls, of the KOSB but he was retired by then.

Sport naturally played a major part in the boys curriculum and we had superb facilities including an excellent swimming pool, fairly rare in those days. Sport was disruptive of training; also, we were determined not to allow it to become too gladiatorial. The balance was about right. Games against our neighbouring units were always nail-biting affairs - The All Arms Junior Leaders at Tonfanau - commanded by my old friend and Army Rugby Captain, Ken Wilson, and The Gunners at Nuneaton (Pat Porteous VC). One competition we did win was the Western Command inter-unit Rugby - the "oldies" of the IJLB were captained by Hugh Greatwood, the Adjutant, an Army player, with support from Gerry Murphy at full-back and the CO making "positively his last appearance" at the age of 42. He swung his rank to be allowed to take the goal kicks.

The big occasions were the Passing Out Parades when the Senior Term marched off the square to "Auld Lang Syne" to join their Regiments all over the world - a very moving moment. The boys, led by the junior RSM, commanded the parade of nearly 1000 men from start to finish; there were no staff on parade at all. So many Mums and Dads came from all over the country that we set up a Dormitory Wing for them - His and Hers. The Dads loved being back in a barrack room (and the NAAFI!) again, and

143

FROM : FIELD MARSHAL THE VISCOUNT MONTGOMERY OF ALAMEIN,
K.G., G.C.B., D.S.O.

TEL: BENTLEY 3126.

ISINGTON MILL.
ALTON.
HANTS.

10 April 1961

My dear Coutts

I must thank you very much for your kind hospitality during my visit to your battalion. I tried to pay my hotel bill but it was not allowed; similarly for lunch at Broadway.

It was most inspiring to see the Junior Leaders and you have worked up a high state of efficiency and enthusiasm. I congratulate you and all your officers and N.C.O.'s.

Good luck to you all — officers, instructors and boys.

Yrs. sincerely
Montgomery of Alamein

the Mums and kiddies looked on it as a novel experience.

The VIP was all-important of course. What about the great "Monty" of the Royal Warwickshire Regiment? Yes; he would be delighted to come provided we picked him up at his Hampshire retreat. No problem. Normally, the Inspecting Officer stayed in the CO's house, but we were now back in the "patch" and we didn't think that was right for The Field Marshal, so he stayed in a hostelry in the town, much to the delight of the Oswestrians. He was marvellous with the boys, but as you would expect, a bit patronising in his speech, and he didn't go down too well with the subalterns. He demanded of them, at a buffet supper on the night before the parade, how many books on military history they had read that term. They looked goggle-eyed. "But, Sir", they protested, "We're at it from 6 in the morning till 10 at night and we have no time for reading". Times had changed since he was a subaltern. The Junior RSM that day was J/RSM Wilson of the Cameronians (Scottish Rifles), son of the Firemaster in Hamilton. He had a distinguished career as an officer in the Small Arms Corps.

Next term, we were honoured by the presence of HRH The Duke of Gloucester. He arrived by helicopter which was a rarity in the 60's and caused great excitement. Unfortunately, it poured with rain and the parade was indoors and limited to The Leavers. Lunch became rather extended, and liquid.

The greatest personal thrill was the occasion when the GOC-in-C Scottish Command and Colonel of The King's Own Scottish Borderers, Lt-Gen Sir William Turner, took the parade with the Military Band and Pipes and Drums of the 1st Battalion KOSB providing the music. General Willow and Nancy spent three days with us in the quarter and we enjoyed every minute of it. The General went way "over the top" in his congratulations.

It wasn't "roses, roses, all the way". The media were always on the look-out for a good story and none too worried about how much damage they could do to our image. *The Daily Mirror* got to hear that we had banned Winkle Pickers in civilian clothes - those ghastly thin shoes with a pointed tip. We stuck to our guns. These boys were Infantrymen and relied on their feet to get them around. Winkle Pickers were positively dangerous to growing boys' feet and the Medical Officer went on record in the strongest way to say so. That was the end of that campaign, but the boys weren't angels of course and "CO's Orders" at 1600 hrs each day was sometimes a mile long. But as often as not they were to get a pat on the back for a good course result as to receive a rollicking or a short spell in the cooler.

2,000 Juniors must have passed through the system between 1959 and 1962, and for the next 10 years I was to meet them in Sergeants (and Officers) Messes all over the world. Once, at the

Mons Officer Cadet School at Aldershot, when Morag's nephew, John Kirkwood, was passing out to join the KOSB, he took me to the Sergeants Mess after the parade (a great privilege), and half the room got up to meet me, all ex-Oswestrians. The system has served the Army well.

Despite school holidays, it was a very tiring and demanding job, and $2^1/_2$ years was enough. I admire Headmasters who go "on and on". Charles Barker of The Gordon Highlanders, who was on General Turner's staff, came to relieve me. To my horror I was posted to Preston as the A/Q of the District there. Much as I admire The Loyals and the other Lancashire Regiments, I protested: "I've been telling these boys what an important job The Infantry is doing all round the world - and you send me to Wigan Pier, I'd look ridiculous". He relented and said I must take the next Grade I job that came up. GSO I Singapore Base District. Just perfect.

The farewell Guest Night in "Oz", which included The Ladies - a new and highly desirable departure from Mess custom - was the most colourful affair with the mess dress of nearly every Infantry Regiment represented. Contrary to Queen's Regulations Charlie Oscar was presented with a beautiful piece of silver.

BIBBY LINE
GOOD MORNING !

BREAKFAST

Chilled Grapefruit

Compote of Mixed Fruit   Stewed Prunes

Grape Nuts
Corn Flakes   Sugar Puffs

Oatmeal Porridge

Smoked Haddock en Milk

Eggs: Fried, Turned or Poached

Grilled Breakfast Bacon

Kidney Saute

Griddle Cakes - Golden Syrup

White & Graham Rolls   Toast
Preserves

Tea   Coffee
Iced Tea   Iced Coffee
s.s."Oxfordshire"   11. 5. 1962.

The girls were now in boarding school at St Hilary's in Edinburgh and we had a wee cottage near Kinross adjacent to my mother's at Balgedie to use as a base. We set off on the *Oxfordshire*, one of the last troopers. National Service had finished and we were now a professional Army. We stopped off at Gibraltar (and immediately met an ex-Junior from the garrison battalion in the main street), at Malta to lunch with Charles and Jean Dunbar of the Highland Light Infantry soon to be The Royal Highland Fusiliers, took on board 40 Royal Marine Commando who were needed urgently in Aden (the Pipe Major of the HLI played us out of Grand Harbour on the Harbour Bar, a tear-jerking departure), and called on 1 KOSB at Aden, now commanded by Alastair Thorburn. As we rounded the Horn of Africa I sent off a cable to Wally and Pip in Uganda, saying it was the nearest we would get. "HE" (His Excellency, Sir Walter, was Governor General) kindly returned fraternal greetings, to the great pleasure of the ship's Captain who wasn't used to such goings-on. It was quite an eventful voyage. We had to turn full circle in the Red Sea to aid a stricken ship and somewhere in the Indian Ocean we had to stop for an air drop, when a child on board had a mysterious ailment which needed some specialist drug.

On arrival in Singapore I presented myself to General "Tommy" Harris, Colonel of The Royal Ulster Rifles, shortly to be part of the Royal Irish Rangers. We were old chums from HQ Scottish Command days where he had been "side-kick" to Alastair Maclean. He shook me warmly by the hand and said: "Congratulations. You have brought distinction to the Head-quarters - you have been awarded the OBE." "That's a bit quick, Sir - I haven't done a day's work yet!"

Fort Canning was a gloomy place, dug into the hillside not far from the spot where Stamford Raffles planted the British flag in 1819. The building was still permeated by the memory of General Percival, that tragic, forlorn figure who went out from Fort Canning to the Ford factory on Bukit Timah road to hand over Singapore to the Japs - carrying a Union Jack and, incongruously, wearing a tin hat.

My predecessor didn't seem to be in any hurry to leave. In our hand-over discussions he had mentioned our responsibilities for North Borneo (where a vast area of Mount Kinabalu was being opened up as a training area), Brunei and Sarawak. I dusted down the operation orders affecting these three territories and reckoned I should take a "look-see" while he was still in the chair and saying his farewells. This was reckoned to be a good idea. The newly formed Malayan Airways were flying Fokker Friendships on that route, stopping at Kuching, Brunei and Jesselton. The plane broke down in Brunei so I had a wonderful opportunity to see The Mosque, which is one of the finest in the world, and get a general idea of the country which was to hit the headlines in a very short time when the Indonesian "war" started. North Borneo was breath-takingly beautiful and I made plans for a holiday which would include the area served by a small single-track railway running out of Jesselton and into the out-back - that trip came into the category of "the best laid plans of mice and men..."!

As the name implies Singapore Base District was responsible for commanding and administering the Singapore Base, a conglomeration of combatant units and a great number of administrative depots which served our diminishing forces in the Far East. Up the road at Tanglin was the grandly named HQ Far East Land Forces. They didn't command much. On top of that, in due course, was a Joint Services HQ, under Admiral Sir Varyl Begg; a classic case of too many Chiefs and not enough Indians. Our own role was principally administrative, but we did have a vital operational role which was the Internal Security of Singapore. Considering the racial mix between the predominant Chinese, and the Malays, and Indians, and the universal desire to get rid of "The Brits" soonest, racial clashes had been very restricted, although the KOSB had dealt with one in '56 from Batu Pahat. But it was a volatile and potentially explosive situation with the emerging Lee Kuan Yew, much farther to the left than he is now, struggling for the dominance of his Peoples' Action Party, and not caring too much about individual freedoms on the way.

The Internal Security operation, code-named *Adam Alpha*, really required nine battalions - an Infantry Division - to make it effective. We never had anything like that and had to make do with improvised units from Nee Soon and other Depots. Every single military person and civilian of all three Services came under command of Singapore Base District for I.S. purposes. It was a good medium for bringing the three Services together and many good friendships were established. We worked hand in glove with the Police - for we were in support of them -

Superintendent Tan Teck Kim, my "oppo", and I were never out of each others' offices and homes, and we went cruising of a Sunday on the General's launch with both sets of children. We still meet home and away.

The fledgling Singapore Government was now in power, though the United Kingdom still remained responsible for Foreign Affairs and Defence. Mr Ong Pang Boon was the Home Minister, and The Chief Constable and I attended his security conference every Wednesday. A lot of it was very "close to the chest" and my report was always eagerly awaited by the British High Commission and the innumerable Headquarters.

In early December 1962 Azahari started the revolt in Brunei. HQ Farelf, led by General Sir Nigel Poett, ("The White Knight", so called because he was prematurely grey) never even looked at the prepared plan lying in our safe. They took immediate control themselves and told us to keep looking after Singapore. The Queen's Own Highlanders were out at Selarang and they were the first to get a Company into the air under Ian Cameron. They landed under fire - and so began the Indonesian confrontation which was to last for three long years. A glance at the map of the Far East will show at once why Indonesia under the leadership of the dictatorial President Soekarno wanted to annex North Borneo (now Sabah), Brunei and Sarawak. They were all part - and a very rich part - of that huge island of Borneo or Kalimantan, the majority of which was Indonesian. As soon as Britain gave intention of withdrawing from her colonies, Soekarno was ready to strike. And strike he did through the usual medium of a "stooge" planted in the supposedly disaffected territory. That was Azahari, an opponent right out of the text-book of Internal Security.

When it came to setting up a Headquarters over the water, Farelf made the classic mistake of disregarding the perfectly good Brigade HQ already in Singapore under "Pat" Patterson and setting up an *ad hoc* Bde HQ under their own Brigadier General Staff with one of my GII's (if you please), Mike Swindells, as Brigade Major. They got the show on the road and then were sensibly replaced by a more conventional Headquarters.

As the Brunei and Sarawak operations built up into a mini-war, Singapore, Malaya and Hong King were denuded of troops. Not for the first time we thanked God for the Gurkhas - and their British officers were as good as they were, which is saying something. We could always rely on the Singapore Guard Regiment, a British unit, composed mainly of Malays and commanded by British and Singaporean officers. The CO was George Dunlop of The Royal Scots, a great ally.

Singapore was now beginning to raise her own forces. Brigadier Peter Bradley had set up the Headquarters at Beach Road, the 1st Battalion Singapore Infantry Regiment was active and the 2nd Battalion was forming under the effervescent Tommy Lamb (my golfing partner, who once had the impudence to beat me 10 and 8 at Muirfield). This eased the pressure on the Internal Security situation - and it was good for Singaporean morale to see their own troops on the streets and not just Gurkhas and Brits. It was vital to keep matters stable as the British Government was now pressing hard for the establishment of Malaysia - a federation of Malaya, Singapore and the three states across the sea, North Borneo, Brunei and Sarawak.

General Alick Williams had now relieved Tommy Harris and we were constantly in touch with Philip Moore, the Deputy High Commissioner in Singapore, (later Secretary to HM The Queen) and the Earl of Selkirk, High Commissioner for South East Asia. As often as not, conferences were in Kuala Lumpur, and we were lucky to have Bill Fargus of the Royal Scots up there to keep us informed.

Lee Kuan Yew was "playing hard to catch" and the British Government were prepared to be very tough with him. He and Tungku Abdul Rahman of Malaya were at daggers drawn, and it was a very tense period before agreement was reached. Lee Kuan Yew was, more than once, within a whisker of being arrested (by the GOC) and the Chief Constable (by me). I typed the Operation Order and kept it in the house. Eventually it was flushed down the lavatory! The Tungku always held the whip hand because 90% of Singapore's water came from reservoirs in Malaya.

Internal security was stepped up which infuriated everyone -

the Services because they couldn't get on with their job, and the civilians because road blocks were thrown up all over the place - and caused horrendous traffic jams. The GI at SBD was not a popular guy. It was almost a relief when I.S. situations developed "for real" and we had to apply night curfews. People could then see the purpose of thing and that we were protecting them. The Intelligence boys were very active. Our man was Donald Lear of the KOSB. His principal job was to keep the General up to date on intelligence and law and order on Singapore Island. It was real cloak and dagger stuff. The Trade Unions of the Army's locally

employed civilians, numbering thousands, were a particular source of trouble at the time, with lightning strikes, sit-ins, and picketing, which could totally paralyse a Base Depot, for example.

Donald writes: "I ran a group of eight agents within the Trade Unions, and encouraged them to become belligerent and become elected to action committees. The agents were paid a small retainer each month for which a signature was obtained. Sometimes there were fierce accusations at union meetings that one or two agents were traitors, but this was equally fiercely denied and never proven. There were some narrow escapes. In order not to blow the agents I also ran a cut-out man who was the only contact. Twelve shady cafes were chosen as meeting places, always in scruffy clothes and dark glasses. The cut-out would ring saying "No 6": the reply would be: "OK, in 30 minutes", taking care never to park the car anywhere near the rendezvous and taking evasive action if followed or observed. By this system we knew everything long before it happened. Several years later, I'm glad to say that I was able to help the cut-out man, through the Foreign Office, to be accepted as an immigrant to UK as two of his children married UK citizens and he wanted to be with his grandchildren."

The only people who would not co-operate were the War Department civilians who had come out from UK at vast expense to operate the essential services in emergency. Their Union in London refused to allow them to work under conditions of danger. What a fiasco.

In a typically British fashion the velvet glove was proffered as well as the iron fist. A full-time staff officer, Lennox Napier (later GOC Wales) was employed to run Operation Concord whose aim was to win the hearts and minds of the Singapore people. A considerable sum of money was allocated to this task and most of this went to the youth clubs which were being strenuously organised by the Singapore Government. Their Social Welfare representative with whom we worked was a cheerful extrovert called Mr Ong Kah Kok. He and Lennox got on like a house on fire. General Tommy and Anne-Marie Harris flung themselves heart and soul into Concord (other staff officers, with an eye to their confidential report, found it advisable to follow suit). It was a fine way of getting to know the locals and a good reason for dodging the constant round of cocktail and dinner party invitations. Every unit on the island adopted an organisation of some kind, and there is no question at all that Concord was a huge success and eased the wheels of the hand-over by the ex-Colonial power.

Nearly 20 years after the war, married quarters were still in short supply. In good old Army fashion, after having a "tied" quarter as a CO one then went to the bottom of the pecking order again and had to accumulate points. On arrival we went to the delightful Gap Hostel high on the Ayer Rajah ridge looking out to sea, then nice Judge "Punch" Coomaraswamee rented us his house in Merryn Road while he went on leave to Ceylon. The girls came out for summer hols - and thereafter, by a superb Government decision, for every holiday. ("We had 15 free cokes on the trip, Mummy"). We had wonderful holidays in the Camerons and Fraser's Hill. Swimming trophies on the mantelpiece multiplied. We all loved living in the tropics. Eventually the Sole Arbiter relented and allocated us a quarter, a jolly nice one, in Rochester Park, at the back of the Royal Signals barracks. When I visited it a year or two back, it had become a rehabilitation centre for young drug addicts. We attended the Presbyterian Kirk in Orchard Road, which was fast becoming a multi-national congregation under hard-working Robert Greer, who was another to have been cruelly treated by the Japanese in Changi jail. Eldership and the choir, under dear Faith Goh, were a good antidote to too much work.

As usual rugby was a "must". Rugger on the padang at the Singapore Cricket Club had a long tradition and the Services played a major part. Games were invariably at 5 pm in the 'cool' of the evening - never less than 80 degrees Fahrenheit. "Mad dogs and Englishmen." I was asked to be manager of a Tri-Service side (6 each RN, Army and RAF) to Perth, Western Australia, and we flew down, courtesy of the RAF, stopping off at the dreamy, picture-book tropical Cocos Islands in the middle of the Indian Ocean. On entry to Australia (on a Sunday, which did not please the Customs) we were sternly warned: "No citrus fruit on any account." Private Jock Black of the Queen's Own Highlanders said to the Customs man in a broad Glasgow accent: "I've nae citrus fruit - just an orange." We were generously hosted by the Australian Navy at HMAS Leeouin and won all three games comfortably against the University, The Services and Western Australia. The boys were fascinated by a game of "Aussie rules" which they called "aerial ping-pong".

Another jaunt, in which Morag was able to join, was to Hong Kong where Tan Teck Khim and I were guest speakers at an Internal Security Seminar. The Duke of Kent, then a Captain in the Royal Scots Greys, was in the audience. As ex-members of the KOSB held most of the top jobs in Hong Kong (Michael Herries at Jardine, Mathieson and Willie Purves at the Hong Kong and Shanghai Bank) we were royally entertained. The General kindly flew us up in his private plane.

The Indonesian war dragged on. We were clearly winning but the Indonesians started a new ploy of dropping parachutists and landing raiding parties in Singapore and Malaya. This kept us busy for a while, until the Gurkhas and Malay Regiments sorted them out. Unusually, the Government went "over the top" in their normally stingy policy for issuing medals; they declared the Malay Peninsula a "war zone" and we were all awarded a thoroughly undeserved "gong".

The Singapore Government had, albeit reluctantly, entered the Malaysian Federation (for a time) and the Singapore Brigade HQ moved into Fort Canning, taking over responsibility for Internal Security. Singapore Base District was shunted into an old POW camp at Tyersall Park, adjacent to the Botanic Gardens and were responsible only for the security of the British enclaves - a considerable slice of real estate and quite a large proportion of the island. But the Base was running down and life began to pall. My "In" tray was empty by lunch-time, an unprecedented occurrence. After $2\frac{1}{2}$ years one's thoughts turned to the future. It is commonly agreed in the Army that after commanding a unit everything falls rather flat. I was lucky to have had such a stimulating appointment. The Army was contracting, the promotion pyramids were becoming more acute, and the future looked bleak when, out of the blue, came a posting as Colonel of Lowland Brigade, which was cancelled a few days later by appointment as Commander 155 (Lowland) Infantry Brigade in Edinburgh. My old mob - I just couldn't believe it.

Chapter Ten
The Army In Scotland
(1965-1973)

The Infantry is the Queen of the battlefield; always spell it with a capital 'I'.
General Wavell

After 20 years of fragile peace the Territorial Army was beginning to fray at the edges. The "knockers" - never any shortage of them - sneered that it was nothing more than a boozing club for Dunkirk and Alamein veterans. They said the same in the 1930's, and whilst not wholly without foundation, it was grossly unfair. Although numbers were low, there was a tremendous volunteer spirit, and the important thing was that the Drill Hall was there in every town and most villages, as recognisable and nearly as important as The Post Office - and very often the principal centre of social activity in the community. Unwise counsels were about to change this.

It was great to be back in Scotland again after 12 years. Jack Monteith of The Black Watch handed over the Brigade in early 1965, and also the delightful residence, *Dunalastair* in Colinton. There were nine bedrooms - and not a stick of furniture! - but the jovial Mike Melvill, the TA Secretary, who had been blown out of his landing craft at Walcheren, came to our rescue.

The Brigade had changed a bit over the years. The Armoured

155

Brigade and the Beach Brigade had been stood down and a composite armoured regiment, The Lowland Yeomanry, (Andrew Monteath) was attached to 155. The Dandy Ninth Royal Scots (Chay Corsar) covered Edinburgh and The Lothians. The two KOSB battalions had been amalgamated to form the 4th/5th KOSB under Sir William Jardine of Applegirth, a brave but impossible experiment. More feasible was the amalgamated 6th/7th Cameronians (Scottish Rifles) (Bob Dobson) which catered for Lanarkshire and the South side of Glasgow.

It was a large area to cover. The Borders were no problem, but Drill Halls, which we were now persuaded to call "TA Centres", at Penicuik, Broxburn, Dunbar, Hamilton, Motherwell, Wishaw, Bellshill and Larkhall were new territory. In addition, The Army Cadet Force had detachments in nearly every hamlet. They all had to be inspected - well, visited - and that meant at least three nights a week on the road. An essential qualification for the Brigade Commander's driver was to know the whereabouts and the opening hours of every Fish and Chip shop between Edinburgh and Stranraer. The Brigade Headquarters, at Wemyss Place in Edinburgh, was itself a very good example of a good TA unit. Nigel Stisted, Royal Scots, was Brigade Major, to be relieved later by Ian Cameron, Queen's Own Highlanders, whom we last met dealing with Mr Azahari in Brunei. The Deputy Commander was Charles Michie of The Cameronians, a 52 Division veteran from the South Beveland campaign and onwards, and now a Glasgow banker. He lived for the TA; his daily telephone call must have cost the Bank of England a fortune. The D/Q was Ronnie Urquhart, an Edinburgh lawyer. But the key man in the organisation was Mr Bill Ritchie, the full-time Chief Clerk, whose enthusiasm brought together a splendid assortment of volunteers who were needed to man the Headquarters - a typical example of the TA at its best.

The location and date for annual camp were always eagerly awaited - so far as the Jocks were concerned, the farther away the better. After all, for many this was part of their annual holiday. Some employers, too few, granted additional holidays in recognition of patriotic duty, but economic times were hard and we were "at peace". As with the Regular Army the principal motive for joining the TA was comradeship and, being brutally frank, an opportunity of getting away from the wife and the weans for a bit!

In 1965 Mr Ritchie's boys purred with pleasure when I announced that we were going to Penhale in Cornwall for a camp on our own as a Brigade Headquarters, while the various units went to separate camps elsewhere in England. This suited me well as it gave us all a chance to practise our procedures without too much interruption.

The hub of Brigade HQ is the "Operations Room", a clumsy command vehicle with the vital communications by radio and sometimes telephone line to the various units under command. The whole "raison d'être" of the Headquarters is to ensure that the Ops Room and its various satellites are in the right place and well camouflaged and protected.

In many ways it was the end of an era for the well-tried vehicles and equipment from 1939-45 were well nigh clapped out. The new range of radios would shortly revolutionise communications and possibly make Brigade HQ redundant, at any rate in a standard Infantry Division. With slick radio orders, there should be no reason why a Divisional Commander shouldn't pass his orders straight down to units.

From deep thoughts on military procedures - to the ridiculous. While we worked hard at TA camp and did with precious little sleep, it had to be fun. On the way up to the Royal Army Medical Corps Depot at Crookham to visit our Field Ambulance, I taught Charles Michie how to play Pub Cricket. As you drive around in England (before the days of motorways) you are constantly passing pub signs. The batsman in play gets the number of runs equivalent to the number of legs on the pub sign. For example: The Canny Man = 2, The Black Bull = 4, and so on. When you reach The Coach and Horses, the game ends in argument and confusion!

Although TA training was confined largely to evenings and weekends, the Powers That Be got their pound of flesh out of us at other times. I was an examiner in the 1965 Staff College

You meet some funny people on the Stanford Training Area

Entrance Exam and, with Mike Harbottle, set and marked the Tactics "C" (Internal Security) paper. Mike's Regiment was the famous Greenjackets who, when later linked with the Light Infantry, gained from us the soubriquet "The Green Mafia" because between them they held most of the top jobs in the Army. He had been very involved in the Aden disturbances and came to the Hong Kong I.S. Conference representing the Aden version of Internal Security. Marking exam papers is a fantastically boring occupation, but all the time one's conscience is imbued with the thought that a young man's future is at stake, which ensures utter dedication and fairness by the examiner.

Camp in 1966 was at the excellent all-arms training centre at Stanford in Norfolk. By this time everyone knew that the TA was to be "re-organised" which is a War Office euphemism for "slashed". 155 Brigade were determined to go out on a high note.

It was a full Brigade camp with the three Infantry Battalions and Field Ambulance. We made extensive use of the excellent facilities and finished with a full Brigade exercise. A combined Retreat by the Massed Bands could have been a tearful occasion - but that is not the way in the Army. It was a celebration of many years of superb comradeship. The last TEWT (Tactical Exercise Without Troops) we had in 155 Brigade was at Biggar in Lanarkshire. It was an Officers' Study Day. The Opening Narrative was that an international flight had crashed in the middle of the village and the TA had been mobilised to help - the identical scenario to Lockerbie some years later. The Police thought we were nuts, but cooperated grudgingly.

Before 155 Brigade finally broke up, I couldn't miss the opportunity of holding a dinner of all the past Commanders of 155 (Lowland) Infantry Brigade, to give it its full title. We had a marvellous turn-out, starting with "Whistling Tom" - twelve of us in all - with the Chief of the General Staff, General Jim Cassells, as guest of honour. We sat down at trestle tables in the East Claremont Street Drill Hall, the home of the Royal Scots TA.

The re-organisation of the TA was carried out in great secrecy at the War Office. The two Generals responsible were most aptly named - Hackett and Carver. It was not a re-organisation, it was a demolition job. General "Geordie" Gordon-Lennox, the GOC-in-C Scottish Command, summoned all his senior officers to a briefing in a blacked-out conference room. When the viewfoil was flashed on to the screen, showing the future establishment of the Territorial Army in Scotland there were gasps from the audience. I thought we might need medical assistance for the Gunners. There were three RA Brigadiers there, each with a "command". The future establishment of the Royal Regiment of Artillery (TA) in Scotland was - NIL.

The Infantry weren't much better. From two Infantry Divisions of 18 battalions, they were reduced to two battalions. One of the problems of the old TA was that there was no clearly defined operational role. No one had the guts to allocate them an overseas role - and in conditions of nuclear war it was debatable whether they would get there anyway. This "re-organisation" had at least faced up to the challenge by earmarking the two - ridiculously named - Territorial and Army Volunteer Reserve II units to reinforce the lines of Communications in Rhine Army. (The name was changed back to "TA" in a few years). The two battalions were to be called The Lowland Volunteers (HQ in Glasgow) and The Highland Volunteers (HQ in Perth). We will be hearing more of them later. Some of the "Young Turks" were delighted. Out would go the World War II boozing club and in would come the ex-National Service whizz-kids who said that they were prepared to accept a very much higher standard of training and readiness for war. One of the attractions was that the considerable financial savings would be used to pay for first-class up-to-date weapons, communications and vehicles. Now, technology in war is important - very important, as the Gulf War has just proved - but the very latest gadget is not the slightest use if the man behind it hasn't his heart in the right place and "sugars off" at the first sight of the enemy. Morale is more important than technology. Wars are won by people, by soldiers with stout hearts and a "bondook" (rifle) in their hands. These stout hearts are born of regimental spirit which has stood the test of 300 years and more. In 1991 we have the ludicrous scenario of the Americans and others trying to copy our regimental system whilst we are in the process of dismantling it!

Unfortunately, this meant cutting across all regimental traditions and attachments and virtually created two new Regiments of "Volunteers". (They now have their own Colours). It also reduced the number of Drill Halls by 90%. On the Borders only three were retained - Galashiels, Dumfries and Stranraer (for the Military Police, not the KOSB) - 27 got the chop, which was a disastrous decision.

Allied to this upheaval was a sop to the Alamein beer drinkers, a Home Defence cadre called TAVR III. It was badly thought out and its implementation only caused a lot of bickering among Britain's thoroughly disgruntled reserve forces. It was no surprise when it died a natural death within a year or two - probably as its originators had planned.

In defence of these cuts the government could claim that

"peace was breaking out all over". Mr Roosevelt's long-cherished dream of the demise of the British Empire was nearly realised, everything East of Suez was to be abandoned, the future was rosy.

The regular Army had already taken painful decisions. In Scotland the agonising amalgamation of The Royal Scots Fusiliers and the Highland Light Infantry had caused the resignation of both Colonels; the situation was only stabilised by the intervention of a "White Knight", none other than our next-door neighbour, the charming and brilliant Brigadier Ian Buchanan-Dunlop. In the Highlands, The Seaforth and Camerons had much in common and they wisely and methodically carved out a great new Regiment, the Queen's Own Highlanders. The saddest blow of all was the demise of The Cameronians (Scottish Rifles) - a piece of the fabric of Scotland's history torn to shreds. Those of us who heard Dr John Fraser, the Padre, and Colonel Leslie Dow, the CO, that sad, sad day at Douglas where they were raised, will never forget it. I was too moved to go to the wake.

Faced with this cataclysm in Scotland's military affairs, one's inclination was to plead "après moi le deluge" and ask for an overseas posting! That was a dishonourable thought, quickly banished by an invitation from General Derek Lang to be his Chief of Staff when he took over at Scottish Command. A great honour. This was followed by a summons to meet the general and his two district commanders at "Fairmount" the official residence of the GOC 51 Division, Major-General Maitland-Magill-Crichton (The Jocks found this a bit of a mouthful and called him "Monday-Tuesday-Wednesday").

General Derek had come from the War Office as Director of Military Training. He had had a most distinguished and gallant career, including a brilliant escape from occupied France. Looking ahead to more peaceful times in Britain's affairs, he envisaged the Armed Forces being employed on useful tasks in aid of local government, such as the construction of much-needed airstrips in the Highlands (ideal training for The Royal Engineers), building small bridges and improving hill tracks by semi-skilled Infantry. This was to be called OpMAC - Operation Military Aid to the Community. As could be imagined, it wasn't wildly popular with the military. But fortune was on General Derek's side, for 1968 turned out to be the only year since 1945 when British forces were not engaged in operations somewhere in the world. "Borneo" was over and Northern Ireland had not quite (re) started. A lot of excellent OpMAC tasks were carried out. The airstrip at Unst on Shetland held a special interest as Morag had relatives there. Another one at Broadford on Skye gave the mist-covered isle its first and only air link with the mainland. There were many other smaller schemes and they continue to this day, unobtrusively.

Sir Derek, as he now was, was a wonderful person to work for, full of charm and enthusiasm, and we backed his scheme to the hilt. But there were a great number of other things to do. The new TAVR set-up had lots of teething problems, besides all the routine work of a large Headquarters. The Chief of Staff system demands that every single piece of paper heading towards the general has to be channelled through the "In" tray and sent up with a recommendation and suggested action.

The "In" tray was always bulging, but there was a strong team to assist - Maurice Mountain as Colonel General Staff, "Raas" Macrae Col A/Q and Tommy Lamb, Recruiting, with Jim McIntyre, Command Secretary, as the financial watchdog, plus the full range of Arms and Services heads, and never forgetting the indispensable "Mrs Mac" who had been Personal Assistant to the Chiefs of Staff at Scottish Command since Bannockburn. Dorothy McKechnie was a pearl of great price. The Chief of Staff's "prayers" on a Wednesday morning were attended by at least 30 people, all with their special problems which they were convinced were more important than anyone else's.

The Chief of Staff had two very attractive "ex officio" appointments - Chairman of the Tattoo Policy Committee and Chairman of the Inter-Services Rothiemurchus Hut Committee. Brigadier Jack Sanderson had taken over from Alastair Maclean as Tattoo Producer. Jack was an unusual combination, an Aussie and a Scots Guardsman. He had been "King of the Castle" for some time and was well astride of the problems - including the annual battle with the residents of Ramsay Garden, for whom we had little sympathy, except the one who had lived there prior to the arrival of the Tattoo; all the others knew what they were in for. I had three particular hates: (1) the attitude of the Festival Committee who looked down their noses at the Tattoo because it is not "kultur"; to this day the Tattoo is shown as a sort of addendum at the bottom of all the other events - whereas it is the main moneyspinner of the whole Festival and the reason why most overseas visitors come to the Festival at all; (2) the exorbitant cost of erecting the stands which took away 90% of the profits. I argued strongly that we should buy our own - and to hell with the cost. It took another ten years to pull that one off. And (3) the outrageous policy whereby military bandsmen - the "oompah" wallahs - received a higher rate of Extra Duty Pay than the Pipers. This was a long and bitter struggle, linked to the history of music in the Army (mainly in England). Once again, it was the pipers who stole the show year after year, not the purveyors of "Colonel Bogey". On productivity, the Lone Piper should have been paid half the takings!

Ski-ing was now being developed on Speyside in a big way, and the Services, through our war-time contacts, had to be involved. The Laird of Rothiemurchus, Colonel Grant, very generously made available a site south of Loch Morlich, quite separated from any of the commercial properties and this was gradually developed by The Navy, Army and Royal Air Force to provide excellent facilities for services skiers and their families. In due course the Nuffield Trust and The Scottish Union Jack Association made funds available to enlarge and modernise the centre. A day out at Rothiemurchus was a wonderful tonic in the clear mountain air.

Since the war, Scotland had not done much for Service rugby football; we provided the odd outstanding player like John McDonald and "Bonzo" Bruce, but they were normally serving in the south. In an attempt to improve Services rugby in Scotland I started a United Services Scotland Rugby Club, based on the Fleet ground at Rosyth. The opening of the Forth Bridge made the link between the Army and the Navy much closer and RAF

Leuchars was no distance in the other direction. There was a lot of good-will and hard work but the constant changes of service life proved a terrible handicap. If defeat is character-forming we must have had strong characters for we got thrashed nearly every Saturday! Friday night was chaos; the phone never stopped ringing with cancellations. It ran for three seasons but the escalation in Northern Ireland eventually forced the club to close.

Further cuts in the Services were due. The two Districts, commanded by Major-Generals, were down-graded to Areas, commanded by Brigadiers, and the staff at Command HQ was to be pruned by some arbitrary percentage. Was I a jinx? The last two appointments - GI Singapore and Commander 155 - had been chopped. Was this to be third time lucky? Not a bit of it. The Chief of Staff's appointment was cut. Quite apart from one's personal position it was a very bad decision. There were a goodly number of full Colonels remaining, and I think they would have welcomed a moderator.

However, there was a silver lining to this particular cloud. Just as the British Government always tried to get Colonial

"I'm in the army now!" Passing out parade at Glencorse Barracks, Penicuik. Lt Col Bill Bewsher toasts the newest recruit.

164

territories to group together in federations (which rarely worked)
so the War Office was always on the look-out for groupings
which would save some money, quite regardless of efficiency.
This time they hit on an idea which was intended to hurt - but in
fact it suited Scotland's situation to a tee. The Scottish Division.
For 300 years and more the British Infantry has been organised
in Regiments. War-time experience proved that training recruits
at individual Regimental Depots was wasteful. After National
Service was phased out Regiments were grouped in Brigades. In
Scotland Lowland Brigade recruits were trained at Glencorse
(Penicuik) and the Highland Brigade at Bridge of Don, Aberdeen.
In each case there was a small Brigade HQ under a Brigade
Colonel who was responsible, in conjunction with the Regimental
HQs, for recruiting, training, and manpower.

Throughout the UK these Brigades were to be phased out and
replaced by six Divisions of Infantry named (like a pack of cards)
Guards, King's, Queen's, Prince of Wales, Light and Scottish.
Behind the War Office proposals, we felt, there was a long-term
threat to form a Corps of Infantry. In Scotland this was anathema
and we were determined that the Scottish Division proposal
would succeed by strengthening the Regimental spirit in every
possible way. But it would require a good deal of give-and-take.
The Divisional Brigadier was given that job so I was moved from
Craigiehall to Edinburgh Castle and set up shop on 1st June
1968. The Lord Lyon King of Arms declared our proposals for
the new Scottish Divisional sign "heraldically impeccable". That
was a good start, followed almost immediately by a splendid
"Opening Ceremony" - the "Big Blaw", a Massed Beating of
Retreat on the Horse Guards in London by the Pipes and Drums
of all the Scottish Regiments in the presence of Her Majesty, The
Queen. It was a magnificent spectacle - superbly managed by
Colonel Claud Moir, Black Watch, the outgoing Highlands
Brigade Colonel and Alastair Thorburn, Lowland Brigade
Colonel. A lot of people complained that the Retreat had been
held in London and not in Scotland. Oddly enough there is no
suitable site in Scotland for such a spectacle. It was tried in 1990
at Bellahouston Park in Glasgow - and failed - whereas the Horse

Guards Parade, with stands provided during the week of The Trooping of the Colour, is ideal.

The appointment of Divisional Brigadier of The Scottish Division was undoubtedly the best job in the British Army and gave enormous satisfaction. One had direct contact and influence with "The magnificent eight" - Scotland's famous Lowland and Highland Regiments of Foot. Higher direction came from the Director of Infantry at Warminster but was implemented through the immensely patriarchal Council of Scottish Colonels: Major-General Bill Campbell, The Royal Scots (The Royal Regiment); Major-General Henry Leask, The Royal Highland Fusiliers; Lt-General Sir William Turner, The King's Own Scottish Borderers; Major-General Henry Alexander, The Cameronians (Scottish Rifles); Brigadier Bernard Fergusson (later Lord Ballantrae), The Black Watch (Royal Highland Regiment); Lt-General Sir George Gordon-Lennox, The Gordon Highlanders; General Sir Peter Hunt, The Queen's Own Highlanders (Seaforth and Camerons); Major-General Freddie Graham, The Argyll and Sutherland Highlanders.

Gone were the animosities of the Lowlands and Highlands which had for generations caused jealousy and distrust. The old Castle rang with laughter as Bernard Fergusson and Geordie Gordon-Lennox argued about "fishing rights in Dundee". The Gordon Highlanders had a thin recruiting area, made worse by the oil boom in Aberdeen, and from time to time they sought permission from The Black Watch to "fish" for recruits in the Dundee area. Co-operation was the order of the day.

A Colonel Commandant had to be elected - The Divisional Brigadier was banished from the room - and they cheerfully proceeded to make the wrong decision. The obvious choice was the GOC-in-C, Lt-General Sir Derek Lang, because Scottish Command and the newly-formed Scottish Division obviously had to work hand-in-glove. They rejected him because he was not Colonel of his Regiment and appointed General Freddie Graham. Now, we all adored Freddie, and worked with him "nae bother", but it was a cruel blow to Sir Derek. Since that day, every single Colonel Commandant has been GOC Scotland - some of them not even members of The Scottish Division!

There were naturally a few suspicions in the early days that Regiments' autonomy would be threatened, When Bernard Fergusson came back from his tour as Governor-General of New Zealand, he bearded me in my office and grilled me for two hours. What was I going to do to his precious "Forty Twa'"? We had a tremendous "natter" (about The Kirk as well as the Army) and when he left I breathed a sigh of relief as he said: "I'll back you to the hilt".

Bernard Fergusson was one of the most colourful characters of our time. Soldier (fanatically Black Watch), fighter (Chindit behind enemy lines), author, poet, Inspector-General of the Palestine Police, TA Brigade Commander in Dundee, Governor-General of New Zealand, he had had the most fantastic career, but I suspect that the appointment which thrilled him most was to be Lord High Commissioner to the General Assembly of the Church of Scotland. The story is told by Sir Charles Fraser, who was then Purse Bearer to the Lord High Commissioner, that Lord Ballantrae arrived at the front steps of St Giles dressed in the full ceremonial dress of The Governor of New Zealand. As the Lord High Commissioner processed down the aisle preceded by the Lord Lyon, Heralds, Pursuivants, the Mace, the Purse and all the panoply of State a young Assistant Minister (with long hair well down over his shoulders) bowed as was entirely proper, The Lord High effectively being The Monarch. A little further on as the formal procession wended its way towards the Royal pew another Assistant Minister again fully robed bowed and this assistant had an exceedingly bushy beard. When the procession had arrived at the Royal pew and was seated Bernard said to Sir Charles: "Order of Service please, Charlie. Pencil please" and he scribbled on the reverse of the Order of Service:

> One's in the Chancel
> One's in the Nave:
> One needs a haircut
> And the other needs a shave.

Poor General Freddie was in trouble again. The Argylls were due to be disbanded like the Cameronians. As Colonel Commandant he had to implement the War Office decisions; as Colonel of The Argylls he would resist to the death. Then started the "Save the Argylls" campaign. Colin Mitchell, "Mad Mitch", had been stirring it up in Aden and was only a whisker off getting the sack for doing so. After he handed over to Sandy Boswell things cooled down. I had the unpleasant task of going to Berlin to interview every officer and sergeant in the Argylls, asking them to say which Regiment they would like to go on disbandment. They treated me with enormous courtesy and there was no one more pleased than I when Northern Ireland came to their rescue and they were spared.

Regular visits to all the battalions were most stimulating. Sometimes Morag was able to join me. When we visited the Royal Highland Fusiliers in Gibraltar, Stuart Green very kindly gave us an unused quarter - and Fiona now at St Andrews University, and her cousin "Kel" came too. Visits to Northern Ireland were more serious and more frequent. The KOSB, under Andrew Myrtle, were in the thick of it. These were the days of the street demos - and the Jocks arranged for me to be near enough the target area to get a brick all to myself. The doc said: "For goodness sake don't tell the CO. He hasn't had one yet". In the next ten years I was able to visit troops in every corner of that unhappy Province. (When an English Brigadier went into a makeshift barrack room in Belfast he said: "Are you fellahs comfy heeah"? The Jocks looked blank and made no reply. After three attempts at the same question, a Jock blurted out: "We dinnae come frae here - we're from Scotland".)

One of the more sensible things said of the Northern Ireland situation during the 1970's (by, surprisingly, Harold Wilson) was: "No one should ever do or say anything about Northern Ireland which will make the situation worse" I go along with that.

The Royal Scots were in Osnabruck, The Gordons in Minden and The Queen's Own Highlanders in Sharjah, the last of the Gulf stations, for a year or two anyway. (In early 1991 practically the whole of the Scottish Division was in Saudi Arabia). If Britain had maintained a presence in the Gulf would Iraq have behaved the way she did towards Kuwait? I doubt it. It's easy to be wise after the event, but these thoughts certainly went through my mind when I left the Queens Own, whose Commanding Officer was Andrew Duncan, now a frequent spokesman for the Institute of Strategic Studies. The Volunteers and Cadets were part of the Division and had to be visited too - what a privilege to be able to shake hands with so many real Scottish soldiers.

The Black Watch were at Ballykinlar in Northern Ireland and they had a tradition of giving young officers fresh from Sandhurst a lively welcome to the battalion. The Adjutant met three of them at Aldergrove airport, warned them of the seriousness of the situation "but don't worry I'm armed to the teeth - you just sit tight in the back of the Landrover". Just short of the camp a furious fusillade of shots rang out from the mock ambush set up by the other officers. The 2nd Lieutenants dived for the ditch and the Adjutant performed heroics in their defence - with blank ammunition. As the firing died away the Commanding Officer arrived on a white charger with his claymore drawn and uttering Gaelic oaths. When he reached the trembling officers he calmly dismounted, sheathed his claymore and welcomed the young men warmly to the battalion.

One of the trickiest decisions was the question of a Scottish divisional Depot which was fundamental to the Divisional concept. The prospect of kilts appearing at Glencorse or trews at Bridge of Don would have caused a riot a few years back. Now it was just too logical. Both Depots were training Juniors and Adults together which was contrary to the *Taylor Report* and wasteful in specialised staff. So we concentrated all the juniors in the lovely Gordon Highlanders barracks at Aberdeen and all the adults at Glencorse. Bingo! No problem, and no complaints.

There was a great character on the staff of Divisional HQ. He was a retired Brigadier called Colin Duncan (proud father of Andrew, above). One of the most important tasks of Division was to plan officers' careers from Sandhurst right through to retiral. Colin did this with total accuracy and complete dedication, as he had been doing in the Highland Brigade for many years. During the war when he was commanding a battalion of The Queen's Own Cameron Highlanders in North Africa they had the misfortune to be captured en bloc by the Germans. Colin asked permission to march his battalion to the POW camp and this was granted. When they marched off a German officer interposed himself between the Pipes and Drums and the Commanding Officer. Without batting and eyelid - and without losing the step! - Colin, an ex-Army boxer, knocked him out cold.

General Turner's time as Colonel of The King's Own Scottish Borderers was running out. One day he shook me rigid by telling me that the regimental trustees had unanimously recommended that I be his successor, and Princess Alice, our Colonel-in-Chief had graciously agreed. The Colonel of a Regiment is unpaid, has no "perks" whatever, works mighty hard, but does it because he knows it is the greatest distinction in any soldier's life to be Head of The Family. For the next ten years some part of every working day was devoted to the KOSB - with outstanding assistance from Philip Harrison and Bill Dunn at Berwick, and Sir Simon Bland and Dame Jean Maxwell-Scott at Kensington Palace.

Five years in Edinburgh had flown by - all in the delightful Dunalastair. Now surely that long-promised overseas posting must be awaiting! Gibraltar or Malta would fill the bill nicely - both Brigadiers commands. Yes, Malta it was, but time was running out on the Base there. On the day the posting was cancelled I was attending what we called a Backward Brigadiers course in Whitehall. The Military Secretary knew how disappointed I would be and he had the decency to break the news himself. Instead it was to be Commander Highland Area in Perth. It was a measure of the trust which had been developed between Lowlands and Highlands that appointments were now virtually interchangeable - and thus it has remained. The Scottish Division was indeed good news. Nevertheless, the legendary "Tartan Tam", General Wimberley, who had commanded the Highland Division with such distinction during the war, was on the phone to give me some advice about commanding Highlanders.

Next to Divisional Brigadier in Scotland, Commander Highlands runs a close second as the best job in the army. There were regular Army units only at Fort George and Aberdeen, but there were a large number of TA and Cadet units spread over a vast area which included the London Scottish and the Liverpool Scottish. The principal responsibility really was as Land Agent for the large amount of land which the Army owns or leases in The Highlands. As the rest of UK became over-developed troops were queuing up all the year round to come to exercise in the Highlands. Iain Stonor spent his entire time negotiating with landowners who were, in the main, only too pleased to give us facilities, maybe for a few bawbees. After all we were responsible people and were answerable for any damage, unlike many other users of the country.

Inevitably there was a great deal of travelling. Although the A9 Perth to Inverness road was still a pretty grim experience, there were other excellent facilities - by train and air. The Army Air Corps Beavers in Yorkshire were always delighted to come to our wide open spaces and get plenty of hours in the flying log books. They touched down at Scone which was only 10 minutes from the Headquarters, in the old Campbell's Dyeworks behind the swimming bath in Perth. Helicopters were pleased to come too, especially useful for the awkward journey to Berwick on regimental business. Sometimes, we had some pretty "hairy" experiences - an over-loaded Beaver struggling up to Wick with all the top brass of the 51st Highland Volunteers, sticking to the cliffs all the way, or flying down from Aberdeen with ice forming on the wings: when I asked the pilot on the intercom why we couldn't lose a bit of altitude he replied: "Can't Sir, the Queen Mum's plane is down there". In thick weather the "chopper" pilots used to follow the M90 from Perth down to the Forth Bridge. I know one young Sergeant Pilot won't use that route again since he came perilously close to an electricity pylon just South of Kelty. Every time I pass that spot I wince.

David Arbuthnott, Black Watch, was making a great job of the Volunteers. One Battalion clearly wasn't enough for an area with four outstanding Regiments, all capable of raising their own TA Battalion. A 2nd Battalion was authorised with HQ in Elgin, and was followed a few years later by a third in Stirling. The Gunners were allowed an Ack-Ack Battery in Arbroath which was part of a Regiment ludicrously based in Belfast (This has now reverted to Scotland). O, Messrs Hackett and Carver, you have a lot to answer for.

Although the main centres of population naturally took up most of the visitations, the "outliers" were always the most appreciative - Wick, Thurso, Portree (O, the problems with the Drill Hall!), Orkney and Shetland. Brigadier Sidney Robertson, whom I entitled "Commander of the Orkney and Shetland Defences" was a Gunner of great charm and influence and, with Elsa at Daisybank, a marvellous host. The Rocket Range at Benbecula was administered by us and a wee plane took off every week from Strathallan airfield with fresh rations. I had the privilege of delivering the mail to St Kilda by air drop - "one good kick - and see you don't go with it" said the pilot.

Our private means of transport was by now a Volkswagen Dormobile so it was possible to combine pleasure with duty, particularly for Cadet inspections in the wilds of Argyll and Islay. I became adept at changing from civvies into uniform and back again in a confined space. When visiting the Cadets at Fort Augustus (Father Vincent in command) I forgot my Sam Browne but Choo Maclagan, now the ubiquitous Colonel Commandant of the Queens Own Highlanders Cadets, saved my bacon. Choo was an inspiration and his Regiment owes him a great debt of gratitude.

As successor to the General Officer Commanding the 51st (Highland) Division, there were a number of important duties to carry out and a good deal of public speaking. Our relations with the City of Perth were excellent. How could they be otherwise with the admirable Lord Provost David Thomson and his charming sister? (In the re-organisation of Local Government in Scotland in 1975, one of the meaner decisions in a bad package was the downgrading of Perth's Lord Provost. Who benefited from that spiteful ruling? No one.) The High Constables' Dinner in Perth was a great annual occasion attended by the Great and the Good, one of the few dinners where they still toasted the

Armed Forces after the Royal toast. That dinner was apt to go on a bit. A newly-arrived Town Clerk, invited to propose the Vote of Thanks at 1am, improved his promotion chances no end by commencing: "When I arrived at this dinner *yesterday* ...." It was a privilege to be asked to give the Remembrance address in the historic St John's Kirk in Perth and also in Arbroath where that notable Black Watch partnership of Brigadier James Oliver and Colonel George Dunn ruled all.

One sign of the Army's increasing involvement with the civilian community was an invitation from the Secretary of State for Scotland to be a member of the newly-formed Scottish Sports Council. Under Lawrie Liddell and Peter Heatly with Ken Hutchison as Secretary this provided a fascinating insight into national and local sporting facilities. It was appalling to find how woefully inadequate they were compared, for example, to our ex-enemy, Germany. We met regularly in different parts of Scotland and were wooed by the local authorities - since we held the purse strings. My particular responsibility was Chairmanship of the Glenmore Lodge Committee - another excuse for skiving up to Aviemore, in company with my boyhood hero, Wilson Shaw, also a member of the committee. Fred Harper and the instructors were a delightful bunch (including Ben Humble and his lovely rock garden). They did a great deal to introduce young people to the joys of the mountains and to improve safety standards in the hills. Army and RAF helicopters did a lot to help, too. Canoeing in the River Spey was a thorny problem which brought me eyeball-to-eyeball with my old boss General Geordie Gordon-Lennox, of Gordon Castle at Fochabers. We each fought our corner pretty hard.

For every six journeys to the North there was one to the South on regimental business. His Grace, Walter, Duke of Buccleuch had always been a tremendous supporter of The KOSB. In August of 1971 he invited "every KOSB officer within 100 miles of Bowhill" to a party attended by Princess Alice. It was a stirring occasion and a few of us stayed the night with an opportunity after dinner to see the priceless paintings and other objets d'art of The Bold Buccleuch. It was a sad day for the Borders and The

Princess Alice, Duchess of Gloucester, Colonel-in-Chief, The King's Own Scottish Borderers, inspects the Guard of Honour at the Freedom of Duns in 1972, with Provost Lennie, Lt Col Bob Riddle, Commanding Officer 1st Battalion, and the Colonel of the Regiment.

Regiment when he was laid to rest in Melrose Abbey in 1973, with the KOSB piper playing the lament.

As the changes in local government became imminent it was clear that most of our Royal and Ancient Burghs would be absorbed in the larger groupings so beloved of The Establishment. Many Provosts and Town Councils were anxious to confer their Freedoms on The King's Own Scottish Borderers, and the Royal Burgh of Duns did so in 1972. Princess Alice, always delighted to return to her beloved Borderland, received the Freedom on behalf of The Regiment and was greeted by "one of us", Willie Swan, the Lord Lieutenant. His Knighthood some years later was welcomed with enormous pleasure by his countless friends particularly in Berwickshire where he knew practically everyone. Another very welcome visitor to The Regiment was Her Majesty Queen Elizabeth The Queen Mother who called at Regimental Headquarters during a visit to Berwick Upon Tweed.

All these galavantings depended on a strong team back at base and that was provided by Ian Cameron (what again?) and Hugh

Mackay, Morag's cousin and son of the legendary 4th Gurkhas Hamish Mackay, Graham Murray, a fine piper, Jack Angus and Mrs Walker, my secretary (who nobly typed Granny Rose's memoirs when I was on leave). For most of my service my mail had been mixed up with another F H Coutts, a Warrant Officer in the Royal Army Service Corps. Somebody with a sense of humour in RASC Records posted him to Highland Area as Chief Clerk. Snap! FH. All these years - Fairmount was our 27th house - Morag had been a fantastic camp follower and enjoyed the copious official entertaining which went with these appointments. She had precious little assistance, but what she had was "gold dust" - Cpl Ray Stirling particularly, Betty Czemerys at Dunalastair and Anna McDairmid at Fairmount. The only time I knew of Morag "blowing the top" was when the Woman's Guild at Barnard Castle said that it was unfair that we should get our quarters and our coal *free*! There were perks. At Dunalastair we had Granny Roses's 80th birthday in a marquee on the tennis court and at Fairmount Sheena's 21st birthday party with sleeping bags 3 or 4 to a room. We evacuated for the night!

The Army sensibly decrees retirement at 55, and it was time to go. After a DIY course at Catterick, which I would have failed if there had been an assessment, and heart-warming farewells with the officers at the George Hotel and the warrant officers and sergeants at the Isle of Skye Hotel I "fell out to dust my medals" on the 8th of July 1973. I still had the precious privilege of wearing uniform as the Colonel of the KOSB for some years yet.

Chapter Eleven
They Shall Grow Not Old
(1973-1983)

They shall grow not old as we that are left grow old
Age shall not weary them nor the years condemn.
At the going down of the sun and in the morning . . .
WE SHALL REMEMBER THEM.
Binyon's lines,
perpetuated by The Royal British Legion

The golden rule of Army resettlement is: "First find your job, then look for a house". Good advice. Fortunately several employers seemed to be interested in "re-treads" from the Services. My No.1 Choice was The Queen Victoria School Dunblane, a superb establishment and the best thing that Scotland does for its Servicemen - but the Commandant's appointment still had a year to run. Another tempting offer was from the person who guides schoolboys keen on the Army towards their best career opportunity. He was "Birdie" Proudlock, the Schools Liaison Officer at Scottish Command who had commanded 186 Field Regiment in our Rhineland battles. Snag about that appointment was that it was still in the Army. As parsons do not retire within their parishes so there is a reluctance among Service officers to go back to their old stamping ground, perhaps under someone whose views, let's say, are not their own.

The most worthy offer came from the Arbroath mafia -

George Dunn and James Oliver - who were looking for a General Secretary for The Royal British Legion Scotland to replace Colonel Colin Macleod of Glendale. The British Legion is, of course, the principal ex-service organisation in Scotland. Of the three offers, it certainly paid the least but offered the most job satisfaction.

There was one catch. George Dunn was Chairman of the British Legion and James Oliver was Chairman of the Earl Haig Fund. The new General Secretary would be required to do the job as Joint General Secretary to both, as soon as Colonel Jock Grant had retired as Secretary of the Haig Fund. Well, that was a real "hornet's nest", for it was common knowledge that there was bad blood between the two organisations. When Field Marshal Earl Haig of Bemersyde founded the British Legion in Scotland (before England) in 1921 he set up The Earl Haig Fund separately to look after the Poppy Appeal money, fearing that very left-wing elements would "get their hand in the till". Particularly in Glasgow, this separation left a legacy of distrust and suspicion which is not entirely eradicated yet. But what a challenge!

Before starting on this crusade, a personal tragedy occurred for Morag whose health had been poor after a back operation. We were living in a third floor flat in Tipperlinn Road when she fell out of a window 60 feet on to a concrete patio. How she survived is a miracle. I was lambasted by Mr Orthopaedics at The Royal Infirmary for not caring for her better. They did a fantastic rescue operation in The Royal and then in the intensive care unit, followed by a grim three months in Ward 6, strung up like a chicken. It was touch and go until the New Year of 1974 when Jimmy Scott ("St James"), a distant relative, who had operated on Morag's back previously, arranged for her to go to The Princess Margaret Rose Hospital. From that moment onwards, she never looked back. The girls were marvellous. Fiona had just returned that day from a three year tour of Voluntary Service Overseas in Grenada. She switched her Teacher Training Course from Aberdeen and came to look after the old man. Sheena rushed up from London where she was Secretary to Lord Shawcross.

After a year the medics said: "What are we going to do now?"
I said: "Go home". That was the one thing they hadn't thought
of. The Dormobile van was a great help and we had two trial
weekends in that before returning - this time to a ground floor flat
in Gillsland Road - purchased without "Hersell" having seen it,
a dangerous move, but "needs must" and it was a huge success.
This was our 29th abode in 26 years of married life.

Let their be no doubt about it, the British Legion has done a
marvellous job for ex-servicemen in the past 70 years. The public
tends only to think of The Legion in terms of the annual Festival
of Remembrance at the Albert Hall followed by the service at The
Cenotaph the next morning, but all the year round The British
Legion is constantly fighting, and fighting again, to get a better
deal for War Pensioners. It seems cruel that ex-servicemen should
have to fight for adequate compensation, for example, for war
widows, but in a democracy every one has to fight his corner and
the ex-serviceman is no exception.

It is a sad fact that the majority of ex-sailors, soldiers and
airmen want very little to do with the Services once they are
"demobbed" with the possible exception of Regiments with
strong regimental associations. As a result The Legion member-
ship in Scotland is well under 100,000. Even allowing for the run-
down of World War II veterans it is a poor response (particularly
among officers I regret to say) and would be much less were it not
for the licensed clubs which many branches run - with constant
pressure from them to admit a higher percentage of associate,
non ex-service members. Many of these clubs in the early days
were badly run and a constant source of worry to the hard-
working and dedicated Assistant Secretary Russell Wight.

The Legion is organised in nine Areas roughly equivalent to
the new Regions (1975), but retaining in many cases the original
county names, such as Angus and Perthshire and Aberdeen,
Banff and Kincardine. Each Area provides five representatives to
the National Council, to which of course are added the national
office-bearers. The National Council has very wide powers and
is closely controlled by its Constitution which is regularly under
review. The honorary legal adviser, George Cockburn in my

time, is a busy man!

How they love the Annual Conference! It is a great talking shop and, also - and very properly - a great social occasion. The administration and entertainment are organised by the Area and the agenda and conference run by the HQ staff. Each Area hosts conference in turn. Accommodation is usually in hotels but twice they were persuaded to try University Halls of Residence - Aberdeen and Stirling - without too many complaints.

Like most organisations the detailed work was carried out by committees - in this case legions of them - General Purposes, Finance, Pensions, Welfare, Clubs and Sports, Publicity and Piping, plus of course the Haig Fund committees and the Officers' Association, which was organised separately. So every Saturday morning, and sometimes the afternoon too, was taken up with committees each requiring a detailed minute. They tended to become rather repetitive. Visits to Area Council meetings and to branch functions up and down the land filled every available moment.

The early years were very much absorbed with the formation of a Joint Secretariat. It took about four years of joint committees to thrash out an agreed solution (and it had been on the agenda for some time before I arrived) - the main bone of contention being "Who pays for what?" A great stimulus to "Jointery" was provided when it was agreed to move from Haig House in Drumsheugh Gardens, where car parking had become almost impossible, to a purpose-built building on ground owned by the Haig Fund in Logie Green Road, adjacent to Lady Haig's Poppy Factory. This enabled us to lay out the offices in a logical way with The Joint Secretariat at the hub and the specialist departments dove-tailed in. It was to be called New Haig House and it was opened by Her Majesty The Queen on 3rd July 1978.

During my service days I had been singularly lucky in serving under congenial people. The Legion and the Earl Haig Fund continued this good fortune - Admiral Sir Peter Reid, Lord Haig, Admiral Sir Nigel Henderson (from whom I got the "quarterdeck" treatment occasionally), George Dunn, James Oliver, Calum Macdonald (an exceptional Legion Chairman) Graeme

Warrack (the medical hero of Arnhem), Andrew Bennett, Hector Maclean in Glasgow, Geoffrey Patterson, Donald Watson, John Burke of The Royal Bank (who died so tragically in a mountain accident) and many others. I particularly admired and liked Earl Haig. For a start, it cannot have been easy growing up as the son of such an illustrious father. Inevitably, he was enlisted into Scotland's Cavalry Regiment, The Royal Scots Greys, and he had the misfortune to be "put in the bag" in the Western desert fairly early on in the war. He was segregated as a VIP prisoner of war - no doubt to be used as a hostage should the need arise. As the war turned against Germany he was moved from Italy to Germany - to the notorious Colditz. By inclination he was a painter and by nature a shy man. How he must have hated the communal life and acute discomfort of the "Kriegies". The only place he could find peace to paint was in the loo. One of his most admired paintings is a self-portrait, achieved in the privy whilst looking into a cracked mirror.

In parallel with his profession as an artist he has devoted the best part of his life to the welfare of ex-servicemen and to the perpetuation of his father's memory. The annual open-air service at Dryburgh Abbey is a most moving occasion. I knew it would rain the year when it was my turn to give the address - and it did! When I was Chief of Staff I had been able to help Lord Haig to move an enormous German gun from his front lawn to its present resting place at Glencorse, where it can be seen by young soldiers and the general public. Since then Dawyck and Frutsy have been most considerate hosts at Bemersyde and happily on return visits to Gillsland Road.

Until it became financially impossible, The Officers' Association ran a Nursing Home in Belgrave Crescent, Edinburgh under the command of Panda Gunn, everyone's favourite. (She could tell a few tales out of school!). The Chairman of the Nursing Home Committee was the eminent surgeon, Sir John Bruce. One of his conditions of service was that the meetings should be preceded by lunch in the New Club when I would brief him on the latest financial situation. Sitting in the library upstairs with a glass of vintage port in his hand he mused: "See Ramsay Garden there? I mind when I was a student in 1928, there were 8 of us in digs there on the ground floor. It was August and we were doing re-sits. We used to rig up a catapult from an old motor car tyre and fire oranges at the polis walking up the Mound. One night retribution arrived. There was a knock at the door and there stood a Police Inspector. We took him into the sitting room quaking at the knees. He surveyed us all and then said quietly: 'Pack it in, boys, you've had a good run'". A good lesson in man-management.

By far the most enterprising thing the Legion did during my tenure as General Secretary was to take the plunge and join up with the Royal British Legion Housing Association in England which for some years had been providing sheltered housing in England and Wales for ex-servicemen and women. Scotland, ever canny, was sure that there must be a catch somewhere. Would the Housing Corporation really put up the capital? John Rivers, its pioneer in England, assured us they would and we were off. Scoring another personnel selection bull's-eye, Lt Cdr Bill Adams of the Fleet Air Arm was appointed Scottish Officer of The Housing Association and he set to work with missionary zeal. In next to no time the first court of 33 homes was opened in Hawick by Princess Alice. It was named Douglas Haig Court after the Founder and the Chairman was John Aitkin, a local Chartered Accountant and KOSB officer, whom we last met in the jungles of Malaya. Soon all the Areas wanted their own Courts and this was quickly realised. At the time of writing there are 24 courts in Scotland housing no less than 999 ex-service people in beautifully warm, modern accommodation. The secret of success was to find good chairmen and committees to run the courts and in this respect the Association has been very well served. We worked so closely with the parent body in England that in due course Bill Adams was invited to be their Chief Executive and John Aitkin the Chairman. In 1990 Scotland were allowed to stand on their own feet and they now have their own Association with Mrs Jean Ann Scott Miller as the Chairman, wife of the Legion Chairman in Scotland, Major Jack Scott Miller - a unique "left and right". I have the honour of being their Hon.

President.

1977 was the "annus mirabilis" when just about everything happened. The first and biggest hurdle was that Scotland had been invited for the first time to host the triennial conference of the British Commonwealth Ex-Services League, which does a very good job in looking after many loyal soldiers of the Commonwealth who rallied to the cause in both World Wars. Many of them are now living in very reduced circumstances. Delegates from 33 Commonwealth countries would meet in Edinburgh for a week under the chairmanship of HRH The Duke of Edinburgh. It was also the year of HM The Queen's Silver Jubilee, so we planned the conference on the week when Her Majesty was in Scotland. By this time, John Pollington a most experienced RAF pilot and Wing Commander, had joined as No 2. He did a marvellous job as conference organiser and, although a Sassenach, endeared himself to the Legion in Scotland for a long period of years. We gave the BCEL a memorable week. What work there was took place in the distinguished Merchants Hall in Hanover Street, The Queen and The Duke of Edinburgh gave a superb Reception in the Palace of Holyroodhouse with the national beverage flowing freely, all the delegates attended an historic service at St Giles when Knights of the Thistle were installed, Scottish Command put on a Combined Retreat in Holyrood Park and on their "day off" the delegates were despatched on a coach trip to the Highlands, with an obligatory stop at a distillery. At the St Giles service the conference representatives were surprised to see the General Secretary in a different role as Falkland Herald Pursuivant Extraordinary, a distinction which The Lord Lyon King of Arms had twice bestowed. The duties were not onerous, merely to escort the Royal equerries to their places - but as there was nothing else happening at the time it attracted rather a lot of attention. By the end of the week the delegates were so imbued with tradition and protocol that a motion to delete the word "British" from the BCEL title was defeated, nem con!

Early in 1976 I had had a phone call from Sir John Orr, the Chief Constable of Edinburgh and The Lothians, saying that he wanted to come and see me. "O, Lord" I thought, "Another Legion Club in trouble". As President of the Scottish Rugby Union he floored me completely by saying that the committee of the SRU were inviting me to be the next Vice-President of the Union in Hector Monro's year as President. I could hardly say "Yes" quick enough before he changed his mind. Although it would mean more absences from Legion/Haig business it was, in a way, a feather in their cap and they made no objection.

The Scottish Rugby Union has 18 committee members, elected annually by the clubs within the six districts - Edinburgh, Glasgow, South, Midlands, North and Anglo Scots. Although unwritten in the constitution, election to the Presidency is automatic by seniority. To prevent the committee changing round too quickly, it has been the custom to elect a vice-President from outwith the committee every second year (now every three years, following a wise amendment introduced by Jimmy Ross). The Union has always believed that the "outside" Presidents have introduced a breath of fresh air and new ideas. I was genuinely surprised to have been selected. Although I had been a life-long fanatic of the game and had given up an immense amount of time and energy to organising rugby after I gave up playing, I had frequently been a stern critic of the SRU in the correspondence columns of *The Scotsman*.

I had a lot to learn in my first year and could not have had a saner, kinder guide than Hector Monro. At the French match in the cauldron which is Parc des Princes, Hector didn't look so kindly; I thought he was going to come to blows with Albert Ferrasse, the perpetual French President. Donald Macdonald had just been felled by a haymaker from Gerard Chollet, the French prop, a notable baddie, butcher and boxer, and this had gone completely unpunished by the referee. Albert then proceeded to order "replacements" on to the field, rather as soccer players are interchanged, completely ignoring the new rule which stipulated that injured players had to be examined off the field by a doctor before they could be replaced.

The French were generous hosts, just as they had been in 1947, and the committees dined in what is reckoned to be the best restaurant in Europe, but they have two idiosyncrasies. Firstly, they flatly refuse to speak English - a hangover from de Gaulle, although in no time we were talking rugby excitedly in Franglais as our schoolboy French didn't operate until after the second brandy. Secondly, when the evening was just warming up, the French committee suddenly exited to a man - no doubt on a pre-arranged signal from Monsieur Albert.

The SRU has a reputation for stick-in-the-mud, diehard, conservatism, an insinuation which has been actively fanned over the years by long-winded musings from such as Norman Mair. In fact, the Union has been in the van of every progressive change in the game, although it sticks firmly to its primary object which is to "promote, encourage, and extend the game of Rugby Football in Scotland". The honour of the Presidency does not, of course, come without responsibilities, and every President can be sure to face some nasty decisions in his tenure. In 1977/78 sponsorship of the game was mooted for the first time and the first deal was signed with Schweppes. The "Old Guard" were horrified. Frank Moffat appealed to me on his death bed to have nothing to do with it. The advertising boards round the sacred turf of Murrayfield had appeared a year or two before - in my opinion an abomination and I would have them removed, even now. What he would have thought about the possibility of players being paid for playing, by ingenious stratagems, I shudder to think. The issue has always been perfectly plain to me, and is well understood on the Borders: "if you want to be paid for playing rugby, go to the Rugby League; Rugby Union is an amateur game". What players in their 20's don't realise is that their time at the top is very short - today you're Somebody, tomorrow you're Nobody. They would reply: "Well, give us our share of the cake while we're at the top". Not so, Buster. As Jimmy Ireland says: "Rugby is all about the 3 Fs - Fitness, Fun and Friendship". Put money into it and the Fun and Friendship will disappear.

The next controversial issue was coaches. Scotland had been in the lead in organising coaching and player-improvement courses, but somehow the thought of an official coach for the national team smacked of professionalism and we shied away. However, an "adviser to the Captain", Bill Dickinson, was approved and soon the flood gates opened. Fitness and ball skills have undoubtedly improved, but it is doubtful if the game is any more enjoyable to the players or the spectators. Certainly, too much time is taken up with preparation. John Rutherford said to me the year before he retired: "Frank, you don't know how lucky you were not to have to sit through these boring video replays".

Playing links with South Africa were high on the agenda of any President. It was a "dead duck" in '77, at any rate for the time being, but that didn't prevent Dannie Craven getting on the phone twice a week to ask what we were going to do about it, a question which might quite properly have been fired in the opposite direction.

The season 1977/78 started with a flourish - a tour to Japan calling at Bangkok and Hong Kong. It was a very happy party and it was a privilege to be with them and to get to know many of the players who were to do Scotland proud in the next decade. Roy Laidlaw and John Rutherford started their long and fruitful partnership there. Jim Renwick, "Twinkle-toes", was the comedian of the party, as always, and his Hawick team-mate, "Toomba", Allan Tomes, was appointed sole judge of off-the-field offences. I was fined a round of drinks for sleeping in after lunch and keeping the bus waiting. Mike Biggar, a family friend, was captain of the side, a real steady hand and a fine player, and he received fierce support from Nairn MacEwan as player/coach. The "Mighty Mouse", Iain McLauchlan, was at the peak of his very considerable form, along with "Barnie", Ian Barnes, Bruce Hay and Colin Deans who had yet to win the first of his many of caps for Scotland.

The Management was no less enlightened. The Team Manager was Tom Pearson, a Fife schoolmaster, assisted by George Thomson ("Lord Myreside"). Although we had a physio, Bobby McNaught, this was in the days before touring sides automatically took a doctor, so poor George spent his time dishing out pills and taking players to hospital. His knowledge of Japanese improved considerably during the tour!

We were most hospitably entertained by the Japanese Rugby Union. As an ex-Serviceman I wasn't too happy about receiving Japanese hospitality after their treatment of our Prisoners-of-war, but we had made it up with the Germans and had to do the same with the Japs. Shiggy Konno, The President of the Japanese RFU, made it easy, for he was utterly charming. He called himself a "failed Kamikaze pilot". They were not supposed to survive! The highlight of our trip was a rest period in a very superior monastery at Tenri. I say superior because one doesn't really expect to have miniatures of whisky besides one's trestle bed in a monastery! But as it was Japanese whisky it was in the nature of a penance. At the farewell dinner in Tokyo we were honoured by the presence of their Patron, Princess Chichibubu, who presented us all with a sample of Japanese wares, far in excess of the maximum value then permitted by amateur regulations.

O, we did play Rugby! The boys won all their games with panache and attracted large crowds to the national stadium in Tokyo and in Kyoto. They scored a lot of points off the field too for they were fine ambassadors. I never heard a cross word throughout. This is no mean feat because the demands of a touring side can be very tiring - travelling, training, being nice to everyone, is quite a strain. They didn't half let their hair down on the return flight from Tokyo "over the top". They didn't look so hot at Anchorage at 4am.

When it came to the Five Nations series we did not do so well. We had a good side well captained by Dougie Morgan, but the opposition in every case were just that much better. So often Internationals are decided by the odd penalty goal or two, or the result of a controversial decision. I became adept at making "gallant loser" speeches after each game. Even the "B" team got beaten. Richie Dixon, that great, and alas uncapped, player will never forget the one at Dieppe which reduced us all to tears!

The stars of that 1978 side had been on the Lions tour of New Zealand while we were in Japan. Andy Irvine was in a class of his own as a ball-player and an entertainer. He had all the skills - running, handling, kicking and tackling (once he had learned to get his man at the right angle) - and charisma. He could also have his off-day. Who will ever forget the French match in 1980 when he was the villain in the first half and the hero in the second, winning the game comfortably on his own - real Boys' Own Paper stuff? Ian McGeechan, now Scotland's coaching "guru", was a sound player in that side, but not yet displaying the tactical finesse which brought Scotland to its second Grand Slam in recent years in 1990. Iain McLauchlan and Sandy Carmichael were prop forwards of world class, in any generation. It was interesting that they should be playing at the same time as the famous Pontypool front row of Faulkner, Windsor and Price. No wonder we lost against Wales! They also had the remarkable Gareth Edwards and Phil Bennett at half back and the kenspeckle JPR Williams at full-back. I'm sure he could have been twice the player if he'd had his hair cut and pulled up his stockings.

That year the French too produced two players who were to make their mark on the world rugby scene - Jean-Pierre Rives, the flamboyant blonde, utterly fearless, usually dripping in blood, and Jacques Fouroux, "Le Petit General" who is now creating as much mayhem in administrative circles as he did at the base of the scrum. Rugby certainly produces great characters. One I had the privilege of sitting beside at dinner was Bill Beaumont, England Captain in '78, who has made such a name for himself as a team captain in *A Question of Sport*.

The best match of the year, as it nearly always is, was against Ireland. We were 3-6 down with two minutes of injury time to go when Scotland were awarded a penalty in front of the Irish posts. As Andy Irvine came up to kick it - a formality which would have ended the match in a draw - Morgan decided to run it and go for a win. Sadly, we fluffed it, but the Lansdowne Road crowd gave the Scots a great ovation for sporting play. But it wasn't to be our year, Rae Tod and I share the dubious distinction of being the only two Wooden Spoon Presidents post-war, a distinction which we toast with great regularity at SRU Dinners. If we couldn't win we could at least give the best dinners of the series with the haggis being piped in with style.

The Presidential year carries a very heavy social programme. The long-standing clubs expect the President to attend their dinner, come what may. With late nights, a surfeit of hospitality and much travelling, it was a very heavy schedule. But what a rich crop of good fellowship as reward!

The meetings were fun and always sparkled with good humour. Our main complaint was that we spent far too much time on administrative detail and not enough time talking Rugby. The laws are constantly under review - a real "jungle", only to be entered by experts. At one meeting I was startled to find that my younger brother Philip, with whom I had shared a storming second-row partnership in the London Scottish, had written an official letter to suggest that the area behind the stand at Murrayfield should be brightened up by planting spring flowers, tulips and daffodils. There was a longish pause, and then a voice said: "Nae daffies for Taffies". Next item, please.

The year was only made possible for an incomer by the help and advice I received from the whole committee, and especially Lex Govan, my "Vice", a war-time colleague, and the ever-faithful John Law, the Secretary, who was very properly honoured not long after that. The SRU are extraordinarily kind to their Past Presidents and we meet regularly at the internationals.

At the same time, The King's Own Scottish Borderers were having a notable decade. The Colonel's job was made a sinecure thanks to a succession of outstanding Commanding Officers in the 1st Battalion during the 70's - Andrew Myrtle, Bob Riddle, Allan Alstead, Mike Thomson and Colin Mattingley. Every one of them made Brigadier and rightly so. With the reduction in the Territorial Army our influence and contacts with the regimental area had been seriously curtailed, we therefore accepted with acclamation the granting of Freedoms of more burghs across the Border. In 1974, between the 3rd of July and the 1st of August (Minden Day) The Regiment was accorded the Freedom of no less than six Border Burghs - Coldstream, Melrose, Wigtown, Newton Stewart, Kirkcudbright, and Hawick. Each burgh had their own way of conducting the Freedom ceremony, but every one was a thrilling occasion characterised by a very warm and spontaneous pride in their local regiment by the large crowds who assembled.

The next year, 1975, saw further excitements. The 1st Battalion received new Colours, presented by Princess Alice on behalf of Her Majesty The Queen, in a unique ceremony at the Deutschlandhalle in Berlin, where the Battalion were again stationed. As most of their burghs were about to fall under the "Wheatley axe" they made it the occasion for a farewell reunion and party. It was rumoured that toasts in German to "Die Grenze Burgomeisteren" were heard in various Bier Kellers off the Ku'damm, followed by stentorian renderings of "Hawick's Queen o' a' The Border", "Jethart's here" and many others. The ringleaders were Provosts Len Thompson of Selkirk, Davie Atkinson of Hawick and Gideon Yellowlees of Jedburgh. The 1st Battalion excelled themselves.

Two further Freedoms followed, those of Jedburgh on a freezing cold evening - never has a dram tasted better than in the Legion Club afterwards - and Sanquhar, in Nithsdale, which took the honour of granting the last Freedom before regionalisation was on us.

The Freedom of Melrose 1974. HRH meets a gallant gunner.

These were the highlights. The "daily bread" consisted of interviewing potential young officers for the regiment, a congenial task and so important for its future well-being. The Regimental Family spreads very wide: constant touch had to be kept with the TA and Cadets, Branches of the Regimental Association in London and Edinburgh as well as the Border towns, and the annual reunions of the 4th, 6th and 7th Battalions. "Once a Borderer, always a Borderer".

After the painful demise of The Cameronians (Scottish Rifles), the KOSB were permitted to recruit in Lanarkshire. Apart from occasional courtesy calls and the provision of Permanent Staff for the Cameronians TA Companies, this was played very low profile. It's like walking on someone's grave. The Old Colours of the 1st Battalion were laid up at the Canongate Kirk in 1976. Our dear Colonel-in-Chief was there as usual with Dame Jean Maxwell-Scott and planted a tree to commemorate the occasion. Accompanying the Minister, the Very Reverend Dr Ronald Selby Wright, who was of course a former KOSB Padre, were four other regimental padres - Dr Neville Davidson, Farquhar Lyall, Douglas Scrimgeour, and Matthew Robertson. It was nice to have Cardinal Gray with us as well.

Although nearly 300 years of KOSB history had been recorded in various volumes there had never been one comprehensive history of the Regiment which a young officer or soldier could pick up and read fairly quickly. This was put right when Robert Woollcombe, an established author and a wartime officer in the 6th Battalion, agreed to write *All The Blue Bonnets*, a most readable account of The King's Own Scottish Borderers from 1689 to the 1970's.

When the time came to say farewell as Colonel the Battalion were at Fort George. The sadness of the occasion was not improved by the fact that we returned to Edinburgh to find that the house had been comprehensively burgled!

Back, broke, to New Haig House. The Legion and The Haig Fund were now talking to each other, the Housing Association was firing on all cylinders (in 1981 alone five new courts were opened) - one more task remained. At Scottish Command

General Lang had often said: "Why are there so many ex-service charities? They all seem to be doing the same thing and they're all after our money". A survey revealed the truth of this. There were no less than 45 different organisations in Scotland caring for ex-service people and there was absolutely no contact or co-ordination between them. Here was another hornet's nest ready for the flame-thrower. A proposed social gathering of all the secretaries received a favourable response and, after lunch, the matter was openly discussed. Naturally, no organisation was prepared to give up its autonomy or funds - nor were they being asked to - but everyone could see the need for more knowledge of "who does what?" and a common approach to ex-service problems. This was not a case of larger groupings or amalgamations, but of closer co-ordination. Under the inspired leadership of Air Marshal Sir Richard Wakeford of the RAF Benevolent Fund and Air Vice-Marshal Calum Macdonald of the Legion, regular meetings were held not just for "waffle", but to plan a

The Diamond Review of the Royal British Legion by their patron, Her Majesty the Queen, accompanied by His Royal Highness, The Duke of Edinburgh and Major The Earl Haig on 11th July 1981 at Holyrood Park, Edinburgh. Jack Scott Miller's braves from Angus and Perthshire are reviewed. Driver, "eyes front!"

new, practical approach to the problems of ex-service welfare. Each organisation would continue its specialist function and funding but would subscribe to a system of joint information and communication. Over the years this has flourished and is now known as SESCO - The Scottish Ex-Service Charitable Organisations. SESCO was tested and proved effective in The Gulf War.

In 1981, The Royal British Legion Scotland celebrated its 60th Anniversary with a parade and march past Her Majesty The Queen, their Patron, in Holyrood Park, Edinburgh. Major Tommy Little, a popular retired KOSB officer, came in to organise everything and did it superbly. It was a glorious day. Her Majesty and Prince Philip received a great welcome from the thousands of old comrades and their families who had come from all over Scotland, particularly our famous disabled organisations - Linburn (War-Blinded), The Erskine Hospital, Whitefoord House and the Lady Haig's Poppy Factory.

When one has done a job for ten years one selfishly hopes that the right chap will be chosen as your successor. They couldn't have done better. They got it absolutely right when they appointed Brigadier Bob Riddle who had recently left the Army as Divisional Brigadier and had just become Colonel of the KOSB - a notable double. I couldn't have been more pleased with the handover and became an OAP on 8th July 1983, a happy man.

Chapter Twelve
Old Soldiers Never Die
(1983-1991)

Old soldiers never die, never die, never die,
Old soldiers never die, they only fade away.
1914-1918 ditty

Free! After 53 years in one kind of uniform or another it was
strange to be a free agent, free to do what one wanted, when one
wanted, no reveille, no bugle calls . . . well, almost free - She Who
Must Be Obeyed was entitled to a larger slice of the cake. At last
the garden would get the attention it deserved, the golf handicap
reduced (with a set of lovely woods presented by the Legion) and
piping classes resumed. All that happened - but the phone kept
ringing and the mail seemed to have increased. This "retiral"
thing seemed to be a bit of a hoax.

A swift review of commitments revealed something of a
horror story:

In the ex-service world:
   1. Royal British Legion Housing Association Executive
      Committee (regular meetings in London).
   2. Soldiers' Sailors' and Airmens' Families Association
      Executive Committee (regular meetings in London).
   3. Scottish Garden Cities Housing Association -

Edinburgh and Lothians Committee and
Executive Committee.
4. President of the Scottish Union Jack Association.
5. President, Edinburgh Branch KOSB Association.

In "Civvie Street":
6. Joint President, The Society of Friends of St Andrew's
Jerusalem.
7. Council of the Glasgow Society of Sons of the Clergy.
8. Elder of Colinton Church.
9. Trustee and Chairman Finance and Fundraising
Committee, Seagull Trust.
10. Trustee, Scottish Rugby Union.
11. Occasional BBC broadcasts and speaking
engagements.

To these would shortly be added a 3-year stint as Chairman
of the VIP and Hospitality Committee of the XIIIth Commonwealth Games in Edinburgh, 1986.

An adjustment was clearly necessary. It followed in slow time.
The important thing was to get something different - no more
committees and minutes please, no more "points of order". The
Seagull Trust provides free canal cruising in Scotland for disabled
people, and its founder, the Rev Hugh Mackay, is a very
persuasive gentleman. He recruited me as Fund Raiser with the
object of clearing off a sizable debt. There's one born every
minute. Despite its ridiculous title, Seagull does a great job,
giving pleasure to over 10,000 disabled people a year on our
delightful inland waterways at Ratho, Falkirk, Kirkintilloch and
Inverness.

It is astonishing how much dedicated work is performed
voluntarily - provided the cause is right. Hats off to:- Norman
Simpson (The Hon Treas), Gladys Hamilton (The Hon Secy),
George Reid (The Monday Boy), Gwen Little and Nigel Stisted
(Tuesday), Isobel Pert (Thursday) and Claud Moir (plus all his
other good works) on Friday. This happy team has stuck together
for 7 years (to date) and raised over £400,000, resulting in two

"Yes, Prime Minister".
Mrs Thatcher visits the Seagull Trust at Ratho.

boathouses and four new narrow boats (or barges) catering for an ever-increasing number of disabled people every year. Mrs Thatcher did us a good turn by cruising with a disabled group from Ratho to Wilkie's Basin on the Union Canal.

Jerusalem The Golden was another novel cause. Bernard Fergusson had asked me to take over from him the Joint Presidency of The Society of Friends of St Andrew's Jerusalem, which acts as a support group, with 500 or so members, all people who have come under the influence of The Holy Land. St Andrew's was opened in 1930 to commemorate the Scots who died in the Allenby campaign of 1917. It is the most lovely building, set on a hill over looking the Valley of Hinnom and the Temple Mount. H. V. Morton said of it:

> "The Scots have a genius for suddenly
> making you want to burst into tears ......

195

It happens in this church in Jerusalem.
I thought it was one of the most beautiful
memorials I had ever seen."

Our grocer in Melrose, Wattie Douglas, used to tell me tales
about the Palestine campaign in which 52 Division, with of
course 4 KOSB, were heavily involved, particularly at the battle
of Gaza with its impenetrable thorn bushes. While Wattie
blethered on, the queue of irate customers holding their war-time
ration books stretched down to the Square. St Andrew's Jerusalem
commemorated these Borderers and thousands of other Scots
killed on foreign soil.

The Church of Scotland has several interests in The Holy
Land. Alongside St Andrew's is an excellent hospice which caters
for visitors of all faiths on their pilgrimage to the holy places; at
Tabeetha, Jaffa, there is a fine international school and up at
Tiberias on the Sea of Gallilee there is another large hospice and
a small kirk. Tiberias was for many years a most successful
hospital, for ever associated with the Torrance family, many of
whose children lie in the cemetery within the garden at the edge
of the lake - a sad reminder of the cruel climate there, hundreds
of feet below sea level. The Kirk has been well served by its
ministers in St Andrews; in our time, the Very Rev Professor
Robert Craig (who was padre with 1 KOSB in Palestine in 1946),
Dr John Miller Scott and now Colin Morton.

Unfortunately, St Andrew's stands right on the border of
Jerusalem and East Jerusalem which was Arab land and it bears
honourable scars from the 7-day war. The majority of the staff
at the hospice are Arabs, many of them living in Bethlehem, in the
occupied West Bank. They are all friendly, good people who have
been loyal to the kirk for years, and they have had a very difficult
time during the "intifada" (Palestinian uprising).

One's first visit to the Holy Land is very inspiring - indeed they
all are. My mother had been very critical of the commercialism
which surrounds the religious sites. (Quoth she: "Cool Siloam?
Huh, its nothing but a pool of muddy water"). It can be off-
putting but certain places like the Garden Tomb are very moving

and leave a lasting impression that someone very special lived and died here.

Morag has a Jewish school friend in Jerusalem. On our last visit we stayed with the Ranans, toured the country with them and got a very good insight into the Palestinian problem, which is not likely to be solved in our time. "The Brits" get the blame for everything, but that didn't spoil a delightful stay at the Red Sea resort of Eilat, with its fascinating under-water exhibitions. At the other end of the country, the Golan Heights are approached via the grandly-named Daughters of Solomon Bridge. It's a bit of a let-down to discover that this turns out to be another of Mr Bailey's splendid bridges - and a gey rusty one at that. Standing at the extremity of Golan and looking over to Damascus one feels a real sense of history. The kibbutzim are beautifully laid out, and the desert blooms. We haven't heard the last of that place.

A bus trip across the Sinai desert to Cairo was another novelty - on the Israeli side most comfortably organised, on the Egyptian side fairly hair-raising. One feels a little insecure handing over the passport to a member of the Hospitality Police, with no laces in his boots, and only about one button on his flies. Apart from the magnificent Son et Lumière at the Sphinx and the usual tourist sites at the Pyramids, the object of the exercise was really to visit a much-cherished war grave near El Alamein, but the Libyans had closed the frontier.

But this is straying far from St Andrew's Jerusalem - which needed a new organ at an estimated cost of £35,000. Another appeal. "Seagull" very kindly allowed us to use their minuscule office and the money was soon raised with a good bit in hand for maintenance and music. The purists were horrified that it was to be an electronic and not a pipe organ. When it pealed out at the dedication service on St Andrew's Day 1987 I for one could not tell that it was not a pipe organ; and I doubt very much whether the purists could either.

The next Joint President of The Society of Friends of St Andrew's Jerusalem is to be Lt-General Sir John Macmillan, whose father General Sir Gordon Macmillan was the last GOC Palestine before the creation of the state of Israel.

One of the great advantages of retiral is the opportunity for foreign travel now made available by reasonable flights and fares from Scotland. The little island of Gozo off Malta GC has always been our favourite in the charming fishing village of Xlendi - now, alas, ruined, by over-development. Two return visits to McGregor Bay in Canada were very special memories and one to Norway to re-visit Utne and dear Ebbe (ex-4th KOSB) and Kirsten Roede in Oslo.

Australia had to be visited more than once for daughter No2, Sheena, had been there for ten years of more, carving out a career with Drake International in Brisbane.

The first visit coincided - surprise, surprise - with a tour of the Scottish Rugby XV. Rugby, Aussie-style, is fun. It's not just a match which is over in 90 minutes; it's a day out with the family. Ballymore, the Queensland ground, is a delightful setting. The party for 30 or so out of the back of Sheena's car in the creek was vastly more entertaining that the First Test which was a scrappy affair won by a neat try by Keith Robertson near the end. The Past President's contribution was to raise the adrenalin by playing the pipes for the boys in blue as they got out of their bus. The Second Test was played at the world's worst international rugby ground, the Sydney Cricket Ground. It rained so hard we could hardly see what was going on which was probably just as well as we got hammered! Fortunately there is an Australian Army Officers Mess adjacent to the ground and there we were revived by Alf Scales and Ian Mackay, who had been the one Australian in the Combined Services side from Singapore to Perth WA in 1963.

Another Aussie connection is the flourishing association with the Royal Queensland Regiment at Toowoomba, up on the Darling Downs about 90 miles from Brisbane. Richard Munt and his officers have more than once given us a marvellous welcome, good touring and lively golf.

The ex-service organisation in Australia is The Returned Services League a powerful body with political clout. I wasn't interested in their politics but I was very interested in their sheltered housing for ex-servicemen and women which was reputed to be streets ahead of ours. I found this to be so, in Brisbane, Sydney and Perth WA. The RSL provide after-care accommodation for those who can no longer cope for themselves and, eventually, Nursing Home facilities, all in the same complex. The British Legion does not, to date, look ahead that far on the very logical grounds that we stick to what we can do best. As the ex-World War II veterans advance into their 70's and 80's, this is a problem which is going to face us very soon.

The Commonwealth Games in Edinburgh were generally written off by the media as something of a disaster, mainly because of the financial difficulties involved. Speak to any of the Commonwealth officials or athletes who took part and you will get a very different opinion. True, there were political problems; the boycott by some of the African Commonwealth countries was disappointing, but made little difference to the sporting side of the Games which went off without a hitch. More serious were the political problems at home. It was iniquitous of the Government to have given no financial support; a little priming of the pump would have made all the difference and given more confidence to sponsors. Kenneth Borthwick tried his level best as Chairman but the back-up team was abysmal, and some very odd appointments were made to the permanent staff. The law of libel prevents elaboration! The real problem was the Edinburgh District Council who were never more than lukewarm and sometimes quite impossible. However, the staff of the Common- wealth Games Federation, under our own genial Peter Heatly, were a great pleasure to work with.

In the Visitors' Division, which was splendidly run by John Mackenzie of Alloa Breweries (that should be worth a pint or two!), these problems did little to discourage us. Gradually an excellent team of volunteers was assembled to run Welcome and Entertainment, The Village (at the Pollock Halls of Residence), Catering, Accommodation and VIP and Hospitality. By the time the VIP group was at its maximum strength, we had to do the briefing on the hallowed turf of Murrayfield; they were nearly 200 strong. General Ronnie Somerville was a tireless operator and Linda Moffat (ex-WRNS) a real find as Executive Officer.

The hostesses, drawn mainly from the Dunfermline PE College were a particular success, and Anne Mathewson made an inspiring Head Girl.

The entire Royal family gave their unstinting support to the games. Every single visit had to be prepared in minute detail. Iain Lowis of the KOSB came in to do this and, apart from one bomb scare, everything went exactly as planned, greatly aided by the charm and efficiency of the Royal equerries.

The arrival of Mr Robert Maxwell caused quite a stir. My brother, Wally, had previously worked for him in Pergamon Press, so I knew what to expect. His offer of a financial life-line was all important, but he was an expert at obtaining every ounce of publicity in return.

The opening and closing ceremonies of the Games, organised by two KOSB Brigadiers, Peter Stephenson and Mike Thomson, were two of the finest outdoor spectacles I have ever seen in Scotland. Just when the biggest Pipe Band of all time had manoeuvred its way into the stadium and played for a while, it was then joined by another Pipe Band, even bigger, comprised of civilian bands. The two combined splendidly and formed a wonderful musical introduction to the principal entertainment of the evening which was pure ballet on a massive scale performed by school children from all over Edinburgh who had been training for weeks and did not even meet each other until the dress rehearsals. The music and choreography was brilliantly devised and the whole presentation was a great tribute to the youth of the host country. It gave us a marvellous start.

No account of our retirement would be complete without recording our pleasure and pride in the McCallum family. Fiona and John McCallum were married in Colinton Church by Dr Bill Johnston on the 29th of March 1975. John is an outdoors man, a Chartered Surveyor, a superb fisherman and never happier than when he is in his native Argyll where they spend every free moment at Tayvallich. Neil (13) is a fine sportsman - the wretched boy can beat me at golf already! - and Kirsty (10) is equally accomplished in music and dance. Our youngest daughter Sheena eventually walked up the aisle at Colinton Church, too, on the 2nd September 1989 when she married Alastair Scott, a travel author. They now live on Skye. As a family, we all owe a great debt of gratitude to Dr Bill Johnston for his distinguished 27 years as minister of Colinton - now sadly coming to its conclusion.

The reader may have gathered that there is another organisation strongly supported by the writer - a Regiment called The King's Own Scottish Borderers. The KOSB were 300 years old in 1989 and set out to celebrate in style. Since the Regiment was raised in Edinburgh for the defence of the City at the foot of the Royal Mile, the first act was a service of thanksgiving on the lawns of Holyroodhouse at which the address was give by the Rev Jim Harkness, Chaplain-General to the Forces and an ex-KOSB padre. The Battalion had assembled there in combat kit and arrived in helicopters in a dramatic and realistic way recapturing the sense of urgency on the 18th of March 1689. After the parade they exercised The Regiment's right to march through the city with "bayonets fixed, drums beating and

Colours flying". Alongside the Lord Provost on the saluting dais was the Earl of Leven and Melville, direct descendent of the sixth Earl who had raised The Regiment in (roughly) the same place.

For the next three months, the 1st Battalion, under the inspiring leadership of Clive Fairweather, organised a series of visits and reunions at our "roots" - the 15 burghs on the Border which have granted their Freedom of entry to the KOSB - (East to West) Berwick Upon Tweed, Coldstream, Duns, Kelso, Jedburgh, Melrose, Hawick, Ettrick, and Lauderdale District, Selkirk, Dumfries, Sanquhar, Kirkcudbright, Newton Stewart, Wigtown, and Stranraer. Two new Freedoms were granted - those of Eskdale and Annandale District (at Annan) and Roxburgh District (at Hawick). At Annan our Colonel-in-Chief braved a cold wind to be with us, as she had on the previous day when HRH opened the latest British Legion Housing scheme at Newcastleton ("Copshawhame") and kindly named it "Frank Coutts Court".

Once again the Border folk gave a terrific welcome to their own Regiment. Nothing was too much trouble. At Sanquhar,

when we suggested to the Police that holding up the traffic on the main Dumfries-Kilmarnock road for 25 minutes while we beat Retreat was a little inconsiderate, the Police Sergeant replied: "Ach, let them wait: it winnae happen for anither 100 years"!

The climax came on Minden Day, 1st August, 1989 when the whole Regiment, with the families who bravely put up with the antics all these soldier laddies, and our Allied Regiments from Canada, Australia, Malaya, America and Sweden, assembled for the grand finale which was a march down Princes Street. It was a glorious day and of course Princess Alice was there to take the salute at the bottom of the Mound, as she had done 50 years previously in 1939 at the same spot. At one point the whole of Princes Street was filled with Borderers from end to end, from the Caledonian Hotel to the NB, a proud and heart-warming moment for Borderers, young and old.

The celebrations which ensued can be imagined. In the early evening there was a band Retreat on the square at Redford barracks. As Drum Major Locke came forward to ask permission from the Colonel-in-Chief to march off, there was a gasp from the crowd. A small plane was flying above the square, carrying a long banner which proudly declared:

"ONCE A BORDERER, ALWAYS A BORDERER".

Epilogue

Under a fig tree,
Gharb, Gozo,
Malta GC
Jan-Mar 91

"...they shall beat their swords into ploughshares and their spears into pruning hooks, nation shall not lift up sword against nation, neither shall they learn war any more. But they shall sit every man under his vine and **under his fig tree**".

Michah 4: vv 3 & 4

Dear Neil and Kirsty

Well, that's my soldier's tale. I'm afraid there's been rather a lot of wars and rumours of wars. Why do the nations so furiously rage together? I dunno. Basically, I suppose, because of Man's inhumanity to Man.

Just when we thought that we were winning against the stupidity of war - fascism and communism on the run - wham! up comes a buffoon like Saddam Hussein and we're off again.

When I was a kid I used to go round houses on a Sunday afternoon dishing out leaflets for an organisation called The League of Nations. Fat lot of good that did! I was in uniform for the next 40 years. Now you've got the United Nations and it must be made to work despite all the jealousy and distrust between the nations of the First and the Third Worlds. When it comes to jealousy and distrust you could say that religion should be our saviour. But which religion? They are even more divided than the so-called United Nations.

You can do your bit by being good citizens. Remember the advice we gave to the Junior Leaders as their rules for living:

1. Keep yourself fit in body and mind. ("Mens sana in corpore sano" - the motto of the Army Physical Training Corps).
2. Know your job better than the next chap.
3. Always try to differentiate between right and wrong.
   And you'll need a bit of luck. GOOD LUCK!

With lots of love,

Grandad

Postscript

As we went to print, Communism collapsed. We had won the Cold War - a satisfying conclusion to 50 years of confrontation - and to this book. Defence cuts were inevitable, and justified - but applied too hastily and too deep. Without a proper defence review the Government, dominated by the treasury and the prospect of a fourth term in office, slashed the Infantry by 17 battalions (out of 51), leaving Tommy as usual grossly overworked:

> *It's Tommy this and Tommy that,*
> *And kick him out the brute.*
> *But it's 'ero o' 'is country*
> *When the guns begin to shoot.*

The remaining commitments for the Infantry Battalions, the workhorses of the Army, considerably exceeded the number of battalions available to fulfil them.

Despite its high level of recruitment (10th out of 51) and proven record of service in peace and war, the KOSB were one of the four Regiments in Scotland to be amalgamated with our good friends The Royal Scots (The Royal Regiment), who are second out of 51 in the recruiting league table and enjoy an even prouder record of 350 years of service to the Crown. The Army Board should reinforce success, not failure.

Although brought up on the adage 'orders is orders', this ministerial injustice was too much for the Top Brass of the Scottish Division. (Not for nothing have they been described as *the Scottish Mafia*). A campaign was immediately set up with the slogan 'Keep Our Scottish Battalions' and I was first in the queue for duty within the Regiment and at Campaign HQ in Edinburgh.

In the week commencing 14th October 1991, nearly every speaker in Parliament condemned the cuts - but Lord Carver in the Upper House opined that they were 'sensible'. That figures!

Time alone will tell. If the worst should befall, we have a fine Regimental team to fight our corner - Colin Mattingley as Colonel of the Regiment, John Kirkwood (Morag's nephew) as C.O. of the 1st Battalion, Clive Fairweather as Divisional Colonel and Colin Grant Hogg (son of 'D.O.') as Regimental Secretary.

Watch this space. Another Blue Bonnet?

Appendix

Officers of the 4th Battalion the King's Own Scottish Borderers 1941-46

Commanding Officers:
Lieutenant Colonels H.A. Kelly
                           J.B. Vans-Agnew
                           W.A.H. Maxwell
                           C.L. Melville BW
                           G.H. Davidson
                           J.B.A. Hankey

From pre-war T.A.

Jock Home Robertson from Paxton (father of the MP) and Horace Davidson from Norham, whose father had been friendly with mine when he was a minister in Coldstream up the River Tweed, Harcourt Rae, a former captain of the Melrose XV, Andrew Stewart from Jedburgh, Jimmy Scott-Noble from Hawick (later transferred to the Highland Division in North Africa), the Hogg Bros, Donald from Kersmains in Roxburgh and Colin, both pipers of note, Jim Bennett from Rulesmains, Duns, Alan Innes of Windywalls, Kelso, a fine amateur steeplechaser, Jock Elliot from Eddington Mains at Chirnside (where Jim Clark the racing driver later farmed), Jack Chapman, a Gala lawyer (for whom Army regulations were irksome), Charles Marrow, a son of the Regiment, Jock Milne Home, now Lord Lieutenant of Dumfriesshire, Jamie Stormonth-Darling, the power behind the National Trust for Scotland post-war, Willie Swan who was later such an outstanding Lord Lieutenant of Berwickshire and David Colville from Earlston.

In 1941 all these TA worthies were supported by an enthusiastic group of war-time officers mainly from Edinburgh schools: Bill Halliburton, Ally Ross, Eddie Dishington, Tommy Gray, Harry Cartner, Viney Scott, Harold Lawrie, Bob Bearpark (a commissioned regular soldier), John Henderson, Alan Sherriff, Allan Hill (Medical Officer), Frank Findlay (Padre), Adam Wyllie (Quartemaster), and not forgetting our two Canadians, Don Urquhart and Phil Carruthers, and our two Norwegians Ebbe Roede and Jimmy Gjendsemsø.

And later, Jimmy Wannop, Peter White, Jock Beattie, Fred Thurgar, Ian Scott, Mark Nisbet, Ken Wilson, Jim McMillan and Frank Clark.

Bibliography

Family

COUTTS, John, *The Life of Francis Coutts (1806-1887)* published1907
COUTTS, Dr John William MA DD, *How to use the Bible*, 1921,
(Student Christian Movement Press)
This My Son, James Clark & Co, London, undated.
The Church and the Sex Question
God and the Old Testament (U. F. Church of Scotland Federation of
Young Peoples Societies)
COUTTS, Mrs Rose, *Horse Trot to Moon Walk*, 1972, unpublished
FLEMING, Sir John, *Looking Backwards 70 years, 1921-1851*,
Aberdeen University Press, 1922
FLEMING, Robert, *Leaves off The Family Tree*, privately published,
Toronto, 1955
COUTTS, Captain J.B.F., MBE
Bothy to Big Ben, 1988, Aberdeen University Press
Highland Air, 1990, Aberdeen University Press
SCOTT, Alastair
Scot Free, 1986
Scot Goes South, 1988
Scot Returns, 1989
Tracks Across Alaska, 1990
(All John Murray, London)
KAMM, Antony and LEAN, Anne
A Scottish Childhood (pp44-47, Sir Walter Coutts)
Collins/Save the Children Fund, 1985
WRIGHT, The Very Rev Dr R.W.V. Selby, CVO ChStJ TD MA DD
FRSE JP and others
Soldiers Also Asked (pp 77-84 *Thou Shalt Not Kill: can a soldier be a
Christian?* by Dr J.W. Coutts), Oxford University Prss, 1943
NEES, Louis A, *McGregor Bay, The Quiet Paradise*, 1976

KOSB

HIGGINS, Captain R.T.
Records of the King's Own Borderers (sic), or Old Edinburgh Regiment.
(Chapman and Hall, 1873)
GUNNING, Captain Hugh
Borderers in Battle, KOSB History 1939-1945, pub. 1948

BLAKE, George
*Mountain and Flood, The History of the 52nd (Lowland) Division,
1939-1945*, Jackson & Co, Glasgow, 1950
WOOLLCOMBE, Robert
All The Blue Bonnets, The History of the KOSB 1689-1980, Arms and
Armour Press, 1980
COUTTS, Major F. H. and others
*War History of the 4th (Border Battalion, The King's Own Scottish
Borderers, 1939-45)*, private publication, 1946, price 2/6d in British
Armed Forces Vouchers (or fags)

British Legion

MALCOLM of POLTALLOCH, Lt Col George
We Will Remember, Royal British Legion Scotland. 1959
LISTER, John A.
Sixty Years On, RBLS, 1982

School

CAMPBELL, Prof C. A. & others
Glasgow Academy, the First 100 Years

Rugby Football

*A Souvenir Book of Scotland v England Services Rugby Matches 1942-
1943* (R.W. Forsyth, 1946)
Scottish Rugby Memories 1946-50 (R.W. Forsyth, 1951)
THORBURN, Sandy
The History of Scottish Rugby, Johnston & Bacon, 1980
OWEN, O. L.
The Barbarians, Welbecson Press, 1955
STARMER SMITH, Nigel
The Barbarians, Macdonald and Jane's, 1978

Index